Perspectives on East and Southeast Asian Folktales

Studies in Folklore and Ethnology: Traditions, Practices, and Identities

Series Editors: Simon J. Bronner, University of Wisconsin Milwaukee, and Elo-Hanna Seljamaa, University of Tartu

Studies in Folklore and Ethnology: Traditions, Practices, and Identities features projects that examine cultural traditions around the world and the persons and communities who enact them. Including monographs and edited collections, the series emphasizes studies of living folk practices, artists, and groups toward a broad understanding of the dynamics of tradition and identity in the modern world.

Recent Titles

Perspectives on East and Southeast Asian Folktales
Edited by Allyssa McCabe and MinJeong Kim
Black Folklorists in Pursuit of Equality: African American Identity and Cultural Politics, 1893–1943
By Ronald Lamarr Sharp
Oral Traditions in Contemporary China: Healing a Nation
By Juwen Zhang
Humor and Rumor in the Post-Soviet Authoritarian State
By Anastasiya Astapova
Prenuptial Rituals in Scotland: Blackening the Bride and Decorating the Hen
By Sheila Young
PTSD and Folk Therapy: Everyday Practices of American Masculinity in the Combat Zone
By John Paul Wallis and Jay Mechling

Perspectives on East and Southeast Asian Folktales

Edited by
Allyssa McCabe and MinJeong Kim

LEXINGTON BOOKS
Lanham • Boulder • New York • London

Published by Lexington Books
An imprint of The Rowman & Littlefield Publishing Group, Inc.
4501 Forbes Boulevard, Suite 200, Lanham, Maryland 20706
www.rowman.com

86-90 Paul Street, London EC2A 4NE

British Library Cataloguing in Publication Information Available

Library of Congress Cataloging-in-Publication Data

Names: McCabe, Allyssa, editor. | Kim, MinJeong, 1977- editor.
Title: Perspectives on East and Southeast Asian folktales / edited by Allyssa McCabe and MinJeong Kim.
Description: Lanham : Lexington Books, [2022] | Series: Studies in folklore and ethnology: traditions, practices, and identities | Includes bibliographical references and index. | Summary: "This volume examines East and Southeast Asian folktales unfamiliar to most Western audiences and highlights similarities to and differences from Western folktales. The discussion includes folktales from Vietnam, Laos, Cambodia, Burma, China, Japan, and Korea"— Provided by publisher.
Identifiers: LCCN 2022026675 (print) | LCCN 2022026676 (ebook) | ISBN 9781666912883 (cloth) | ISBN 9781666912906 (paperback) | ISBN 9781666912890 (ebook)
Subjects: LCSH: Tales—East Asia—History and criticism. | Tales—Southeast Asia— History and criticism. | Comparative literature—Oriental and Western. | Comparative literature—Western and Oriental.
Classification: LCC GR330 .P47 2022 (print) | LCC GR330 (ebook) | DDC 398.2095—dc23/eng/20220624
LC record available at https://lccn.loc.gov/2022026675
LC ebook record available at https://lccn.loc.gov/2022026676

Allyssa McCabe and MinJeong Kim would like to dedicate this book to the members of the Burmese, Vietnamese, Cambodian, and Laotian communities of Lowell, Massachusetts, who welcomed us and shared their wonderful, favorite folktales with us. We also want to thank our own families. Allyssa wants to thank Charlie, Jessamyn, Nick, Luke, and Vince. MinJeong wants to thank Chung, Yura, and her grandmother, Oklim Shin, the best storyteller she's ever known.

Contents

List of Tables   ix

1 Introduction: Perspectives on East and Southeast Asian Folktales   1
Allyssa McCabe and MinJeong Kim

FOLKLORISTIC PERSPECTIVE   **17**

2 Folk and Fairy Tales as Expressions of Identity in Cross-Cultural
Communication: A Folkloristic Perspective   19
Juwen Zhang

CULTURAL PERSPECTIVE   **45**

3 Morals Take Precedence Over Resolution: An Exploration
of Chinese Idiom Stories in Mandarin   47
Allyssa McCabe, Fangfang Zhang, and Chien-ju Chang

4 Collectivism in Asian versus Western Folktales
of (Extra)ordinary Companions   67
*Juwen Zhang, Allyssa McCabe, MinJeong Kim,
and Charlotte L. Wilinsky*

PSYCHOLOGICAL PERSPECTIVE   **81**

5 A Developmental Perspective on Violence in Southeast Asian
Folktales   83
Charlotte L. Wilinsky and Allyssa McCabe

6 What You Hate Becomes Your Fate: Researcher Reflexivity
in Encounters with Southeast Asian Folktales   99
Allyssa McCabe and George Chigas

EDUCATIONAL PERSPECTIVE 115

7   Japanese Language Socialization through Folktales 117
    Masahiko Minami

8   Educational Implications of Buddhist Values in Vietnamese
    Folktales 141
    Tham Tran and MinJeong Kim

9   Learning *Nunchi*: Folktales as Tools to Teach
    Emotional Competence in Literacy Learning in Korea 157
    MinJeong Kim and Min-Young Kim

Index 175

About the Editors and Contributors 187

List of Tables

Table 1.1	Number of Participants and Number of Folktales	3
Table 3.1	Number and Percentage of Mainland Chinese Middle-Class Children Who Provided Resolutions in Their Personal Narratives	48
Table 3.2	Number and Percentage of Middle-Class Taiwanese Children Who Provided Resolutions in Their Narratives about Frightening Experiences in the Past	49
Table 3.3	Idiom Stories ($n = 21$) with No Resolution in Collection of 100 Common Chinese Idioms and Set Phrases	54
Table 4.1	Gifts of Companions in Several Tales, ATU 513, Collected by Multilingual Folktale Database	69
Table 4.2	Specific Features of Collectivism in *Kongjwi and Patjwi* Modified from Cha (1994)	72
Table 6.1	Interesting Topics Included in Cambodian Print Collection (Number of Tales that Mentions Topic)	103
Table 6.2	Functions of Scatology in Published Cambodian Folktales	105
Table 9.1	Types of *Nunchi*	160
Table 9.2	Themes of the *Hare's Liver* Play Script	164

Chapter 1

Introduction

Perspectives on East and Southeast Asian Folktales

Allyssa McCabe and MinJeong Kim

In this Introduction of Perspectives on East and Southeast Asian Folktales, we present a folktale project that gave rise to a number of contributions to this volume, as well as synopses of included chapters. We employ several different perspectives to examine folktales for children from East Asian and Southeast Asian countries.

What is a folktale? There are many efforts to define this term precisely yet comprehensively. Bottigheimer (2004, 270), for example, writes that "The definition of folk tales is more fluid than that of fairy tales and tales about fairies. The term 'folk tale' normally embraces a multitude of minor genres, like nonsense tales . . . jests, burlesques, animal tales and never ending tales." She also notes that they are generally short tales. We generally will use the term *folktale* in this volume, as it is more comprehensive.

Overall, this collection discusses various aspects of Asian language, culture, societal beliefs, and educational processes reflected in folktales with a specific focus on various kinds of narration. Narration is a linguistic meeting ground of culture, cognition, and emotions (McCabe 2017). Folktales—a particularly beloved form of narration—have been honed over countless generations and are, by dint of that fact, accessible and memorable repositories and promoters of cultural values both in terms of their content and form. More importantly, folktales in Asian contexts are not mere artifacts and value systems from the past but also cultural, educational, sociopolitical, and communicative practices that are constantly challenged, negotiated, and reshaped within various sociocultural contexts (Ben-Amos 1993; Zhang 2015). Throughout this volume, we will point out similarities and differences in values and practices among various Asian countries in order to reflect on the richness and complex nature of storytelling within various geographical and sociocultural contexts. In sum, this volume will analyze folktales from China, Japan, Korea, Cambodia, Vietnam, Laos, and Burma. While much has been written about folktales in China, Japan, and Korea, considerably less addresses those from Southeast Asia.

SOUTHEAST ASIAN FOLKTALE PROJECT

Four of the contributions on Southeast Asian folktales are based on a community storytelling project, called simply the Southeast Asian Folktale Project. The editors of this volume, McCabe and Kim, collected oral folktales from Southeast Asian immigrant families from Cambodia, Vietnam, Burma, and Laos in the city of Lowell, Massachusetts, the United States (Kim, McCabe and Uy 2016). These articles examine the forms and the functions of the folktales reflecting on their culture of origin, religion, and developmental perspectives on culture and cognition in narratives, an important form of socialization of children throughout the countries. Some of the contributions explicitly link folktales to pedagogical practices in those countries.

McCabe and Kim have had a long-standing interest in collecting culturally relevant materials for use in various educational contexts, primarily in elementary education. They are aware that bilingual children perform better when they are provided with culturally relevant materials (Goldenberg et al. 2006; Snow 2006). McCabe (1996) argued that *all* children should have their sense of story matched some of the time. Despite the fact that the city in which we teach has a wonderfully diverse population and that we have long searched for stories culturally relevant to that population, we consistently came up virtually empty-handed. Lowell High School students were 30.6% Asian in 2019 (NCES.ed.gov)—well above the typical representation nationally, which in 2017 was determined to be 5% (NCES.ed.gov). Yet despite the population of the schools in our city and despite our long-standing search, we had only a handful of books relevant to Southeast Asians, in particular. The city of Lowell is home to the second-largest population of Cambodian Americans in the United States. The 2010 US Census Bureau estimated that 13,000 Lowell residents are of Cambodian descent, and the total Southeast Asian American (SEA) population, including significant Laotian, Burmese, and Vietnamese populations, in Lowell to be near 50,000.

In 2016, we applied to and were granted money to remedy this problem (Kim, McCabe and Uy 2016). In particular, we conducted two types of interviews with members of the Southeast Asian communities: (1) Focus groups (or what we called *Family Literacy Nights*), and (2) individual interviews with parents and grandparents in those four communities. In four Family Literacy Nights, we met with groups of members of each of the four communities, arranging for food to be served and recording favorite folktales. We audiotaped these tellings, along with translators' versions in English, and took supplemental notes. Audio recordings were subsequently transcribed verbatim and folktales identified. Individual interviews followed a similar process but, of course, were with one or two members of a community instead of larger groups. Interviews took place in situations chosen by each group and included participants' homes and community centers (e.g., The Cambodian Mutual Assistance Association). Table 1.1 shows the results of our interviews.

In collaboration with members of each community, we selected six of the thirty-eight folktales to turn into a book to be given to members of the community, the Lowell Public Schools, and available to anyone anywhere who wishes to purchase one. We mildly edited those stories (e.g., eliminating *ums*). Undergraduate art majors at the University of Massachusetts Lowell illustrated each story under the supervision of a professional illustrator, Anne Sibley O'Brien. Each story was presented both in English and in the language of origin.[1]

Shortly after we received copies of the book, we held a publication party for members of the communities and the University of Massachusetts Lowell community, which was very well attended and a great deal of fun. Members of each community read briefly from a story that they contributed to the illustrated volume—both in the original language and in English. We also held an in-service training session for teachers in the Lowell schools. It was after that session that we determined a need to provide more information to educators interested in using our book and other

Table 1.1 Number of Participants and Number of Folktales

Number	Southeast Asian Immigrant Groups			
	Burmese	Cambodian	Lao	Vietnamese
Participants in focus group	5	7	5	5
Folktales from focus groups	4	5	6	6
Individual interviews	5	6	4	3
Folktales from individual interviews	4	5	5	3
Total folktales	8	10	11	9

folktales from East Asian communities. We decided we needed to provide more information to educators about aspects of those communities, and hence this project began.

While all children should be provided culturally relevant stories, all children also should have their sense of story challenged some of the time by reading stories from cultures other than their own. There is evidence that reading even one story from a culture other than their own significantly reduces racism in children who have been found to be racist (e.g., Katz and Zalk 1978). In a country such as the United States that has seen near-constant racial strife, such a goal is critical.

SUMMARY OF CONTRIBUTIONS TO THIS VOLUME

General Remarks

Asian Folktales Are Distinctive

In the present volume, we compare Asian and Western cultures in order to problematize the use of the Western standard to interpret Asian folktales. For example, in discussing the legacy of the Grimm brothers, Zipes (2015, 4) notes that they deliberately downplayed moralistic and didactic tones in German folktales. This stands in marked contrast to most of the Asian folktales discussed in the present volume. Moral instruction is prominent, explicit, and pervasive in Asian folktales.

Folktales and Asian Aesthetic Values

Another unique feature of this volume is that many of the contributions link aspects of Asian folktales to cognitive practices and aesthetic values of discourse. Socialization of children involves not only moral content but also preferred styles of storytelling—explicit or implicit, resolved or unresolved, elaborative or sparse. Socialization involves implicit instruction in aesthetic preferences regarding desirable numbers (e.g., four is valued in Western folktales and culture but shunned in a number of Asian cultures because the words for death and four are similar). Folktales both embody discourse styles of various cultures and, in turn, help promote them in children and adults alike. For example, Chinese idiom stories often cut off a story at the emotional climax rather than, as many, many Western stories do, go on to say how things worked out in the end. In other words, instead of a resolution, there is an idiom, a moral, a lesson to be learned.

Summaries of Specific Sections and Chapters

Folkloristic Perspective

The folkloristic perspective, like others below, is complex, multifaceted. Zipes (1988) has forcefully argued that folktales should be understood within their historical, social, and political contexts.

In the second contribution, Juwen Zhang addresses the topic "Folktale as Expression of Identity in Cross-cultural Communication: A Folklorist Perspective." Folktales as a genre of folk literature and a major component in folkloristics have been increasingly used by various parties in cross-cultural communication. In this globalizing age, folktales have also revealed their roles beyond the often-discussed basic functions like moral education and entertainment. In our own everyday practice, to understand Asian folktales in the US context is to learn to live a meaningful life within diverse cultures and to seek harmony with differences. This contribution first discusses the general functions of folktales from folkloristic perspectives. It then looks at different uses of folktales based on different ideologies and cultural values and examines some misconceptions with examples of Chinese folktales in the West. Finally, this contribution argues that folktales are not only essential in cross-cultural understanding and tolerance, but they also play a unique role in reconstructing and expressing identities for individuals and groups in multicultural interaction.

Cultural Perspective

Folktales are shaped by many aspects of the cultures that give rise to them and, in turn, play a key role in shaping children as they grow and adapt to their cultures of origin. Two of our chapters foreground key components of Chinese and Southeast Asian culture as these are exemplified in folktales.

In the third chapter, Allyssa McCabe, Fangfang Zhang, and Chien-ju Chang address a particular form of Chinese folktale. As noted, folktales are stories which have been passed down generation by generation through the years in the oral tradition. The authors are unknown, but the stories hold universal truths and timeless appeal and often address and reflect the values of a group of people (Almerico 2014). This contribution examines whether the style of Chinese folktales has some impact on the structure of preschool Chinese children's narrative components and patterns, an endeavor that has not been considered in past research. Zhang, McCabe, Ye, and Wang (2018) found that Chinese children, when narrating personal stories, for the most part do not use narrative resolution (i.e., telling how an emotionally climactic situation concludes). Unlike English-speaking children who do resolve many of their personal narratives at age six (Peterson and McCabe 1983), even at age six, 70% of the Chinese participants do not resolve their narratives. Similar results have emerged from a study of Taiwanese personal stories.

Previous studies show young children's independent narrative skills originate in dialogic contexts between children and competent adults—in many cases their mothers (Fivush 1991; Fivush and Fromhoff 1988; McCabe and Peterson 1991; Reese and Fivush 1993). Miller et al. (1997) observed that Chinese mothers, unlike non-Chinese mothers, had a tendency to emphasize social rules and moral standards when reminiscing with their children.

Until the early twentieth century, Chinese folktales were primarily spread through word of mouth and mainly consisted of a series of events, orientation, evaluation, and reported speech—without dwelling too much or at all on how things worked out in the end, namely the resolution of a story. Chinese folktales are avidly read to children today, and these usually contain metaphorical meanings or moral lessons. Among these, idiom stories are a very common form of story mothers share with their children in China. Each such story explains an idiom, and these are to be memorized by children in school, who often receive extra points when they include them in essays at school. For example, there is one idiom story about a man who dropped his sword in the water while rowing in a river. He marked the side of the boat where the sword had sunk. When the boat reached the shore, the man jumped from the spot he marked into the water to look for his sword. The story ends there with the idiom "to mark the boat to find one's sword," which means trying to solve a problem in an ineffective way. Instead of resolution about whether or not he ever found his sword, then, there is the idiom—the moral of the story. In sum, we argue that Chinese mothers' and educators' greater emphasis on social rules and moral standards in various idiom stories told and read to their children contributes to fewer resolutions in Chinese children's personal narratives.

In the fourth contribution, Juwen Zhang, Allyssa McCabe, Minjeong Kim, and Charlotte Wilinsky address "Collectivism in Asian versus Western Folktales of (Extra)ordinary Companions." One Cambodian folktale we collected (included in the illustrated book), "Why the Rabbit Doesn't Drink from the Pond," describes a race around a pond between a snail and a rabbit to see who has the right to drink from that pond. Faced with this seemingly impossible challenge, the snails organize. They disperse themselves around the pond. Whenever the rabbit calls out to see where the snail is, a snail replies, "Coo, I am here"—ahead of the rabbit. This continues until the rabbit concedes that he has been beaten when a snail calls out from the finish line ahead of him.

What is now known as the Aarne-Thompson-Uther (ATU) Classification System is an index of types of folktales told in Europe and Western Asia used by folklorists since the early twentieth century. The rabbit-and-snails folktale is a variant of the ATU type 513, "The Extraordinary Companions" (Zipes 2015, xiv). This is a type of tale told in many countries around the documented folklore world (Zipes 2015). In the Grimm brothers' tale, "How Six Made their Way in the World," a penniless soldier gathers a strong man who can rip up trees, a sharpshooter who can hit targets miles away, a blower who can rotate windmills miles away, a runner, and a man who can make the air freeze if he takes off his cap. Together, the six outwit and defeat a King and make off with his riches. Most of the ATU type 513 tales involve a similar set of individuals whose special and distinctive talents combine to collectively defeat an evil enemy. Zipes (2015) notes that such collective action in the interests of promoting social justice has perhaps found its contemporary zenith in the wildly popular superhero comic books and movies in American culture.

Our snails, however, differ from the extraordinary companions by virtue of the fact that they are simply ordinary snails, each so much like the others that the rabbit is satisfied they are simply one snail. These identical snails prevail as a group.

Much has been written about the contrast between individualistic societies that value independent selves, like the United States, and collectivist countries, like many Asian countries, that value interdependent selves. This contribution addresses the notion that this may be a somewhat exaggerated contrast, given the Grimm story about "How Six Made their Way in the World" and others like that.

But we also address the fact that there are very real differences in preferences for collectivism and individualism in Eastern versus Western countries, along with concomitant values such as a preference for versus against copying, a topic explored at length by Gish Jen (2017). That is, some Western readers of our snail and rabbit story might see the snails as cheaters; Jen elaborates why that notion represents a very incomplete understanding of collectivist cultures. Finally, we will explore the motif related to collectivism: Little creatures can together achieve great power. That cooperation can triumph over a single individual who has an enormous competitive advantage is a value of many Asian cultures.

Psychological Perspective

Psychologists study the way individuals think, feel, and behave. Psychologists employ quantitative, qualitative, and mixed methods to observe behavior. Two chapters look at two very important aspects of human behavior addressed by folktales, namely violence and hatred.

Violence is prominent in folktales from around the world and continues to provoke strong and varied reactions from those listening to or reading the tales. In the fifth article, Charlotte Wilinsky and Allyssa McCabe present "A Developmental Perspective on Violence in Southeast Asian Folktales." The broad focus of this contribution is to explore the implications of violence in folktales for the development of children. Specifically, this contribution examines violence in Southeast Asian folktales and its implications for the social, emotional, and moral development of children who read/hear those folktales. Violence in folktales, and in media in general, has long been a controversial issue (e.g., Boudinot 2005), triggering concerns about the effect of violence on childhood aggression and antisocial behavior. However, and perhaps paradoxically, violence in folktales is often used as a vehicle through which the protection of children from harm is enacted (e.g., Boudinot 2005). For example, a cautionary folktale may use violence or tragedy to instill fear in children in order to warn them about some danger (Boudinot 2005; Isaacs 2013). Additionally, this violence or evil provides a counterpart to the peaceful or good aspect of the folktale, creating a moral dilemma in the story (Bettelheim 1989). This moral dilemma then encourages children to develop independent judgment (Boudinot 2005) and advance their moral thinking. As these examples show, violence in folktales may have positive functions and effects on development, though these remain understudied in the context of Southeast Asian tales.

Using a developmental framework, this contribution seeks to answer questions regarding the diverse manifestations and uses of violence in Southeast Asian folktales, and their implications for the social, emotional, and moral development of children. The article also documents the applicability of the ATU tale type index to Southeast Asian folktales, which counters an important critique of that index as being Eurocentric (Dundes 1997).

The sixth contribution is entitled "What You Hate Becomes Your Fate: Researcher Reflexivity in Encounters with Southeast Asian Folktales" by Allyssa McCabe and George Chigas. This contribution addresses what is seemingly a striking difference between Eastern and Western folktales: the inclusion of scatological references in folktales from a number of Asian countries. For example, one of the most distinctive and profound folktales to emerge from our project was told in our meeting with elders from the Cambodian community. One man told an elaborate story about a man who was afraid of lawsuits going off to farm in a tree. He slipped one day and was hanging by his hands, calling for help. Another man heard him, a man so afraid of poop that he rode an elephant so as not to encounter it more closely by walking on the ground. He positioned himself under the man who was afraid of lawsuits and grabbed the man by the ankles. Unfortunately, he also startled the elephant who galloped off, leaving the man who was afraid of poop hanging on to the ankles of the man who was afraid of lawsuits. This frightened the man who was afraid of lawsuits so much that he pooped on the man below him. After they were rescued, the man who was afraid of poop sued the man who was afraid of lawsuits.

The narrator explained this tale as, "If you hate something, you will meet that kind of thing." Another member of the Cambodian community extended the conversation with an example from her own life:

> [For a long time I thought] I'll never marry [a tall person]—because I see people married: short person married to tall person, fat people marry skinny people. It's like, "'Why are you married to opposite all like that?' So I told myself as a kid. Guess what my husband is? Six foot eight."

So there we have it: a matter-of-fact reference to what has been a taboo subject of conversation from the first author's American childhood days: poop. While thinking about the profound implications of the folktale itself, the first author squirmed. What is more, this was far from the only story about poop and pee that we collected in our project on tales from Southeast Asia. How were we going to deal with this issue, especially since one of the early goals of our project was to prepare illustrated versions of some of those tales for teachers to use in their classrooms? In fact, in a teacher training session, teachers (primarily from European North American backgrounds) literally dropped the picture of a dog pooping on an alligator's back when they realized what it was.

Unless we educators come to terms with this issue, we will shy away from stories like the above one and other excellent tales. This means that an element of Cambodian culture is not only misunderstood but also censored because it is beyond Western expectation and understanding. And censorship of any culture is not acceptable when you are seeking to understand it.

What to make of the frequent mention of poop in Southeast Asian folktales, then? For one thing, this mention reflected a fact of Cambodian life. When we made inquiries on this topic, one member of the Cambodian community noted that there were no public toilets in Cambodia for many years, so there were poops to be found everywhere. He said that's why it was common in the settings of many old stories. In addition, scatological references serve several different roles in Asian folktales, which we document.

In fact, some of the differences between Eastern and Western folktales may well be the result of the extensive editing of the latter that has taken place over the centuries. Folktale scholars (e.g., Harries 2001; Zipes 2015) have documented how carefully scrubbed of bawdy or scatalogical content Western folktales were in their many iterations in print, a point we will explore in some detail in the present contribution.

Another factor explaining the presence of poop in Southeast Asian folktales is that it has symbolic value. Several members of these communities talked about how it has superstitious value connecting it with wealth, a superstition shared by other Asian cultures (e.g., Korean). This symbolism of poop and wealth is shared in Western cultures as well. While few American or European folktales at present include the explicit mention of poop, not all writers from such backgrounds have been so fastidious. In fact, Freud, in his seminal work, *Interpretation of Dreams* (p. 439), wrote:

> Dreams with an intestinal stimulus throw light in an analogous fashion on the symbols involved in them, and at the same time confirm the connection between gold and faeces which is also also supported by copious evidence from social anthropology.

Freud discusses the symbolic meaning of defecation in dreams throughout that book. In general, then, this contribution will explore the mention of poop as a prime example of the need to be vigilant about and to explore instances of researcher reflexivity:

> A researcher's background and position will affect what they choose to investigate, the angle of investigation, the methods judged most adequate for this purpose, the findings considered most appropriate, and the framing and communication of conclusions. (Malterud 2001, 483–484)

Finally, the contribution explores the symbolic functions of the mention of feces in various Cambodian folktales, systematically exploring these in a multi-volume collection of 244 Cambodian folktales.

Educational Perspective

An educational perspective looks at how folktales are used as educational tools in and out of school to socialize children into using a particular type of narrative style that is valued in their communities. In addition, how educational values are reflected in folktales for children is discussed in this section. In the seventh contribution, Masahiko Minami addresses "Japanese Language Socialization through Folktales." Adults implement their goals for child development in a wide variety of ways. As a result, in addition to basic grammar and vocabulary, children acquire knowledge of the appropriate social use of language beginning in early childhood. In this way, culture-specific patterns of communication play a pivotal role in children's interpretation of how to interact with people around them.

It is well known that the Japanese communication style is intuitive and indirect and that interpersonal communication, at times, relies on intuition, empathy, and feeling. Previous studies (e.g., Minami and McCabe 1991) have demonstrated that the structure of Japanese children's narratives can be understood within the larger context of *omoiyari* (i.e., "empathy") of Japanese children. Empathy training nicely accounts for the production, comprehension, and appreciation of implicit discourse in Japanese society.

Through examination of folktales, this study reveals how children learn an intuitive, indirect style of communication. The study focuses on a story entitled "Gon the Fox," a longtime staple in national-language readers for elementary school children. "Gon the Fox," a famous children's story written by Nan-kichi Niimi, is said to be based on a folktale from the author's hometown, but Niimi's additions altered the content to make it more of a story of apology, which nicely fits adults' expectations of how Japanese children should behave, and how their language and social development should proceed.

Tham Tran and MinJeong Kim address "Educational Implications of Buddhist Values in Vietnamese Folktales" in the eighth contribution. Folktales have long been recognized as a source of learning (Hanlon 2000) and a means of transmitting moral values from generation to generation (Leimgruber 2010). Folktales also depict the cultural and social values of the countries that they come from (Shaŵa and Soko 2013; Hourani 2015). Through the diffusion of approved values, folktales modify behaviors and promote proper and beautiful mindsets (Hourani 2015). While significant secular values of folktales have been explored through many research studies, research on spiritual values in folktales is still limited. Southeast Asian folktales analyzed in this contribution were collected in interviews with adult Southeast Asian immigrants in the project mentioned above. Social semiotic and symbolic aspects are used to pinpoint Buddhist values ingrained in the folklore of Vietnam (though they could also apply to folktales from other Asian and Southeast Asian nations).

With a long and profound influence of Buddhism since the early centuries AD on Southeast Asian culture, folktales from these countries also reflect the spiritual values of Buddhist teachings. Two basic principles in Buddhism include Interdependent Co-arising and karma. These are depicted in many of these folktales as a means of teaching people to avoid doing evil things and to encourage them to do good deeds and nourish compassion and loving-kindness in order to attain a good life with peace and happiness in the present and future. These Buddhist principles are also used to express the culture's wishes of justice and equality in the face of injustice and evil forces. Evil characters with bad qualities (such as being greedy, harsh, or unsympathetic) usually end up with adverse consequences because of their evils. In contrast, righteous characters, who are usually poor and/or orphaned and possess good qualities (such as being kind, hard-working, diligent, honest, helpful), usually attain happy and successful endings at the end of the story. The law of cause and effect in Interdependent Co-arising is evident in most Southeast

Asian folktales. According to this concept, everything is a result of multiple causes and conditions (Thich Nhat Hanh 1998). One thing to note is that the effect of wholesome or evil conduct is indicated immediately in each folktale so that people can witness it. Readers can see that the folk authors want to affirm strongly and transparently the law of cause and effect as a proposition, thereby encouraging the improvement of personality and human morality.

Karma, according to Mackenzie (2013), is a semantically complex and contextually fluid notion. Karma can be comprehended in quite different ways depending upon the context. According to Buddhism, everything is impermanent, so characters in folktales also move along with that law; good or evil has its results as a definite proposition. While Western folktales also contrast good and evil, and usually portray good triumphing over evil, the influence of Buddhism lends a distinct flavor to Southeast Asian folktales. This contrast is explored in some detail.

MinJeong Kim and Minyoung Kim address "Learning *Nunchi*: Folktales as Tools to Teach Emotional Competence in Literacy Learning in Korea" in the ninth chapter. As textbooks provide milestones not only for teaching and learning of content knowledge but also for acquisition of cultural values and societal norms practiced by the members of the society (Curdt-Christiansen 2017), Kim and Kim view textbooks as one of the important resources and a medium for cognitive, cultural, and emotional socialization. They examine, in the chapter, the third-grade Korean Language Arts textbook in order to see how children's folktales are used as tools for emotional socialization. The *Tale of Hare's Liver* in the textbook is not the original version of the tale. It has been completely dramatized and reconstructed as a play script to be included as mentor text to meet the goal of the unit titled "Understanding Characters' Emotions." The unit of "Understanding Emotions" is one of the five major units in the textbook to achieve the Korean Language Arts standards of the national curriculum. This is a culturally distinctive feature of the Korean national Language Arts curriculum; the US English Language Arts standards (e.g., Common Core Standards suggested by the Massachusetts Department of Elementary and Secondary Education) mainly suggest that teachers teach cognitive and structural aspects of narrative texts (e.g., retelling of beginning, middle, and end in proper order).

Kim and Kim analyze the way that the *Tale of Hare's Liver*, in the form of a play script in the textbook, is presented and types of comprehension questions asked about the tale to teach children *nunchi* as a form of emotional competence. In its literal meaning, *Nunchi* is "eye-measure" or "sense of eye" that captures what's hidden between the lines of the uttered words by observing and feeling the air of the scene without explicit verbal and nonverbal cues. *Nunchi* is considered as a major determinant for successful communication with others (Kim 2003) in Korea and is particularly valued as a communicative skill in collectivistic societies such as Korea, Japan, and China where there is more emphasis on interpersonal communication and group harmony than on individuals' self-expression and problem solving.

Kim and Kim specifically analyzed two key aspects of how the folktale the *Tale of Hare's Liver* was presented as mentor text in the textbook. First, they analyzed the content and structure of the play script (e.g., the main plot of each scene and stage directions), focusing on the emotional and symbolic aspects of the main characters' behaviors to resolve the main problem associated with the Dragon King's illness (e.g., obtaining the hare's liver as a cure). Second, along with the analysis of the characters' behaviors related to *nunchi*, they analyze the prompts and questions for comprehension following the play script for children to discuss. Kim and Kim found that *nunchi* presented in the textbook was similar to "empathy" and "other-centered" concepts, but went beyond those concepts. For example, in addition to the simple definition of *nunchi* as the ability to understand others' feelings, desires, and intentions, *nunchi* requires the interlocutor to have an understanding of the social position and emotions of the self. Furthermore, it requires not only an understanding of the other person's emotional status but also behaving properly based on such an understanding. Thus, in the textbook, *nunchi* is embedded in the mentor text as a multilayered and multifaceted concept that is highly context-dependent and key to discussing the discussion prompts. Given the nature of *nunchi* and emotional competence presented in the mentor text, Korean third graders are asked to acquire the competence to successfully infer interpersonal relationships among the characters in the text, intercontextual and intertextual cues. In short, intersubjectivity and intercontextuality are central to emotional socialization through folktales in Korea.

CONCLUSION

In short, many of the contributions to this volume on Eastern and Southeast Asian folktales exemplify Emile Durkheim's (2002, 64) famous dictum that "We are moral beings to the extent that we are social beings." In this respect, for all their cultural specificity and uniqueness and differences from their Western counterparts, Eastern and Southeast Asian folktales show key similarities with cultures everywhere: they seek to instill morality in listeners at the same time as they socialize them into a particular culture. Similarities and differences between any entities are the inevitable two sides of the same coin. One cannot notice one without noticing the other.

NOTE

1. The book *A Long Long Time Ago in Southeast Asia* is available at: umlseada .omeka.net/items/show/1241.

REFERENCES

Almerico, G. M. 2014. "Building Character through Literacy with Children's Literature." *Research in Higher Education Journal*, 26, 1–13.

Ben-Amos, Dan. 1993. "'Context' in Context." *Western Folklore*, 52, 209–226.

Bettelheim, Bruno. 1975. *The Uses of Enchantment*. New York: Vintage.

Bottigheimer, Ruth B. 2004. "Fairy Tales and Folk Tales." In Peter Hunt (Ed.), *International Companion Encyclopedia of Children's Literature* (pp. 261–274). Routledge.

Boudinot, David. 2005. "Violence and Fear in Folktales." *Looking Glass: New Perspectives on Children's Literature*, 9(3).

Dundes, Alan. 1997. "The Motif-Index and the Tale Type Index: A Critique." *Journal of Folklore Research*, 34, 3.

Durkheim, Emile. 2002. *Moral Education*. Translated by Everett K. Wilson and Herman Schnurer. Mineola, NY: Dover.

Fivush, Robyn. 1991. "The Social Construction of Personal Narratives." *Merrill-Palmer Quarterly*, 37(1), 57–81.

Fivush, Robyn and Fayne A. Fromhoff. 1988. "Style and Structure in Mother-Child Conversations about the Past." *Discourse Processes*, 11(3), 337–355.

Golden, Joanne M. 1990. *The Narrative Symbol in Childhood Literature: Explorations in the Construction of Text*. New York: Mouton de Gruyter.

Goldenberg, Claude, Robert S. Rueda, and Diane August. 2006. "Sociocultural Influences on the Literacy Development." In Diane August and Timothy Shanhan (Eds.), *Developing Literacy in Second Language Learners* (pp. 269–318). Mahwah, NJ: Erlbaum.

Hanlon, T. 2000. *General Guidelines for Teaching with Folktales, Fables, Ballads and other Short Works of Folklore*. Virginia, USA: Ferrum College.

Harries, Elizabeth. 2001. Tw*ice Upon a Time*. Princeton: Princeton University Press.

Hourani, R. B. 2015. "Folktales, Children's Literature and National Identity in the United Arab Emirates." *Looking Glass: New Perspectives on Children's Literature*, 18(1).

Isaacs, David. 2013. "Sex and Violence in Fairy Tales." *Journal of Paediatrics and Child Health*, 49(12), 987–988.

Jen, Gish. 2017. *The Girl at the Baggage Claim: Explaining the East-West Culture Gap*. New York: Knopf.

Katz, Phyllis A., and Sue R. Zalk. 1978. "Modification of Children's Racial Attitudes." *Developmental Psychology*, 14(5), 447–461. doi.org/10.1037/0012-1649 .14.5.447.

Leimgruber, Walter. 2010. "Switzerland and the UNESCO Convention on Intangible Cultural Heritage." *Journal of Folklore Research*, 47(1–2), 161–196.

MacKenzie, M. 2013. "Enacting Selves, Enacting Worlds: On the Buddhist Theory of Karma." *Philosophy East and West*, 63(2), 194.

Malterude, Kirsti. 2001. "Qualitative Research: Standards, Challenges, and Guidelines." *The Lancet*, 358, 483–488.

McCabe, Allyssa. 1996. *Chameleon Readers: Teaching Children to Appreciate All Kinds of Good Stories*. New York: McGraw-Hill.

McCabe, Allyssa. 2017. "Children's Personal Narratives Reflect Where They Come From, Reveal Who They Are, and Predict Where They Are Going." In Natalia Kucirkova, Catherine E. Snow, Vibeke Grover, and Catherine McBride (Eds.), *Routledge International Handbook Series* (pp. 308–324). Routledge: London.

McCabe, Allyssa, and Carole Peterson. 1991. "Getting the Story: A Longitudinal Study of Parental Styles in Eliciting Narratives and Developing Narrative Skills." In A. McCabe and C. Peterson (Eds.), *Developing Narrative Structure* (pp. 217–253). Hillsdale, NJ: Lawrence Erlbaum Associates.

Miller, Peggy J., Angela R. Wiley, Heidi Fung, and Chung Hui Liang. 1997. "Personal Storytelling as a Medium of Socialization in Chinese and American Families." *Child Development*, 68(3), 557–568.

MinJeong, Kim, Phitsamay Uy, and Allyssa McCabe. 2016. *Reviving the Forgotten Tales of Childhood: Turning Narratives of Southeast Asian Families into Children's Multicultural Literature*. UMass President's Office 2016 Creative Economy Initiatives Fund.

National Center for Education Statistics (NCES). https://nces.ed.gov/.

Peterson, Carole, and Allyssa McCabe. 1983. *Developmental Psycholinguistics: Three Ways of Looking at a Child's Narrative*. New York: Plenum.

Reese, Elaine, and Robyn Fivush. 1993. "Parental Styles of Talking about the Past." *Developmental Psychology*, 29(3), 596–606.

Shaŵa, Lester B., and Boston Jaston Soko. 2013. *Tumbuka Folktales: Moral and Didactic Lessons from Malaŵi*. Mzuzu: Mzuni Publications.

Snow, Catherine. 2006. "Cross-cutting Themes and Future Research Directions." In Diane August and Timothy Shanhan (Eds.), *Developing Literacy in Second Language Learners* (pp. 631–651). Mahwah, NJ: Erlbaum.

Suzuki, Daisetsu T. 2017. *An Introduction to Zen Buddhism*. New York: Grove Press.

Thich, Nhat Hanh. 1998. *The Heart of the Buddha's Teachings*. Broadway Books: New York.

Uther, Hans-Jorg. 2004. *The Types of International Folktales: A Classification and Bibliography, Based on the System of Antti Aarne and Stith Thompson*. Helsinki: Suomalainen Tiedeakatemia, Academia Scientiarum Fennica (OF Communications).

Zhang, Fangfang, Allyssa McCabe, Jiaqui Ye, Yan Wang, and Xiaoyan Li. 2019. "A Developmental Study of the Narrative Components and Patterns of Chinese Children Aged Three to Six Years." *Journal of Psycholinguistic Research*, 48, 477–500. press. doi.org/10.1007/s10936-018-9614-3.

Zhang, Juwen. 2015. "Chinese American Culture in the Making: Perspectives and Reflections on Diasporic Folklore and Identity." *Journal of American Folklore*, 128(510), 449–475.

Zipes, Jack. 1988. *The Brothers Grimm*. Routledge.

Zipes, Jack. 2015. *The Oxford Companion to Fairy Tales, 2nd ed*. Oxford University Press.

FOLKLORISTIC PERSPECTIVE

Chapter 2

Folk and Fairy Tales as Expressions of Identity in Cross-Cultural Communication

A Folkloristic Perspective

Juwen Zhang

In this globalizing age, folktales have also revealed new roles in reconstructing and maintaining identity in cross-cultural communication, beyond the often-discussed basic functions like moral education and entertainment in a relatively stable society. In our own everyday practice, to understand Asian folktales in the US context is to seek harmony with differences and to live a meaningful life within the diverse cultures. As our societies develop, folktales also change in their symbolic meanings to reflect social changes. Subsequently, storytelling has become ever more popular and meaningful in our daily artistic communication through various new forms of media. Therefore, our perspectives toward folktales must also be dynamic to grasp these changes.

In folkloristic studies, folktales are a genre of folk or oral literature and constitute an important research area in the discipline. Through a folkloristic perspective, this chapter first discusses the aspects of folktales (used here to mean folk and fairy tales in a broad sense) as ways of communication. Then it looks at contexts, namely, various uses of folktales based on different ideologies and cultural values, with examples of how Chinese folktales were introduced in the West. Finally, this chapter argues that folktales, along with other folklore forms, are essential not only in understanding and tolerating different cultures, but also in reconstructing, maintaining, and expressing our own identities at individual, group, and national levels. Although the term "Asia" is used in this discussion, it mostly refers to "East Asia" where a culture-circle has been historically informed based on the common Confucian ethics and family-centered cultural values, as well as various Buddhist and other religious and philosophical ideas and practices, which are all expressed through folktales. Consequently, when "Asian American" is used, it is to be understood that there is great cultural connection as well as diversity, for example, among and within the Asian American groups.[1]

FOLKTALES AS WAYS OF COMMUNICATION

Function

The use of folktale has been a central question for folkloristic studies. Influenced by the structural-functionalist ideas in early anthropology represented by Radcliffe-Brown (1935) and Malinowski (1939), William Bascom (1954) once summarized four functions of folklore in a culture: (1) to escape from repressions imposed upon them by society; (2) to validate culture and justify its rituals and institutions; (3) as a pedagogic device, reinforcing morals and values; (4) as a means of applying social pressure and exercising social control. However, this particular approach, although influential to folkloristics, tends to explain or interpret a society/culture from a static view and lacks the capability to explain the dynamic changes within a society, as the folklorist Elliott Oring (1976) criticizes. While the ideas about the function of folklore in general can certainly be applied to the use of folktale in particular, cautions are necessary in explaining versus interpreting a folktale or a folklore practice, and in understanding an insider's view versus an outsider's view, particularly in a cross-cultural context.

Today, as we experience the increasingly globalized interactions in our own lives on a daily basis, we find that the use of folktale can be understood from broader and more dynamic cross-disciplinary perspectives. At the very least, the following aspects can be considered in addition to the aforementioned traditional views:

1. Maintaining one's group identity through folktales, among other oral and material folklore forms like myths and foodways, in order to enhance the sense of one's origin and history;
2. Maintaining personal and group/regional identity in relation to their national identity (within a multiethnic state) and their shared folkloric identity through everyday practices (e.g., common folklore practices like table manners or etiquettes, food, tales, and jokes) in order to enforce moral ethics and cultural values;

3. Transmitting and educating certain cultural or religious values by coordinating the relations between material life and spiritual life, and by maintaining one's own tradition while adopting cultural elements from other cultures;

4. Mitigating social conflicts, tensions, and pressure in everyday practice, whether it is at home, at work, in school, or in other circumstances;

5. Adjusting or healing personal and social psychological or mental afflictions by providing channels for releasing the pressure or stress, and escaping from a real material world of disparity to an imagined world of hope by such means as tales or jokes;

6. Bridging cross-cultural communication and paving the road for the formation of new cultures, most obviously seen through the formation and development of diasporic cultures in the United States. For example, fortune-cookies lore, which originated from Chinese American restaurants in the late twentieth century with various "legends" or "folktales" and was similar to the chop-suey lore informed in the late nineteenth century (both in California as symbols of the new Chinese American cultural identity emerged from cross-cultural interactions in certain historical periods), has become a symbolic means and a practical expression of the Chinese American identity, and a folkloric identity for all those who share the tales and jokes (e.g., the ways of reading the fortune—adding "in bed" to the end of the printed omens), while eating and talking together, in reconstructing their own personal identity.

Genre

In studying folklore, the first step is to identify the categorization or classification of the various forms. Genre is often used as an analytical system to categorize different folklore forms such as folktale, proverb, and joke. Within the genre of folktale, for example, different types of tales like fairy tales, tall tales, and other forms of oral narratives can be referred to as "subgenres."

This methodological approach has its Eurocentric origin in nineteenth-century Europe. Clearly, the concept about a particular genre or sub-genre is only meaningful to its own cultural practitioners, and different cultures have different concepts or terms about their categorizations. What is called "myth" or "legend" in one culture may well be believed as "history" or "experience" in another. As a result, for example, all attempts to define "fairy tale" as a universal genre have been "irrelevant" (Ben-Amos 1971, 4) and "failed" (Zipes 2011, 222). It was not until the late 1960s when the folklorist Dan Ben-Amos (1969) reflexively developed the concept of "ethnic genre" to recognize this reality. Consequently, the concept led to a paradigmatic shift in studying folktales or oral narratives in particular, and folklore in general. This idea has also let folklorists be aware of the difference between analytical categorization and practical conceptualization of local genres and, furthermore, move away from the colonialistic imposition of Eurocentric values upon interpreting folktales from other value systems (Zhang 2020a). Thereafter, folklorists began to pay attention not only to the context of a particular storytelling event (e.g., text-performer-audience) but also the broad social and historical context (Ben-Amos 1993), or "context of situation" and "context of culture" (Malinowski 1946 [1923], 307; 1965 [1935], 18). Furthermore, largely due to this idea, the performance-centered approach has been developed to study storytelling or verbal arts as performance (Bauman and Babcock 1977), which is valuable in understanding the role of folktales or oral narratives in the making of identity through oral communication.

Tale-type

The next step, particularly in folktale study, is to identify the tale-type of folktales. According to Stith Thompson (1977), a tale-type is "a traditional tale that has an independent existence. It may be told as a complete narrative and does not depend for its meaning on any other tale. It may indeed happen to be told with another tale, but the fact that it may be told alone attests to its independence. It may consist of only one motif or of many" (415).

The current Aarne-Thompson-Uther (ATU) Index (Uther 2004) is based on the cumulative efforts of the Finnish folklorist Antti Aarne (1867–1925) and American folklorist Stith Thompson (1885–1976), known as the AT Index (Aarne 1961). The AT system contains about 2500 basic plots of tales representative of Europe and Indo-European regions. The updated ATU system has more than 250 new types and subtypes. It is a step forward, though it still lacks the inclusion of tales from other places like Africa and Asia. For this reason, scholars from some specific cultures have published tale-type indexes (sometimes including motif), mostly based on the AT system, to supplement studies of the folktales from their own cultures. For example, about Chinese tale-type, there are indexes by Eberhard (1937a), Ting (1978), Qi (2007), and Jin (2007); about Japanese tale-type, Seki (1966), Ikeda (1971), and Kobayashi (2015); about Korean tale-type, Choi (1979); about Arabic tale-type, El-Shamy (2006) and Gary and El-Shamy (2005).

The ATU Index system is structured to contain such categories with designated numbers and letters as:

Animal tales (1–299)
Tales of magic (300–749)
Religious tales (750–849)

Realistic tales (novelle) (850–999)
Tales of the stupid ogre (giant, devil) (1000–1199)
Anecdotes and jokes (1200–1999)
Formula tales (2000–2399)
Unclassified tales (2400–2499) (Uther 2004)[2]

Thus, within the ATU Index system, some well-known tales are labeled as Rapunzel (310); Hansel and Gretel (327A); The Three Hairs of the Devil (461); The Fisherman and his Wife (555); Little Snow-White (709); The Little Peasant (1535); The Emperor's New Clothes (1620). The tale of Cinderella is identified as 510A, containing such motifs as [S31, L55] a young woman is mistreated by her stepmother and stepsisters; [B450] she accomplishes an impossible task with the help of birds; [D1050.1, N815] she obtains beautiful clothing from a supernatural being, or [D815.1, D842.1, E323.2] a tree that grows on the grave of her deceased mother. With this system, researchers can scrutinize the historical and geographical changes of a tale, particularly through the migration of folktales.

Another important analytical approach to folktales through identifying the structure or tale-type is the theory developed by the Russian folklorist Vladimir Propp (1895–1970). His *Morphology of the Tale*, first published in 1928, was not known to the rest of the world until it was translated into English in 1958, and many other languages thereafter. In fact, there has been a general misunderstanding caused by the English translation that Propp's model on what he defined "fairy tales" was taken as a model for all "folktales." Propp is seen as "the first theoretician of folklore who realized that textual analysis should start with setting up strict procedures of segmentation" (Dundes 1976, 87–88; Liberman 1984, xxviii). Therefore, in studying folktales, particularly fairytales or wonder tales, he articulated a set of 31 key elements, or motifs, that he called "functions" in the structural composition of a typical tale, such as:

> 1. Absentation; 2. Interdiction; 3. Violation of interdiction; 4. Reconnaissance; 5. Delivery; 6. Trickery; 7. Complicity; 8. Villainy or lacking; 9. Mediation; 10. Beginning counteraction; 11. Departure; 12. First function of the donor; 13. Hero's reaction; 14. Receipt of a magical agent; 15. Guidance; 16. Struggle; 17. Branding; 18. Victory; 19. Liquidation; 20. Return; 21. Pursuit; 22. Rescue; 23. Unrecognized arrival; 24. Unfounded claims; 25. Difficult task; 26. Solution; 27. Recognition; 28. Exposure; 29. Transfiguration; 30. Punishment; 31. Wedding. (Propp 1968)

Out of the 31 functions (or, key elements in tales), Propp also concluded that there were typically 7 characters in a tale, such as the villain, the dispatcher, the helper, the princess or prize, the donor, the hero, and the false hero. Today, however, Propp's fairy-tale model has been well recognized and applied by scholars of fairy tales all over the world (e.g., *The Morphology of Folktale* was published in Italian translation *Morfologia della fiaba* in 1966, in French translation *Morphologie du conte* in 1970, in Spanish translation *Morfología del cuento* in 1998, and in Chinese translation in 2006).

Motif

The study of tale-type is inseparable from the study of motif, and thus the latter is the necessary third step in studying folktales. A motif is "the smallest element in a tale having a power to persist in tradition. In order to have this power it must have something unusual and striking about it" (Thompson 1977, 415). While this definition is generally accepted in folk narrative studies, it has also received criticism. One particular argument by Ben-Amos (1995) is that "in folklore there are no motifs but symbols" because, as he proposes, "the shift from motifs to symbols involves not merely a terminological substitution but a more comprehensive turn in scholarly inquiry" (81). His conclusion is to suggest that in folktales studies, it is the cultural symbols, but not the formalistic motifs, that constitute and sustain the meaning of a tale so that it embodies and transmits the cultural values of the culture. This argument is significant and sheds light upon our studies of folktales in cross-cultural contexts; that is, even though we may still use the term "motif," we should understand it as "symbol" from cultural perspectives (Zhang 2019b).

In this structural approach, Thompson's six-volume *Motif-Index of Folk Literature* (1955–1958) has served as the most fundamental tool in studying folktales. The subtitle of this index is: *A Classification of Narrative Elements in Folktale, Ballads, Myths, Fables, Medieval Romances, Exempla, Fabliaux,* which suggests that folktales are inseparable from other subgenres of oral narratives in terms of understanding the "smallest element" in their formation.

Thompson's *Motif-Index* is structured with letters from A to Z, under which each letter is further divided with numbers for more subcategories, for example,

A: Mythological Motif
  A0-A99: Creator
  A100-A199: Gods
  A200-A299: Gods of the upper world
  A300-A300: Gods of the underworld
  A400-A499: Gods of the earth
B0-B99: Mythical animals
C0-C99: Tabu connected with supernatural beings

D0-D699: Magic: transformation

E0-E199: The Dead: resuscitation

F0-F199: Marvels: otherworld journeys

G10-G399: Ogres: Kinds of Ogres

H0-H199: Tests: identity tests: recognition

J0-J199: The Wise and the Foolish: acquisition and possession of wisdom (knowledge)

K100-K299: Deceptions: deceptive bargains

L0-L99: Reversal of Fortune: victorious youngest child

M. Ordaining the Future

N. Chance and Fate

P. Society

Q. Rewards and Punishments

R. Captives and Fugitives

S. Unnatural Cruelty

T. Sex

U. The Nature of Life

V. Religion

W. Traits of Character

X. Humor

Z. Miscellaneous Groups of Motifs (Thompson 1955–1958)[3]

Identity

As seen in the above-mentioned approaches, the functionalist idea would lead to a negligence of the social and cultural dynamism within a society, and the structuralist idea tends to isolate folktales from their broad social and cultural contexts. By integrating different approaches, it is helpful to connect a tale's *content, structure,* and *purpose* as a necessary "tripod" in the context of storytelling as an *event* in understanding folktales. Therefore, the ultimate goal of a methodology for studying folktales should be understanding the mechanism with which the tales and the telling of these tales help construct and reconstruct the identities of the practitioners and their groups. After all, the awareness of identity is what makes one's life meaningful, and "the concept of identity has always been central in folklore studies" (Oring 1994, 226). Further, as Wilson (1988) argues, folklore studies are "at the very center of humanistic study" (158).

Identity in folklore studies can be seen from at least these three levels: personal (individual); group (collective); and national. Personal identity is inseparable from its group identity. Group identity is often used to draw boundaries with such concepts as ethnicity or ethnic identity and cultural identity. However, what fundamentally informs a group is its shared folklore, that is, common lifestyle, beliefs, and values that are most often sustained and continued through storytelling or other forms of oral communication. The essence of such practices within a group constitutes its folkloric identity which is essential for living a meaningful life for the individuals within a group (Zhang 2015, 2020b).

The study of a folktale often begins with structural or textual analyses, then extends to broad contextual studies of the storytelling event in relation to its broad historical, social and cultural context, and finally ends at the understanding of the process of how a tale and its storytelling plays a role in reconstructing and maintaining identities for the storyteller and the audience. In this sense, folktales studies are to "make sense of nonsense" (Dundes 2002, 137) in everyday communication. Folktales, whether in form or in content, are representative of all genres of folklore. While folklore is defined to be "artistic communication in small groups" (Ben-Amos 1971, 13), the meaningful question about how to understand such traditional face-to-face small groups in today's digital or Internet age is a challenge we cannot shun away.

FOLKTALES IN DIFFERENT CONTEXTS

Context

The idea of context, as mentioned above in relation to the ideas of "context of situation" and "context of culture" (Malinowski 1946, 1965) and "'context' in context" (Ben-Amos 1993) can be understood at several levels, and each contains different content and meaning, and serves different purposes:

1. The context of generating the (written) text of a tale: it is about how an oral tale is collected, recorded, edited, printed, and translated. Today, the changing social context also requires us to find proper ways to deal with various new forms of texts like musical notations, digital images, and other nonverbal signs, to seek new methods and attitudes in collecting texts through fieldwork (Schoemaker 1990), and to examine new media forms like the popular films "*Mu Lan*" (1998) and "*Kung Fu Panda*" (2008). As the text is generated, its categorization has much to do with the researcher's ideological and methodological orientation, as seen in the studies of genre and motif.

2. The context of performing the text (i.e., storytelling event) within its group: It looks at the interaction and relationship among the storyteller, the tale (content), and the audience. In such an event, the texture (e.g., how the time and place affect the storyteller and audience, how the

storyteller changes his/her tones or gestures) should not be ignored (Dundes 1964; Bauman and Babcock 1977; Jason 1997).

3. The context of storytelling in cross-cultural milieu: It relates to the questions about how an insider or an outsider of a culture tells a tale from within or outside of that person's own cultural group, and, specifically, what tales (i.e., text) are chosen and how (i.e., context) they are told. It also deals with the concepts of explanation and interpretation from different ideological or disciplinary perspectives. At this level, folktales are represented or retold in various forms or means, but always express the storyteller's and interpreter's worldview and cultural values.

4. The context of studying the text with certain goals: It deals with the fundamental question of "so-what?" in both telling/using and studying a tale, particularly in cross-cultural context. For example, folktales in Asian societies versus in Asian American communities play different roles in the construction of identity, and thus require different methodological approaches.

Uses of Folktales in the East and the West

The uses of folktales in the Eastern (mostly in East Asia in this discussion) and the Western (Europe and the United States) cultural traditions are matters not only related to storytellers and audiences but also to the researchers (including translators and teachers) who, with certain cultural attitudes and purposes, interpret folktales through a different language to a different public. In this regard, at least these methodological and ideological aspects should be considered in using Asian folktales:

1. Structural studies by means of comparing such components as motif, tale-type, and genre: As discussed above, the previous Eurocentric theoretical framework in classifying motif, tale-type, and genre, has been corrected by some cultural-based classifications and new concepts. There is certainly a long way to go to establish an equal discourse on Asian folktales between Asians and Westerners. The power of language, English in this case, is a self-evident example in representing other cultures. The fact that there is no such a thing as a common "genre" or "folktale" requires the researcher to first understand the local or native concepts about those narratives and the embedded beliefs and values before conducting comparative structural studies or interpretations. For example, when a Chinese tale is told in its native group by its insiders, it functions in certain ways. But when it is told in a different regional, cultural, linguistic, or religious group, it would certainly bear different meanings to the receivers, not to mention issues of textural translation.

2. The beliefs and cultural values hidden in the tales: A folktale is created to express and enforce a certain cosmology, belief, and lifestyle, while serving to reconstruct the group identity. Although there are structural similarities among folktales world-wide, each tale carries its own distinctive historical, cultural, linguistic, and social messages or metaphors. This fact remains true when tales are adapted to films or other artistic forms. The popularity or commercial success of the films of *"Mu Lan"* and *"Kung Fu Panda"* in the United States versus their criticism or less-popular acceptance in China is an example of different uses of folktales in different contexts and different messages for different audiences. While *Mu Lan* is often discussed from modern social and gender perspectives in the United States, the tale is continued in China largely due to its (hidden, implicit) traditional values about filiality (children's respect to parents) and patriotic loyalty, in accordance with Confucian familial ethics. By the same token, the commercial success of films like *Kung Fu Panda* in China shows that it is mostly due to the artistic presentation and the impact of American culture (spread through Disney and Hollywood alike) itself, rather than any cultural interpretation of the social and family values expressed in the tale.

3. Translation and its uses: The continuity of a tale, particularly in cross-cultural context, has much to do with translation and its uses. Two inseparable aspects must be considered: One is about semantic or linguistic issues, which affect the readability or popularity of a tale; the other is about the ideological stand of the translator and the users (or re-tellers) of the tale. While each folktale has its cultural identity, so does the translator or the user. A choice of word is often beyond the consideration of semantic equivalency, and the choice of using one tale over another is always determined by the purpose of the user with a certain ideological agenda.

At the translation level, the translator's age, gender, intellectual interest, personality, linguistic competence, religious belief, and social status, among others, determine to what extent the values of a tale, or its cultural identity, can be conveyed to the reader. At the user level, what translated tales or versions are chosen for what audience reveals the user's purposes, and thus inevitably demonstrates the user's identity and attitude toward the *other*, as seen in the examples mentioned below.

1. Exploring the representation and interpretation of tales within and beyond their cultural backgrounds in order to think through the "so-what" question. Given the fact that the discourse on folktales has historically been based on Eurocentric theories and methods, and that

the targets of studies are mostly European tales or the selected tales from other cultures that are translated into English (often by non-local scholars), it is essential to be reflexive in today's folktale studies. For this purpose, this author insists that a culture-centered holistic approach may be necessarily useful (further discussion below). Otherwise, misconceptions or misled understandings could even enhance existing (negative) stereotypes, as seen in the following examples from the studies and translations of Chinese folktales in the West, which should be perceived in a historical perspective as such, with a number of successive stages:

Stage One of the developmental history of recording and translating folktales includes a period from remote ancient times until the sixteenth century. This period is marked by limited records by adventurers, religious ministers, and traveling merchants, often related to the exploration along the Silk Road which began more than two thousand years ago and connected China with Central Asia and Europe. For example, a number of European translations of *The Travels of Marco Polo* since the fourteenth century have continuously stirred up European curiosity toward China and Chinese folktales.

Stage Two is marked by numerous missionary works from the sixteenth century to the late nineteenth century in China, when many Chinese folktales were translated into Western languages. Those translations have shaped the image of the Chinese people and culture to the West, and are still responsible for the stereotype against the Chinese known to the public today: for example, *Some Chinese Ghosts* (Hearn 1887), *The Chinese Boy and Girl* (Headland 1901), *Chinese Fairy Stories* (Pitman 1910), *Chinese Fairy Tales* (Giles 1911), *Chinese Fairy Tales: Forty Stories Told by Almond-Eyed Folk* (Fielde 1912), *Gleanings from Chinese Folklore* (Russell 1915), *A Chinese Wonder Book* (Pitman 1919), and *The Chinese Fairy Book* (Wilhelm 1921).

The problems with these translations were obvious almost from their inception. Even in the early twentieth century, scholars in China were aware of the fact that the tales were mostly taken from classic texts without acknowledgment of the oral element of presentation; there was no clear distinction between folktales, fairy tales, myths, and legends, and no identification of regional differences (given the diversity in China); and the "Chinese elements" were generalized by even adopting Western plots to tell "Chinese" stories (Li 2018, 34–35). However, these books have been reprinted and are still widely read today. One conclusion can be drawn from this reality: there is a great need for more Asian folktales, old and new, to be translated, along with comprehensive contextual information, because Asia is more and more important in world affairs, and Asia can be better understood through its folktales.

One example of how even a word can bear an important historical message is seen in a translation about Chinese folklore by a British colonial official in Hong Kong for the British journal of *Folk-Lore* in 1890, in which the term *coolies* was freely used to refer to the worker or peasant in a folktale (Lockhart 1890, 363). Although the translator was not a missionary and had a good master of the local language/dialect, he inevitably carried the historical notion of *coolie*, a derogatory and discriminatory term widely used in the United States at the peak of the anti-Chinese movement that resulted in the Chinese Exclusion Act (1882–1965).

Clearly, the stereotypes shaped in the West toward the "inferior" East (or the *other*) during the colonial period had much to do with folktales translated into European languages. Similarly, ethnological and anthropological works were also used to justify European colonialistic and imperialistic movements. The impact of colonialism in the colonizing countries, as well as the colonized countries, is doubtless continuing, a phenomenon of "the coloniality of folklore" (Briggs and Naithani 2012) that reflects the unconscious habitual actions of the native groups with an effort to accord with colonial ideology. Thus the readers and researchers of the new generations must be alert to the environment in which their attitudes and values take shape.

Stage Three began with academic studies of Chinese/Asian folktales in the early twentieth century. The folklorist Richard Dorson (1965) once pointed out that "Earlier purveyors of purportedly Chinese folktales to Western audiences either had translated art stories which differed considerably in style and purpose from the true folktale or had Europeanized the Chinese texts," but "a landmark in the history of Chinese folktale studies" (xxix) was Wolfram Eberhard, who was "the one Western scholar who has made the oral Chinese folktale his specialty" (xxviii).

Wolfram Eberhard (1909–1989) played an important role in introducing Chinese folk and fairy tales to the West, though he was certainly not the first one to do so. In fact, before Eberhard published his translations of *Chinese Fairy Tales and Folk Tales* (first in German and then English 1937b) and *Folktales of China* (1965), R. D. Jameson (1896–1959) published his *Three Lectures on Chinese Folklore* (1932), in which he first introduced to the English world the ninth-century Chinese version of Cinderella, Ye Xian, as the earliest written record of the tale-type 510A in the world.

At least two problems in Eberhard's translations can be mentioned here to illustrate his uses of Chinese folktales: (1) His idiosyncratic generalization of genres (or subgenres) out of local/native context. For example, in Eberhard's 1937 collection, there are 137 tales (60 as "fairy tales" and 77 as "legends, myths, jokes, anecdotes"), and his categorization is not based on the Chinese categorization. (2) His diminishing the role of the local/native contributors. For example, the 1937 English collection says that it is "collected and translated by Wolfram Eberhard." However, in the Introduction, Eberhard did not explain how he "collected" those tales. He even said that "I have taken them [the tales] down as they were related to me, as nearly word for word as possible, and I have only altered enough to be sure that a fairy tale appears and not a scientific treatise" (Eberhard 1937, xiv). But the fact is that 86 of the 137 tales were translated from a series of publications whose editor's name was not mentioned at all in the Introduction. In Eberhard's 1965 collection with 43 of the 79 tales from the same series, the local Chinese collector/ publisher was not introduced either (Zhang 2020c).

Interaction and conflict between East and West became more ideological in the twentieth century than previous centuries. In Europe, fantasies about China generated a spectrum of prejudices and curiosities toward Chinese culture. At the one end of the spectrum was the propaganda that, in turn, enhanced European ethnocentric superiority (as seen in the still widely promoted/ needed market through Amazon.com and other venues for the books on Chinese folktales produced in the nineteenth century along with the wave of the Yellow Peril against Chinese); at the other end was curious adoption of Chinese arts, poetry, and music. For example, Tang China (seventh to tenth century) poetry led the composer Gustav Mahler (1860–1911) to complete his significant symphonic song, *The Song of the Earth* (*Das Lied von der Erde*). Certainly, there were other uses of Chinese folktales for different purposes. An example of this kind is Béla Balázes's (1884–1949) *The Cloak of Dreams: Chinese Fairy Tales* (2010), in which all the tales were imaginatively created by the author to meet the public's fantasies about China as a wonderland.

In the United States, the popular tales that largely shaped stereotypes against Chinese/Chinese Americans in the beginning of the twentieth century (in addition to such proverbs/jokes/films like "No Tickee, No Washee" emerged in the late nineteenth century and the early twentieth century) were those with such protagonists as Fu Manchu and Fah Lo Suee, who were depicted by Hollywood films as the evil of evils. Films of that kind were rampant for almost the entire twentieth century. This phenomenon has demonstrated a typical use of folktales for a particular ideological agenda by means of entertainment through mass media. Fortunately, some translations of and introductions to Chinese folktales in the late twentieth century began to pay attention to broad social and cultural contexts (Roberts 1979; Chin, Center and Ross 1989; Miller 1995; Faurot 1995; Giskin 1997; MacDonald, McDowell and Degh 1999; Zhang 2018).

In Stage Four, as we are experiencing today, face-to-face cross-cultural communication is becoming routine, and cultural diversity is celebrated. But the previously shaped stereotypes will not disappear quickly. For this reason, a culture-centered holistic approach toward Asian folktales is particularly meaningful.

This approach emphasizes the analysis of *the smallest unit of meaningful actions*, that is, a sequence or group of actions or symbols that constitutes a specific meaning in a specific cultural event, rather than "the smallest element in a tale" (i.e., motif) which denotes a single action or object. For example, the action of kowtow/bowing can be a motif as the smallest element in a tale, but its symbolic meaning in one tale can be different from its meaning in another tale due to related actions or elements immediately before or after the action of kowtow. The different meanings of kowtow/bowing in a wedding, a funeral, a festival celebration, a church, or other situations are determined by the smallest unit of a sequence of actions in each specific situation. Examining the smallest unit of actions allows a culture-based interpretation of the actions as symbols, and also underscores the nature of multiple meanings of a single symbol in different contexts (Zhang 2020c).

A holistic approach to folktales emphasizes multiple (cultural or disciplinary) perspectives, which consider a folktale as a part of an organic cultural entity. Such an approach is seen in Chinese cosmic views about the relationships between humans and nature, family and society, and within a human body. In traditional medicine, for example, each prescription is different depending on the patient's individual situation even though a symptom might seem to be in common. In folktale studies, each tale, even though the structural elements may seem alike, has different meanings to different audiences, and thus needs to be studied within its own contexts, including the context of retelling in a different language or culture, in order to avoid stereotyping, generalizing, or imposing interpretations. This is the right way to maintain healthy communication in cross-cultural interactions and to understand the process of reconstructing identity that is central to our lives.

At a semantic level, perspective can be seen through the choice of a word in translation. In most translations of Chinese folktales, the Chinese concept of *tian* (sky, or upper world) has been rendered into *heaven,* largely due to the early missionary influence. The problem of this translation is that the monotheist concept of "heaven" is used to convey the polytheist concept of *tian* which denotes a world of many gods mirroring the human world. As a result, one system of beliefs and cultural values is imposed upon another—in effect eclipsing the original—in translating a tale.

At a social level, besides the above-mentioned popular films like *Mu Lan, Kung Fu Panda*, and those about Charlie Chan and Fu Manchu, there are also tales that are retold to meet the needs of different audiences with different purposes and thus exert different social impact or stereotypes. For example, the Chinese folktales retold in Maxine Hong Kingston's popular book *The Woman Warrior* (1976) in the US context eventually led to a warning by the

San Francisco Association of Chinese Teachers that "Especially for students unfamiliar with the Chinese background, [*The Woman Warrior*] could give an overly negative impression of the Chinese American experience" (Yin 2006, 242). Some criticisms are that her deliberated mistranslation of some terms was to "suit white tastes so that her book would sell better" (Wong 1988, 3), and that her biased commentary regarding Chinese culture resulted in her "Orientalist effect" (Shu 2001). Another popular children's picture book, *Tikki Tikki Tembo* (Mosel 1968), created a false stereotype about children's naming tradition in China and provided inaccurate representations of Chinese culture (e.g., the characters dressing in Japanese kimono and sandals and eating rice cakes instead of mooncakes on the Mid-Autumn Festival) (Yamate 1997; Cai 1994, 2002, 108), which eventually showed the ideological superiority toward the inferior *other*. As social context has been changing, tales are retold with new purposes. For example, Amy Tan's *The Joy Luck Club* (1989), *The Kitchen God's Wife* (1991), and *Sagwa, the Chinese Siamese Cat* (1994), are relatively better received by the public in the United States than some others' literary retellings due to the fact that her representations of Chinese culture were of "authority of authenticity," even though she also bears the burden of "the American-born writer's heavily mediated understanding of things in China" (Wong 1995, 181). However, one has to be warned of the fact that Chinese Americans have been building a unique culture, a "Third Culture" (with its own experiences and narratives, or identity), that should not be seen as an equivalent or a continuum of the culture practiced in China (Zhang 2015).

Regarding the role of folktales in reconstructing national identity, a representative example is about how the Brothers Grimm collected, edited, and (re)published their *Kinder- und Haus-Märchen* (*Children's and Household Tales*), first edition in 1812, and last edition in 1857. The central purpose for the Brothers Grimm was to help reconstruct a new nation with its own tradition that was carried and demonstrated through tales. Their action was inspired by the spirit of romantic nationalism influenced by such thinkers as Johann G. von Herder (1744–1803) and Clemens W. Brentano (1778–1842). Eventually, their tales indeed played a meaningful role in the birth of a nation state of Germany in 1871. It was such a nationalistic spirit that also inspired folklorists in many other countries, including China and Japan, to use folklore as a path to seek national essence or spirit in order to build a nation equal to and as strong as the West in the twentieth century. As a result of this particular historical and national context, the Brothers Grimm, as Zipes (2015, 4) points out, deliberately downplayed moralistic and didactic tones in German folktales. In China, the Brothers Grimm nationalistic spirit (i.e., to use tales as a means to trace the history of a nation so as to help reconstruct a new national identity) was adopted in the late nineteenth century and early twentieth century to seek national independence (resulting in the establishment of the Republic of China in 1912) (Zhang 2020c, 2022). Folktales were collected and published to promote children's education and women's education as part of the effort to build a modern nation following the Western example. It is true that folktales were traditionally used primarily for promoting familial and social ethics, and didactic moral power in Asian folktales was/is particularly strong and common (Grayson 2001; Lwin 2009, 78). However, the cross-cultural aspect in reviving folktales is a new question.

Obviously, folktales also carry fundamental religious beliefs in a society, as well as political ideology of a certain historical age. Therefore, it is necessary to understand and study a tale from a culture-centered holistic perspective based on specific situations. Since the differences along the stages of collecting, editing, publishing, translating, and interpreting folktales are often confrontational in cross-cultural communication, it becomes clear that methodological questions are also ideological ones.

FOLKTALES AS A MEANS OF RECONSTRUCTING AND MAINTAINING IDENTITIES

The Continuity of Tradition through Folktales in China

Folktales are the media of tradition, not only connecting the past to the present in strengthening group, regional, and national cultural identities but also relating different socioeconomic realities to a common imaged world of fantasy, nostalgia, and, more meaningfully, hope, in order to help people live a meaningful life. The former aspect exhibits synchronically geographical and historical characters; the latter reveals diachronically some universal human desires and longing. This point can be illustrated by the example of how folktales are transmitted in the parallel and interactive written and oral traditions in China (Zhang 2022).

Chinese written records have shown a dynamic and parallel tradition of oral telling and text printing and reprinting for at least the past two thousand years. This echoes the commonly known developmental history of Chinese culture through the dichotomy of the folk tradition carried by the great mass through oral narration and the official tradition represented by China's intellectual elite, a minority of the population, through written literature. The two aspects have interacted as the yin-yang forces, or the two sides of a coin. For example, most tales collected in the early twentieth century can be traced back to their original records decades or centuries ago, and most tales collected in the late twentieth century and recent years are directly related to the variants a century earlier (Jiang 2007; Zhang 2014, 2019a, 2020b).

For example, the numerous written records from the sixth to the tenth centuries have been retold through various written collections until today. The tale of Ye Xian (ATU 510A) was recorded in the ninth century and continues in both written and oral traditions (Jameson 1932; Waley 1947; Beauchamp 2010). The tale of Mu Lan (or Hua Mulan) (ATU 514) has been rewritten and retold since the fifth century (Kwa and Idema 2010). The tale "Predestined Wife (ATU 930A)," from which the image of the match-maker in the moonlight (*yuelao* or Moon Man, symbolic of the yin-yang transformation and arranged marriage system) was depicted in the ninth century (Taylor 1959), is still popular today (e.g., in metaphorical speech referring to a male match-maker, and the Temples of Yuelao in various regions), while the oral telling of *yuelao* tale is continuing in everyday life, as seen in an event of storytelling by Tan Zhenshan in his village in Northeast China (Zhang 2014, 2022).

Tan Zhenshan (1925–2011) is a representative of traditional storytellers in modern China (Zhang and Jiang 2021). As a peasant for his whole life, Tan could tell 1062 tales and was well-known in the neighboring villages for decades (Jiang 2007). It was due to the movement of Safeguarding Intangible Cultural Heritage (ICH) launched by the UNESCO in 2003 that China reacted with a nationwide campaign of collecting and publishing folktales, along with other folklore genres. As a result, Tan was discovered as a traditional storyteller, a national treasure as the representative of the bearers of traditions. His tales were then listed on the first List of ICH at the national level in 2006, and Tan himself was on the first List of National Intangible Cultural Heritage Bearers in 2007. Subsequently, hundreds of traditional storytellers across China have been enlisted as ICH Bearers thus far, and storytelling events are also performed in places beyond home or village. Tan's example shows that folktales have been important for the reconstruction of regional identity because he was a local peasant and his tales are his variants of traditional tales integrating local identity markers. Studies have also shown that most of his tales can be traced to the tale-types commonly told in China for centuries; for example, his telling of the tale "Yuelao Peihun" (Yuelao arranging marriage) is essentially identical (e.g., the plot and figures) to the "Predestined Wife" (ATU 930A) recorded in the ninth century (Jiang 2002, 2007; Zhang 2014, 2020).

Another example demonstrates how a body of folktales and the protagonists has been used for the reconstruction of national identity in addition to regional identity. The Liu Bowen Legends as an ICH item was listed on the second National List of ICH in 2008, and Liu Ji (aka Liu Bowen) Ancestral Sacrifice was listed on the third National List of ICH in 2011. Liu Bowen (1311–1375) was a historical figure from a village in Wenzhou, Zhejiang Province. He became legendary in the region due in part to his contribution to the establishment of the Ming Dynasty (1368–1644) as the strategist for the founding emperor Zhu Yuanzhang (1328–1398), but mostly for his practices of traditional Chinese virtues like loyalty and righteousness. Over the years, Liu became the protagonist of many tales of history, mystery, *fengshui,* and other genres of local narratives and performances.

These two cases clearly exhibit the use of folktales in transforming a group and regional identity marker into a national identity marker, a phenomenon only possible and meaningful in the current national and international contexts. They also demonstrate a new role of folktales in China's effort to establish a discourse with the world through ICH and a discourse within the nation to revive traditions and celebrate cultural diversity within China itself.

At present, a key national project, the *Compendium of Chinese Folk Literature* (*Zhongguo minjian wenxue daxi*) was launched in 2017 by the China Federation of Literary and Art Circles. It is expected to be completed in eight years with 1,000 volumes covering such genres of folk literature as ethnic myths, legends, tales, ballads, proverbs, epics, folk operas, and narrative and singing texts. This *Compendium* includes written and oral materials of the past century. The intention is to collect what was not included in the previous national project (i.e., *Three Grand Collections, santao jicheng, 1984–2009*), which contained 298 volumes of three genres: folktales, ballads, and proverbs.

Obviously, the tradition of telling, collecting, and publishing folktales in China is continuing as it has been in the past millennia. Yet, the purposes have not been exactly the same since the historical and social contexts have changed. For example, collecting tales and songs was to find out common people's reactions to the rulings of the emperors/kings, as seen in the extant earliest collection of folksongs, *The Book of Songs* (Shi Jing), known to have been edited by Confucius (551–479 BCE). However, the recent national project of collecting folk literature in China, as mentioned above, is largely an effort to revive the traditional values in order to reconstruct a new Chinese national identity by taking advantage of the ICH movement in the world. Nevertheless, the unchanged cultural core of all folktales and the event of storytelling remain the means of creating a world of fantasy, imagination, magic, and hope to compensate what is missing and what people are longing for while living a meaningful life in this world.

Multi-identity in Multicultural Context

The concept of identity itself was developed from psychology and then extended to sociological, anthropological, and some other disciplinary studies. The term "ethnic identity" has transformed to become a replacement of "racial identity" since the 1960s in the United States, and is closely related to studies of diasporic identity. However, it is important to make a distinction between ethnic identity and cultural identity because they are two different concepts (Bausinger 1997); the former has racial and racist connections, and the latter refers to the core of humanities. Today sciences have proved that the concept of "race" as a social categorization was constructed to serve racism. Thus we need to seek new paths in understanding our diverse cultures. Clearly, studying folkloric identity through folktales is a promising approach because it is essential for reconstructing and maintaining identity in everyday life (Zhang 2015, 2020b).

With the social, political, and cultural changes in the world after the 1960s, particularly in the United States, general attitudes toward personal identity have changed from enforcing single-identity to tolerating and accepting multiple identities. The old "melting-pot" idea was replaced by the newer "salad-bowl" metaphor. Ideas of multiculturalism and cultural diversity are increasingly absorbed in everyday life across the world, along with advocacy of safeguarding ICH and diverse human cultures. These efforts have paved the road for cross-cultural communication as well as brought awareness of maintaining the identities of distinctive cultures.

Even in cognitive psychology, cross-cultural studies have demonstrated that people of different cultures, particularly between East Asians and Americans, think differently (Nisbett 2004). In other words, different ways of knowing and telling among peoples of the world must be recognized in cross-cultural communication so that we can avoid conflict and learn to coexist in harmony. Folktales are certainly representative of such differences.

The role of folktales in reconstructing identity has to be considered with clear understanding of the complex contexts of identity, including the context of reconstructing diasporic identity in the United States. Asian American cultures are new cultures and are integral to American culture, though they have close relations with Asian cultures. Similarly, Asian folktales should be treated differently from Asian American folktales, though their connections are obvious. An extreme example is the recently published *Asian American Folktales* (Green 2009), which includes a number of Chinese folktales from those books by the missionaries at the turn of the twentieth century as mentioned above, an incongruous connection between the Chinese/Asian and the Chinese/Asian American cultures.

Thus, one fact has to be taken into account: Asian American folktales are substantially generated in the American English language, while Asian folktales (known to us) are translated into (American) English. A language carries a unique set of cultural values, expressed through its folktales, jokes, and proverbs. Cultural nuances go beyond semantic translation. In this sense, the study of Asian folktales would be significantly more beneficial with a relevant understanding of the original languages and cultures. Although appropriate research of the related background of a folktale through different languages is not impossible, the condition is that there have to be enough translated materials to research. Furthermore, while publications of the translated Asian folktales and related studies are rapidly increasing in this new age of technology, the ideological issues in translating and interpreting Asian folktales should not be ignored.

The study of folktales today needs also to consider new ways of storytelling (e.g., through films or animation) other than traditional face-to-face interaction. For example, the two films, *The Year of Fish* (2007) and *Crazy Rich Asians* (2018), can be analyzed as variants of the Ye Xian (Cinderella) tale adapted primarily for the American audience. There are also variants of animated or RPG (role-playing game) computer or online games (e.g., *Total War: Three Kingdoms*, RPG series of the *Square* and *Xuanyuan Jian*) that are essentially based on Asian folktales, which transmit and transform traditions and are integrated into local cultures. The audiences or consumers of these new cultural products are consciously or unconsciously using them as a means of reconstructing and maintaining their own identities in a new environment.

Obviously, folktales are used today in various ways to integrate the unfamiliar "once-upon-a-time" into the familiar in our own lives. In this process of reconstructing and expressing identity, we should also be aware of both intra-group and inter-group diversity and complexity. Such diversity and complexity are often best revealed in the school education system, in which students learn to accept the unfamiliar or the *others*. In the process, folktales may be the most accessible means to both students and teachers.

In fact, storytelling is already part of curricula in schools at all levels, as seen in these guiding books: *The Greenwood Encyclopedia of Folktales and Fairy Tales* (Haase 2007), *The East Asian Story Finder* (Elswit 2009), *Living Folklore: An Introduction to the Study of People and Their Traditions* (Sims and Stephens 2011), *Storytelling Animals* (Gottschall 2013), *Fairy Tales Transformed?* (Bacchilega 2013), *Teaching Fairy Tale* (Canepa 2019), and *The Fairy Tale World* (Teverson 2019). The use of Asian folktales in classroom teaching would tackle at least such questions as: How do the translated terms or concepts (or even names) help us understand a different culture? How do they potentially enforce (or positively change) the stereotypes against those people who have "weird" foods, clothes, looks, names, speeches, and different religions? How can folktales help students learn to be open to differences?

For example, a young student may use an eraser with a (Disney) Mickey Mouse image, a notebook with a (fairy tale) Snow White image on the cover, a backpack with (Chinese legend) Mulan image, a T-shirt with (Chinese wonder tale) Monkey King image on the chest, or a sweater with (Disney's African folktale) Lion King image on the back, while being able to tell stories about those images. Through these communicative symbols and actions, students' "school" identities are constructed among their schoolmates. Then, in after-school life, students may use some of those stories/connectors to build cultural or ethnic group identities in a multicultural neighborhood. Still, students may speak one language at home and another in school. These practices certainly help inform the students' multiple identities through folktales. After all, personal identity does not exist alone in a vacuum; personal identity is part of group identity. A cultural group is also a folk group that shares common values and lifestyles through such means as telling and retelling folktales so as to maintain that group identity.

However, the universal structure and the distinctive cultural symbols (rather than motifs) of folktales are not to be confused. Similarly, methods developed in studying one culture are not to be blindly applied to the study of another culture. In studying Chinese folktales, for example, the goal is to explore the Chinese cosmos, ideologies and beliefs, ethical values, and ways of knowing as the roots of Chinese culture have developed as a system different from that of the West. We need to understand how different systems have co-existed throughout history.

After all, the ultimate goal of telling and studying folktales is to obtain and maintain harmony with differences in our own lives. This goal is particularly meaningful in today's unprecedented globalized communication. A culture is always the result of multiple cross-cultural interactions, but the temporal and spatial dimensions of such interactions have never been so broad in human history. Therefore, in studying Asian folktales we should consider their new dimensions of reconstructing and maintaining multiple identity in multicultural contexts, because the cultural values in folktales are essentially the driving force in the making and maintaining of all our identities.

In conclusion, folktales or folk narratives are at the very center of folkloristic studies, but they are not limited to this discipline's interpretations. In fact, the disciplinarity of folkloristics lies in its cross-disciplinary approaches by adopting different theories and methods to understand the creativity of humanities through everyday life. By the same token, some concepts and ideas in folkloristic studies such as function, genre, tale-type, motif, identity, context, and performance can well be used in other disciplinary fields, particularly in education and psychology where a goal is to understand identity as a key to the body-mind-heart growth of individuals and groups in a society. For this reason, this chapter first provides a general picture of folkloristic approaches to folktales in order to broaden the readers' interpretations of folktales from other perspectives. Then, by focusing on the ideas of context and identity in cross-cultural communication in this globalizing age and by using the examples related to Chinese folktales, this chapter argues that folktales are not only expressions of individual and group identities in context but also the means or mechanism of (re)constructing and maintaining identity, and creating new culture through cross-cultural interactions (e.g., a diasporic culture like Chinese American culture is a "Third Culture" different from Chinese culture). Indeed, how can one live a meaningful life without integrating folktales from diverse cultural backgrounds into one's own personal identity?

NOTES

1. It is expected that through studying how to analyze Asian folktales one can learn to be inclusive and also gain the rational lens to understand Asian American people and their culture—the inseparable part of American culture as a whole—in our own everyday life. This point is particularly meaningful, though it is not elaborated in this essay. The rampant anti-AAPI movement in the United States during the COVID-19 pandemic is only the superficial expression of the latent ideologies and racism which are maintained by stereotyping *others* through picture books, folk and fairy tales, and other popular culture forms in and outside schools.

2. See also this website, sites.ualberta.ca/~urban/Projects/English/Motif_Index.htm. Accessed Nov. 20, 2021.

3. See also this website, sites.ualberta.ca/~urban/Projects/English/Motif_Index.htm. Accessed Nov. 20, 2021.

REFERENCES

Aarne, Antti. 1961. *The Types of the Folktale: A Classification and Bibliography* (Stith Thompson, trans. & enlarged). 2nd rev. ed. Helsinki: Suomalainen Tiedeakatemia.

Bacchilega, Cristina. 2013. *Fairy Tales Transformed?: Twenty-First-Century Adaptations and the Politics.* Wayne State University Press.

Balázes, Béla. 2010. *The Cloak of Dreams: Chinese Fairy Tales* (Jack Zipes, trans. & intro.). Princeton: Princeton University Press.

Bascom, William. 1954. Four Functions of Folklore. *Journal of American Folklore,* 67: 333–349.

Bauman, Richard and B. Babcock, eds. 1977. *Verbal Art as Performance.* Prospect Heights: Waveland Press.

Bausinger, Hermann. 1997. Intercultural Demands and Cultural Identity. *Europaea: Journal of the Europeanists,* 3(1): 3–14.

Beauchamp, Fay. 2010. Asian Origins of Cinderella: The Zhuang Storyteller of Guangxi. *Oral Tradition,* 25(2): 447–496.

Ben-Amos, Dan. 1969. Analytical Categories and Ethnic Genres. *Genre,* 2(3): 275–301.

————. 1971. Toward a Definition of Folklore in Context. *Journal of American Folklore,* 84(331): 3–15.

————. 1993. "Context" in Context. *Western Folklore*, 52: 209–226.

————. 1995. Are There Any Motifs in Folklore? In Frank Trommler, ed. *Thematics Reconsidered: Essays in Honor of Horst S. Daemmrich.* 71–85. Amsterdam: Rodopi.

Briggs, Charles and S. Naithani. 2012. The Coloniality of Folklore: Towards a Multi-Genealogical Practice of Folkloristics. *Studies in History,* 28(2): 231–270.

Cai, Mingshui. 1994. Images of Chinese and Chinese Americans Mirrored in Picture Books. *Children's Literature in Education,* 25(3): 169–191.

————. 2002. *Multicultural Literature for Children and Young Adults: Reflections on Critical Issues.* Westport, CT: Greenwood Press.

Canepa, Nancy, ed. 2019. *Teaching Fairy Tales.* Wayne State University Press.

Chin, Yin-Lien, Yetta S. Center, and Mmidred Ross, eds. 1989. *Chinese Folktales: An Anthology.* M. E. Sharpe.

Choi, In-Hak. 1979. *A Type Index of Korean Folktales.* Seoul: Seoul Myong Ji University Publishing.

Dorson, Richard. 1965. Foreword. In W. Eberhard, ed. *Folktales of China.* xv. Chicago: University of Chicago Press.

Dundes, Alan. 1964. Texture, Text, and Context. *Southern Folklore Quarterly,* 28: 251–265.

————. 1976. Structuralism and Folklore. In J. Pentikainen and T. Juurikka, eds. *Folk Narrative Research.* 79–93. Helsinki: Suomalaisen Kirijallisuuden Seura.

————. 2002. *Bloody Mary in the Mirror: Essays in Psychoanalytic Folkloristics.* Jackson: University Press of Mississippi.

Eberhard, Wolfram. 1937a. *Typen chinesischer Volksmärchen* (FF communications; no. 120. Helsinki: Suomalainen Tiedeakatemia, Academia Scientiarum Fennica.

————. 1937b. *Chinese Fairy Tales and Folk Tales.* English tr. by Desmond Parsons. London: K. Paul, Trench, Trubner & Co.

————. 1965. *Folktales of China.* Chicago: Chicago University Press.

El-Shamy, Hasan M. 2006. *A Motif Index of the Thousand and One Nights.* Bloomington: Indiana University Press.

Elswit, Sharon B. 2009. *The East Asian Story Finder: A Guide to 468 Tales from China, Japan and Korea, Listing Subject and Sources.* Jefferson: McFarland & Co.

Faurot, Jeannette L., ed. 1995. *Asian-Pacific Folktales and Legends.* New York, NY: Simon & Schuster.

Fielde, Adele. 1912. *Chinese Fairy Tales: Forty Stories Told by Almond-Eyed Folk.* 2nd ed. New York, NY: G. P. Putnam's Sons.

Garry, Jane and Hasan El-Shamy, eds. 2005. *Archetypes and Motifs in Folklore and Literature: A Handbook.* Armonk, NY: M. E. Sharpe.

Giles, Herbert A. 1911. *Chinese Fairy Tales.* London: Gowans & Gray, Ltd.

Giskin, Howard. 1997. *Chinese Folktales.* Lincolnwood, IL: NTC Pub.

Gottschall, Jonathan. 2013. *The Storytelling Animal: How Stories Make Us Human.* New York, NY: Mariner Books.

Grayson, James H. 2001. *Myths and Legends from Korea: An Annotated Compendium of Ancient and Modern Materials*. London: Routledge.

Green, Thomas, ed. 2009. *Asian American Folktales*. Westport, CT: Greenwood Press.

Haase, Donald, ed. 2007. *The Greenwood Encyclopedia of Folktales and Fairy Tales*. 3 Vols. Westport, CT: Greenwood.

Headland, Isaac T. 1901. *The Chinese Boy and Girl*. New York: Fleming H. Revell Co.

Hearn, Lafcadio. 1887. *Some Chinese Ghosts*. Boston: Roberts Brothers.

Ikeda, Hiroko. 1971. *A Type and Motif Index of Japanese Folk-Literature*. Helsinki: Academia Scientiarum Fennica.

Jameson, R. D. 1932. *Three Lectures on Chinese Folklore*. Peking: North China Union Language School.

Jason, Heda. 1997. Texture, Text, and Context of the Folklore Text vs. Indexing. *Journal of Folklore Research,* 34(3): 221–225.

Jiang Fan. (江帆). 2002. The Inseparable Marriage. In S. Liu, ed. *The Studies of Chinese Folktale Types*. 433–443. Wuhan: Central China Normal University.

———. 2007. *A Highlight of the Stories Told by Tan Zhen Shan* (谭震山故事精选). Shenyang: Liaoning Jiaoyu Chubanshe.

Jin Ronghua (金榮華). 2007. *Folktale Type Index* (民間故事類型索引). 3 vols. Taibei: Zhongguo kouchuan wenxue xuehui.

Kingston, Maxine H. 1976. *The Woman Warrior: Memoirs of a Girlhood among Ghosts*. New York, NY: Alfred A. Knopf.

Kobayashi, Fumihiko. 2015. *Japanese Animal-Wife Tales: Narrating Gender Reality in Japanese Folktale Tradition*. New York, NY: Peter Lang.

Kwa, Shiamin and Wilt L. Idema. 2010. *Mulan: Five Versions of a Classic Chinese Legend, with Related Texts*. Hackett Publishing Company.

Lwin, Soe M. 2009. Revisiting a Structural Analysis of Folktales: A Means to an End? *Buckingham Journal of Language and Linguistics*, 2(1): 69–89.

Li, Liang. 2018. *The Chinese fantasy and Heart-Mind: The Structure and Meaning of Lin Lan Fairy Tales* (中国人的幻想与心灵：林兰童话的结构与意义). Beijing: Shangwu yinshuguan.

Liberman, Anatoly. 1984. Introduction and Notes. In A. Liberman, ed. *Theory and History of Folklore*. ix–lxxxi. Tr. A. Y. Martin and R. P. Martin. Minneapolis: University of Minnesota Press.

Lockhart, J. H. Stewart. 1890. Chinese Folk-Lore. *Folklore*, 1(3): 359–368.

MacDonald, Margarae R. ed. 1999. *Traditional Storytelling Today: An International Sourcebook*. London and NY: Routledge.

Malinowski, Bronislaw. 1939. The Group and the Individual in Functional Analysis. *American Journal of Sociology*, 46: 938–964.

———. 1946 [1923]. The Problem of Meaning in Primitive Languages. In C. K. Ogden and I. A. Richards, eds. *The Meaning of Meaning*. 296–336. NY: Harcourt, Brace and World.

———. 1965 [1935]. *The Language of Magic and Gardening. Coral Gardens and Their Magic*. Vol II. Bloomington: Indiana University Press.

Miller, Alan. 1995. The Woman Who Married a Horse: Five Ways of Looking at a Chinese Folktale. *Asian Folklore Studies*, 54: 275–305.

Mosel, Arlene. 1968. *Tikki Tikki Tembo*. Illustrated by Blair Lent. NY: Holt, Rinehart and Winston.

Nisbett, Richard E. 2004. *The Geography of thought: How Asians and Westerners Think Differently... And Why*. NY: Free Press.

Oring, Elliott. 1976. Three Functions of Folklore: Traditional Functionalism as Explanation in Folkloristics. *Journal of American Folklore*, 89(351): 67–80.

———. 1994. The Arts, Artifacts, and Artifices of Identity. *Journal of American Folklore*, 107(424): 211–233.

Pitman, Norman H. 1910. *Chinese Fairy Stories*. NY: Thomas Y. Crowell.

———. 1919. *A Chinese Wonder Book*. NY: E. P. Dutton & Co.

Polo, Marco. 1934. *The Travels of Marco Polo*. New York: Heritage Press.

Propp, Vladimir. 1968 [1928]. *The Morphology of the Folktale* (Laurence Scott, trans.). 2nd ed., Revised by Louis A. Wagner. Austin: University of Texas Press.

Propp, Vladimir (普罗普). 2006. 故事形态学 (*Gushi Xingtaixue*). Trans. Jia Fang (贾放). Chinese translation of *The Morphology of the Folktale*. Beijing: Zhonghua shuju.

Qi, Lianxiu. 2007. *Tale Types of Ancient Chinese Folktales* (中国古代民间故事类型). 3 Vols. Shijiazhuang: Hebei jiaoyu chubanshe.

Radcliffe-Brown, A. R. 1935. On the Concept of Function in Social Science. *American Anthropologist*, 37: 394–397.

Roberts, Moss. 1979. *Chinese Fairy Tales and Fantasies*. NY: Pantheon.

Russell, Nellie N. 1973 [1915]. *Gleanings from Chinese Folklore*. Compiled by Mary H. Porter. Detroit: Singing Tree Press.

Schoemaker, George, ed. 1990. *The Emergence of Folklore in Everyday Life: A Fieldguide and Sourcebook*. Bloomington: Trickster Press.

Seki, Keigo. 1966. Types of Japanese Folktales. *Asian Folklore Studies*, 25: 1–220.

Shu, Yuan. 2001. Cultural Politics and Chinese-American Female Subjectivity: Rethinking Kingston's Woman Warrior. *MELUS*, 26(2): 199–223.

Sims, Martha C. and M. Stephens. 2011. *Living Folklore: An Introduction to the Study of People and Their Traditions*, 2nd ed. Logan: Utah State University Press.

Tan, Amy. 1989. *The Joy Luck Club*. NY: G. P. Putnam's Sons.

———. 1991. *The Kitchen God's Wife*. NY: G. P. Putnam's Sons.

———. 1994. *Sagwa, the Chinese Siamese Cat*. NY: Simon & Schuster Children's Publishing.

Taylor, Archer. 1959. The Predestined Wife (Mt. 930*). *Fabula*, 2: 45–82.

Teverson, Andrew, ed. 2019. *The Fairy Tale World*. London: Routledge.

Thompson, Stith. 1955–1958. *Motif-Index of Folk-Literature*. 6 vols. Revised and enlarged edition. Bloomington: Indiana University Press.

———. 1977 [1946]. *The Folktale*. Berkeley: University of California Press.

Ting, Nai-Tung. 1978. *A Type Index of Chinese Folktales*. Helsinki: Suomalainen Tiedeakatemia Academia Scientiarum Fennica.

Uther, Hans-Jörg. 2004. *The Types of International Folktales: A Classification and Bibliography Based on the System of Antti Aarne and Stith Thompson*. 3 Vols. Helsinki: Academia Scientiarum Fennica.

Waley, Arthur. 1947. The Chinese Cinderella Story. *Folklore,* 58(1): 226–238.

Wilhelm, Richar, ed. 1921. *The Chinese Fairy Book.* NY: Frederick A. Stokes Company Publishers.

Wilson, William. 1988. The Deeper Necessity: Folklore and the Humanities. *Journal of American Folklore,* 101(400): 156–167.

Wong, Sau-Ling C. 1988. Necessity and Extravagance in Maxine Hong Kingston's The Woman Warrior: Art and the Ethnic Experience. *MELUS,* 15(1): 3–26.

———. 1995. Sugar Sisterhood: Situating the Amy Tan Phenomenon. In D. Palumbo-Liu, ed. *The Ethnic Cannon: Histories, Institutions, and Interventions.* 174–210. Minneapolis: Minnesota University Press.

Yamate, Sandra. 1997. Asian Pacific American Children's Literature: Expanding Perceptions About Who Americans Are. In V. Harris, ed. *Using Multiethnic Literature in the K-8 Classroom.* 95–128. Norwood, MA: Christopher-Gordon Publishers.

Yin, Xiao-Huang. 2006. *Chinese American Literature since the 1850s.* Chicago: University of Illinois Press.

Zhang, Juwen. 2014. Cultural Grounding for the Transmission of the "Moon Man" Figure in the Tale of the "Predestined Wife" (ATU 930A). *Journal of American Folklore,* 127(503): 27–49.

———. 2015. Chinese American Culture in the Making: Perspectives and Reflections on Diasporic Folklore and Identity. *Journal of American Folklore,* 128(510): 449–475.

———. 2018. Folklore in China: Past, Present, and Challenges. *The Challenge of Folklore to the Humanities,* 7(2), 35. Retrieved from http://www.mdpi.com/2076 -0787/7/2/35/htm.

———. 2019a. Fairy Tales in China: An Ongoing Evolution. In A. Teverson, ed. *The Fairy Tale World.* 335–346. London: Routledge.

———. 2019b. Motif as Symbol in Context. In S. Bronner and W. Mieder, eds. *Contexts of Folklore: Festschrift for Dan Ben-Amos.* 355–365. NY: Peter Lang Publishers.

———. 2020a. The Concept of Ethnic Genre as a Paradigm Shift. *Western Folklore,* 79(1): 13–44.

———. 2020b. Folkloric Identity Is the Thing. Archer Taylor Lecture at the 2019 Western States Folklore Society annual meeting. *Western Folklore,* 79(2/3): 215–250.

———. 2020c. Rediscovering the Grimms of China: Lin Lan. *Journal of American Folklore,* 133(529): 285–306.

———. 2022. *Oral Traditions in Contemporary China: Healing a Nation.* Lanham: Lexington Books.

Zhang, Juwen and Jiang Fan. 2021. Fairy Tales from Tan Zhenshan in Contemporary China: An Introduction to 'The Paper Maid Turned to a Real Bride' Translation. *Marvels & Tales: Journal of Fairy Tale Studies,* 35(1): 182–186.

Zipes, Jack. 2011. The Meaning of Fairy Tale within the Evolution of Culture. *Marvels & Tales,* 25(2): 221–243.

———. 2015. *The Oxford Companion to Fairy Tales,* 2nd ed. London: Oxford University Press.

CULTURAL PERSPECTIVE

Chapter 3

Morals Take Precedence Over Resolution

An Exploration of Chinese Idiom Stories in Mandarin

Allyssa McCabe, Fangfang Zhang,
and Chien-ju Chang

When does a story end? How do we know a story has ended? This ability to know when a story is finished is an important pragmatic skill. Not only do children need to recognize when others have finished telling a story; they need to be able to clearly mark the end of the stories they themselves tell so that listeners will know when not to interrupt (during story) and when they are themselves expected to respond. Folktales are stories which have been passed down generation by generation through many years in the oral tradition. The authors are unknown, but the stories hold universal truths and timeless appeal and often address and reflect the values of a group of people (Almerico 2014; Zipes 1983). Other chapters in this volume address a number of ways in which Asian folktales socialize children to be interconnected and to avoid doing dangerous things, for example. This chapter examines a very different type of socialization—specifically whether the style of some Chinese folktales socializes Chinese children about how they should end their personal stories, an endeavor that has not been considered in past research to the best of our knowledge. Specifically, we examine Chinese *cheng-yu* as a broad cultural phenomenon (Wu 1995, 65).

Standard Western conceptions of narrative and folktale suggest that resolutions are a crucial part of the structure of those, but not all cultures place equal emphasis on resolution, as we will see. First, William Labov (1972) famously established six major components of a fully developed narrative, with better narratives containing all six components:

1. *Abstract*—a sort of headline given at outset of a narrative that summarizes what the upcoming narrative is about.
2. *Orientation*—information about the setting of an experience, including who participated in an experience, what objects were involved, when that experience occurred, and where it happened.
3. *Complicating action*—past-tense events narrated in the sequence in which they occurred and that build to a climactic event.
4. *Evaluation*—ways in which a narrator conveys the point of the narrative, what things meant to him or her.
5. *Resolution*—past-tense events just like complicating action that tell how the experience was concluded.
6. *Coda*—clauses at the ends of narratives that clearly show a narrator has finished the story (e.g., "It's over.").

CHILDREN'S STRUCTURE OF NARRATION IN CHINESE VERSUS ENGLISH

English-speaking children resolve many of their personal narratives beginning at age seven years (48%–58% of narratives from seven- to nine-year-old children are resolved; Peterson and McCabe 1983), as do many six-year-old Spanish-speaking children (Wishard Guerra 2008). In contrast to this, Zhang, McCabe, Ye, Wang and Li (2019) found that Mandarin-speaking children in mainland China for the most part do not use narrative resolution (i.e., telling how an emotionally climactic situation works out). Three year-olds did not provide any resolutions in their narration. Only one 4-year-old child among 20 children offered resolution when telling personal experiences, and only 20% of the 5-year-olds included resolutions in their narratives. Even at age six, 70% of the Chinese participants did not resolve their narratives, as was the case in the first narrative below. Also see table 3.1 as follows:

Table 3.1   Number and Percentage of Mainland Chinese Middle-Class Children Who Provided Resolutions in Their Personal Narratives

Age	N	Resolution (Number of Children)	Resolution (Percentage of Children)
3	20	0	0
4	20	1	5
5	20	4	20
6	20	6	30

NARRATIVE 1 (CHILD: 5:11 GIRL)

EXP[1]:* 你 讲 一下 有 一 次 你 去 看 医生 的 事情 [^c]. Please tell me one of your experiences of seeing a doctor.

*CHI: 嗯 # 我 去 看 医生 的 时候 呢 [^c] +…When I went to see a doctor,

*CHI: +, 爸爸 就 打 的 [=打出租车] [^c]. Dad called a taxi.

*CHI: 我 不敢 去 [^c]. I didn't dare to go.

*CHI: 爸爸 叫 我 上去 [^c]. Dad asked me to get on the bed (in the hospital).

*CHI: 他 打 得 <我 就 吓> [//] <我> [/] 我 就 吐 [=呕吐] 死 了 [^c]. Then I vomited to death.

*CHI: 我 就 哭 了 [^c]. Then I cried.

*EXP: 喔 好 的 [^c]. Oh, ok.

*CHI: 我 就 是 不敢 把 屁股 露 出来 [^c]. Then I didn't dare to show my rear end.

*CHI: <因为> [/] 因为 打 下去 太 重 了 [^c]! Because the shot is too heavy. (Here the child thinks the shot may cause great pain.)

The phenomenon of ending personal narratives without resolutions of action is not limited to children in Mainland China. Mandarin-speaking children in Taiwan show a similar tendency to forgo resolutions in personal narratives (elicited in the same fashion as those in China; using the procedure detailed in McCabe and Rollins 1994). As did the children in Mainland China, about 70% of the six-year-olds and the seven-year-olds did not provide resolutions in their personal narratives. Only 40% of the eight-year-olds and the nine-year-olds included resolutions in their narratives (Chang 2009). See table 3.2 as follows:

The fact that school-aged Chinese children's narratives often do not end with a resolution is of importance, particularly in the context of the American educational system. In the 1970s in America, several different teams of psychological researchers (e.g., Stein and Glenn 1979) discovered

Table 3.2 Number and Percentage of Middle-Class Taiwanese Children Who Provided Resolutions in Their Narratives about Frightening Experiences in the Past

Age	N	Resolution (Number of Children)	Resolution (Percentage of Children)
4	24	3	12.5
5	30	6	20
6	30	10	33
7	30	9	30
8	30	12	40
9	30	12	40

Vladimir Propp's influential *Morphology of the Folktale* (2015, 86), based on an analysis of Russian folktales. This is the second major conception of narrative structure, and it (like Labov's approach) sees resolution as an essential component of a complete story. Stein and Glenn (and the other teams) developed what they called story grammars to analyze the narratives produced by children. In that system, narratives that lack explicit mention of aims and, to the present point, resolving consequences of attempts to achieve those aims were deemed "incomplete episodes." Story grammar values have permeated the American Educational system since that time. Children from a Chinese family background who have been encouraged to value Chinese storytelling would therefore be at risk of having many of their stories devalued in American classrooms.

Below are two of the few Chinese children's narratives that did in fact end with resolution:

NARRATIVE 2 (CHILD: 5:7 GIRL)

*EXP: 请 问 你 记 不 记 得 你 有 一 次 去 看 医 生 的 事情 啊 [^c]? (Do you remember one of your experiences of seeing a doctor?)

*CHI: 嗯 嘛 <我 有 一 次> [//] 那 次 好像 我 发烧 [^c]. It seems once I had a fever.

*CHI: <那> [//] 第一 次 挂水 我 有 点 害怕 [^c]. The first day I was scared of dripping.[2]

*CHI: 但是 第二 次 挂水 我 就 不 害怕 了 [^c]. But the next day I wasn't afraid.

*EXP: 好 的 [^c]. En.

*CHI: 就 是 那 天 护士 小姐 给 我 打针 [^c]. It is (then) that day the nurse gave me a shot.

*CHI: 他 先 给 我 呢 一 个 牌子 [^c]. She first gave me a pass with a number.

*CHI: 我 坐 那 # 位子 [^c]. I sat on a chair.

*CHI: 嗯 然后 呢 # 嗯 护士 小姐 可以 看到 你的 牌子 [^c].Then the nurse could see your pass.

*CHI: 二 十 二 号 [^c]. My number is 22.

*CHI: 帮 你 挂水 [^c]. (The nurse) helped you with the dripping.

*CHI: 嗯 # 第一 次 挂水 时候 [^c]. When it's the first day

*CHI: 我 很 害怕 [^c]. I was very scared.

*CHI: 但是 第二 次 挂水 时 [^c]. But when it's the next day

*CHI: 我 一点 都 不 害怕 了 [^c]. I was not scared at all.

*CHI: 因为 第一 次 挂水 时候 [^c]+...

*CHI: +, 就 是 今年 一 天 好 几 个 都 没 挂水 了 [^c]+... Because when it's the first day, it's a long time since I took the dripping.

*CHI: +, 所以 我 很 害怕 [^c]. So I was very afraid.

*CHI: 但是 第二 次 挂水 时 [^c]. But when it's the next day

CHI: 不是 那 一 天 已经 挂 过 水 了 嘛 [^c]! I've taken it the first day.

CHI: 所以 我 很 勇敢 [^c]. So I was very brave.

CHI: 所以 没 哭 一 声 [^c]. So I didn't cry a sound.

EXP: 喔 所以 没有 哭 # 对 吧 [^c]? So you didn't cry, right?

CHI: 对 [^c]. Yes.

EXP: 那 后来 呢 [^c]? Then later?

CHI: 后来 呢 # 我的 病 就 好 了 [^c]. Later I recovered.

CHI: 因为 重新 上 幼儿园 了 [^c]. Because I went to kindergarten again.

EXP: 喔 # 好 的 [^c]. En.

EXP: 谢谢 [^c]. Thank you.

The child resolves her story about going to the doctor by noting that she recovered and went back to kindergarten.

NARRATIVE 3 (CHILD: 5;0 BOY)

EXP: 喔 那 你 就 跟 我 讲 [^c] 有 一 次 你 跟 别人 吵架 [^c]. Please tell me one of your experiences of quarreling with others.

CHI: 呃 好吧 [^c]! En, ok!

EXP: 好 来 说说 看 [^c]. Ok, go ahead.

CHI: 有时候 我们 两个 打来打去 的 [^c]. Sometimes we hit each other.

EXP: 嗯 然后 呢 [^c]? Then?

CHI: 然后 我们 就 一边 打 [^c] 一边 吵架 [^c] 生气 的 要 死 了 [^c]. Then we hit each other as we quarreled. We were mad.

EXP: 真的 啊 [^c] 然后 呢 [^c]? Really, then?

CHI: 然后 啊 [^c]+...

CHI: +, 就 生气 的 [^c] 我们 就 打来打去 的 [^c] 踢来踢去 [^c]. Then we were angry. Then we hit each other; kicked each other.

EXP: 嗯 然后 呢 [^c]? Then?

CHI: 然后 踢来踢去 [^c] 打来打去 [^c]. Then kicked each other; hit each other.

CHI: <然后>[//] 后来 老师 看见 [^c] 就 不 让 [^c] 我们 两个 打 了 [^c]. Later the teacher saw. Then didn't allow us to hit.

CHI: 就 不 打 了 [^c]. Then we stopped.

EXP: 是吧 [^c] 然后 怎么 了 啊 [^c]? Then what happened?

CHI: 然后 [^c]+...

CHI: 我们 两个 <u>相亲相爱</u> 地 玩 [^c]. Then the two of us played lovingly.

EXP: 喔 是 吧 相亲相爱 地 玩 啦 [=! laughs] [^c]. Oh, you played lovingly.

EXP: 好的 好的 嗯 非常 好 [^c]. Good, good.

This third narrative is of particular interest because it ends with a particular type of resolution—a *cheng-yu*—echoing an idiom the teacher told the children when she broke up their fight. The four-character idiom (相亲相爱)

means roughly "be kind and love each other." This tendency to end with a moral rather than a resolution to action per se, we argue, is a form of narration valued in Chinese storytelling.

We turn now to a common type of folktale that we believe is in no small part responsible for this tendency to end narratives without resolving them. Much as *Haiku* serves as a discourse regulation device for Japanese speakers (Minami and McCabe 1991, 577), we will argue that a particular ubiquitous folktale, *Cheng-yu*, serves a similar function in Mandarin. We should also note at the outset of this investigation that while idioms are frowned on in formal English writing,[3] they are very much valued in Mandarin writing.

CHINESE IDIOM STORY (*CHENG-YU GUSHI*)

For *Cheng-yu*, there have been definitions given in various representative dictionaries, for example, *Ts'u-yuan* (1915); *Ts'u-hai* (1936); *Hanyu cidian* (1936) (*Chinese dictionary*); *Xiandai hanyu cidian* (1959) (*Modern Chinese dictionary*), or in representative works, e.g., *Xiandai hanyu zhishi* (1973) (*Modern Chinese knowledge*); *Xiandai hanyu* (1975) (*Modern Chinese*). Here, we adopt the most recent accepted definition provided in *Xiandai hanyu* (1975): "An idiom is a set phrase, shaped through the practice of the language for ages of constant use. Its meaning cannot be simply inferred from its constituents. Its structure cannot be freely changed, nor could its constituents be replaced by any other elements unless it is required for a specific need" (Wu 1995, 64). The sources of idioms are mainly classic works of literature, poems, and other standard works, or ballads and common sayings "*suyu*" or "*suyan*" (Wu 1995, 65). Shi (1979) argued that colloquialisms and writings are two primary origins of idioms, which are mutually dependent. Idioms are used more frequently in Chinese than in English (Zhang 2009). They are different from both English phrases and clauses. In English grammar, the phrase is distinguished from the clause; it is composed of a group of two or more associated words, not containing a subject and predicate. However, Chinese idioms can be either the counterpart of an English phrase or a short sentence (Wu 1995, 66).

Cheng-yu are considered aesthetically pleasing (Stellard 2011, 12). Use of *cheng-yu* is considered a sign of intelligence and knowledge among native speakers of Mandarin Chinese (Bai 2010, cited in Zhang 2012, 10), and many can be traced back to ancient written records (Zhang 2012, 25). A large number of metaphors are derived from idioms that once described or illustrated a popular or known historical event. These metaphorical uses of four-character idioms are no doubt unique in Chinese and not to be found in other cultures (Su 2004, 63). There really is no exact counterpart to idiom stories in English.

Until the early twentieth century, Chinese folktales were primarily spread through word of mouth and mainly consisted of a series of events, orientation, evaluation, and reported speech—without dwelling too much or at all on how things worked out in the end, namely the resolution of a story. Chinese folktales are avidly read to children today, and these usually contain metaphorical meanings or moral lessons. Among these, idiom stories—primarily four-character *cheng-yu*—are a very common form of story parents share with their children in China and Taiwan.

Each such story explains an idiom (*Cheng-yu*), and these are to be memorized by children, who often receive extra points when they include them in essays at school (Louie 1996). For example, there is one idiom story about a man who dropped his sword in the water while rowing in a river. He marked the side of the boat where the sword had sunk. When the boat reached the shore, the man jumped from the spot he marked into the water to look for his sword. The story ends there with the idiom "to mark the boat to find one's sword," which means trying to solve a problem in an ineffective way. Instead of resolution about whether or not he ever found his sword, then, there is the idiom—the moral of the story.

To ascertain whether such non-resolved idioms are common, we consulted two collections of *cheng*-yu that are available in English. The first collection is *One Hundred Common Chinese Idioms and Set Phrases* (Yin 2003), which was developed to assist individuals learning Chinese as a second language at a relatively advanced level. The second collection, *Five Hundred Common Chinese Idioms* (Jiao, Kubler, and Zhang 2011), is based on the frequency with which they were found in a national newspaper, textbooks, and several other corpuses. That collection was also compiled to assist individuals acquiring Chinese as a new language. In fact, the need for explicit instruction of these idioms for foreign Chinese-language learners has been noted by others as well (e.g., Stellard 2011; Zhang 2012).

We listed all those unresolved idioms we found in the two published collections. As table 3.3 shows, there are many *cheng-yu* that end without resolutions.

ORIGINS OF NARRATION IN (MATERNAL) INPUT

Previous studies show that in any country examined to date, young children's independent narrative skills originate in no small part in dialogic contexts between children and competent adults, in many cases their mothers (Cristofaro and Tamis-LeMonda 2008; Fernandez and Melzi 2008; Fivush 1991; Fivush and Fromhoff 1988; McCabe and Peterson 1991; Reese and Fivush 1993).

Wang (2013) noted that Chinese parents emphasize what she calls "narrative economy," meaning that a prevailing aesthetic value is on saying

Table 3.3 Idiom Stories (n = 21) with No Resolution in Collection of 100 Common Chinese Idioms and Set Phrases

Idiom Stories	Literal Meaning	Figurative Meaning	Resolution That Is Missing
班门弄斧bānménnòngfǔ Lu Ban was supposed to be a great carpenter in ancient times. It is said that he once carved a wooden phoenix that was so lifelike that it actually flew in the sky for days.	Showing off one's proficiency with the axe before LuBan the Master Carpenter	Rebuking those who display slight skill in front of experts	What happened to masterful wooden phoenix?
吹毛求疵chuīmáoqiúcī Long ago, there was a man who was a notorious nitpicker. Once he went to buy a fur cloak. To check the fur, he blew the hairs apart, looking for trivial defects.	Blow apart the hairs upon a fur to discover any defect	Looking for tiny faults (is undesirable)	Did the man find flaws or not? Did he buy fur or not?
打草惊蛇dǎcǎojīngshé Once there was a county magistrate who was corrupt and took bribes. One day, somebody sent him a letter accusing his secretary of practicing graft and taking bribes. The magistrate trembled when he read the petition. He wrote on it: "You have beaten the grass and frightened a snake."	Beating the grass and flushing out the snake	Inadvertently letting your intended victim know your plan	Was magistrate convicted of crimes?
囫囵吞枣húlúntūnzǎo A physician once told a group of people: "Dates are good for the spleen, but harmful for the teeth." On hearing this, one man said, "I have a good idea: When eating dates, we should just swallow them whole without chewing them. Then we can both enjoy the advantage and avoid the disadvantage."	Gulping down a whole date	Absorbing information without understanding or analysis	Did the man swallow date whole or not?
精卫填海jīng wèi tián hǎi Long ago, King Yan had a daughter. One day she went to the East Sea to play, and was accidentally drowned. After her death she became a brave and beautiful bird, and was called the jingwei bird, in imitation of her cry. She was determined to fill up the sea. So every day she would pick up twigs and pebbles from a mountain and drop them into the sea.	Jingwei fills up the sea	Having a great will to succeed at something	Was sea ever in fact filled up?

刻舟求剑kèzhōuqiújiàn			
Long ago, a man had a sword which he cherished very much. One day, when he was crossing a river in a boat, the sword suddenly fell into the water. The man made a mark or the side of the boat at the spot where the sword had fallen overboard. When the boat reached the shore, he jumped from the spot he marked into the water to look for his sword.	Notching the boat to find the sword	Satirizing those who do not take changing circumstances into account	Was sword found or not?
临渴掘井lín kě jué jǐng			
Long ago, Duke Zhao of the State of Lu fled to the State of Qi, following palace turmoil. He admitted his mistakes to Duke Jing of Qi. Duke Jing advised him to go back to Lu, as he might become a wise ruler, since he recognized his faults. But Yanzi, an official of Qi, said, "It is too late to make weapons when one is encangered, and to dig a well when one is choked in eating and needs water desperately."	Not digging a well until one is thirsty	Be prepared.	What happened to Duke Zhao of the State of Lu after admitting mistakes? Did he go back to Lu?
盲人摸象mángrénmōxiàng			
A group of blind men gathered around an elephant, trying to find out what the creature looked like. One of them happened to touch one of the tusks and said: "An elephant is just like a turnip." Another touched one of the elephant's ears and said: "It is a big fan." One put his arms around one of the beast's eg, and said: "It is a column." One who happened to place his hands on the body of the elephant said: "It is like a wall." But the one who got hold of the tail said, "It's like a snake." They then fell to arguing with each other.	Blind men touching an elephant	Satirizing those who only know part of a thing	Famously, we never discover what blind men eventually realized; tale ends with their unresolved argument.
怒发冲冠nùfàchōngguān			
Long ago, Lin Xiangru, chief minister of Zhao, was sent as an envoy to the State of Qin to ask the ruler of Qin to return a fine piece of jade to Zhao. But the ruler of Qin was rude and unreasonable. Lin was angry, and his hair stood up so stiffly on his head that it lifted up his hat.	So angry that one's hair lifts up one's hat	Referring to being extremely angry	Was anger ever resolved? Was fine piece of jade ever recovered?

(continued)

Idiom Stories	Literal Meaning	Figurative Meaning	Resolution That Is Missing
日暮途穷 rìmùtúqióng Long ago, Duke Ping of Chu was misled by malicious gossips and had Wu Zixu's father executed. Wu Zixu fled to the State of Wu. More than ten years later, Wu Zixu took his revenge by helping Wu conquer Chu. Yet he suffered agonies of remorse, because his countrymen called him a traitor. He protested, "I'm just like a traveler. It's already late, but I still have a long way to go. I simply don't know what to do."	The day is waning and the road is ending	Referring to being in a tight spot	Character aimlessly wandering at end: "I simply don't know what to do."
如火如荼 rúhuǒrútú Long ago, Duke Fuchai of Wu led a huge army against the State of Jin. He ordered his men to form three square contingents. The middle one was dressed in white and holding white flags, which looked from afar just like the flowers of a field full of reeds. The left unit was in red and holding red flags, which looked from afar like flaming fire all over the mountains. The right unit was in black and holding black flags, which looked from afar like thick black clouds covering the sky. Fuchai was trying to present to the enemy a show of overwhelming force.	Like a raging fire	Describes scene of great momentum and exuberance	We never discover whether the use of all those flags worked to fool opposing army.
丧家之犬 sàngjiāzhīquǎn Long ago, Confucius led his disciples on visits to various states. They went offering their services everywhere, but were always rebuffed. One day, in the State of Zheng, Confucius lost his disciples. He stood outside by himself, not knowing what to do. A citizen of Zheng then mocked Confucius: "Look at him," he said. "Isn't he like a stray cur?" Hearing this, Confucius smiled, and said uncaringly: "Yes, yes, indeed."	A homeless dog	Refers to people with nowhere to go and no one to turn to	Confucius himself acknowledges that having lost his disciples, he is like a homeless dog. The story ends with Confucius' reaction, but is not resolved. Was Confucius ever reunited with his disciples?

甚嚣尘上shènxiāochénshàng Long ago, the State of Jin was at war with the State of Chu. Duke Gong of Chu stood on a high platform built on a chariot and watched the movements of the Jin army. After watching for a while, he said, "It's quite noisy over there and a cloud of dust has been stirred up." His aide answered, "The enemy are filling up wells and destroying their cooking stoves. They are preparing to fight."	Making a great clamor	Making a big fuss over nothing, hearsay	We do not discover what in fact noisy army *was* up to or whether they fought or not.
守株待兔shǒuzhūdàitù Long ago, a farmer in the State of Song was one day working in the fields, when he saw a rabbit bump into a tree stump accidentally and break its neck. The farmer took the rabbit home and cooked himself a delicious meal. That night he thought, "I needn't work so hard. All I have to do is wait for a rabbit each day by the stump." So from then on he gave up farming, and simply sat by the stump waiting for rabbits to come and run into it.	Sitting by a stump, waiting for a careless hare	Waiting for luck instead of working to get what one needs	Did man waiting for hares to run into stump starve for lack of effort or return to using more effective means of farming and hunting?
图穷匕见tú qióng bǐ jiàn Long ago, Jing Ke was ordered by the crown prince of the State of Yan to assassinate the ruler of the State of Qin. In order to be able to get close to the latter, Jing Ke pretended to want to present to him a valuable map. The assassin had hidden a dagger in the rolled-up map. When the map was unrolled, the dagger was revealed.	When the map is unrolled the dagger is revealed	In the end, a person's true intention is revealed.	Did person with dagger in map assassinate the ruler of the State of Qin or not?
亡羊补牢wángyángbǔláo A man who raised sheep once noticed that there was a hole in the wall of his sheepfold. But he neglected to repair it. A few days later, several sheep were missing. His neighbor advised him: "It is not too late to mend the sheepfold."	Mending the fold after the sheep have been stolen	It is never too late to prevent further loss.	Was fence mended? Did mended fence work to protect sheep?
为虎作伥wèihǔzuòchāng An ancient legend has it that a tiger ate a man, and the man's soul could not be freed until it found another man for the tiger to eat.	Helping the tiger to pounce upon its victims	Doing evil things in the service of the wicked	Did man free his soul by feeding another man to tiger?

(continued)

Idiom Stories	Literal Meaning	Figurative Meaning	Resolution That Is Missing
掩耳盗铃 yǎn'ěrdàolíng Long ago, a man in the State of Jin took a fancy to a bronze bell and wanted to steal it. The bell was too large and heavy to be moved away, so he decided to smash it to pieces. But when his hammer struck the bell, it gave out a deep booming sound. Fearing that he might be heard, he covered his ears, and carried on with the work.	*Plugging one's ears while stealing a bell	Satirizes those who think they are smart but deceive themselves	Was man smashing bell and plugging his ears successful or was he caught due to the noise?
偃旗息鼓 yǎnqíxīgǔ Long ago, during a battle between Cao Cao and Liu Bei, the latter ordered his generals Zhao Yun and Huang Zhong to capture Cao Cao's supplies. Cao Cao led a large force against Zhao Yun, who retreated as far as the gates of his camp. There, he ordered that banners be lowered, the war drums silenced, and the camp gates be left wide open. Zhao Yun then stationed his troops in ambush nearby. When Cao Cao arrived and saw the situation, he immediately suspected a trap and withdrew his forces.	To lower the banners and silence the drums	Halting an attack or ceasing all activities	Which side won in the end?
夜郎自大 yèlángzìdà Once there was a tiny country called Yelang on the southwestern border. Small though it was, its ruler was quite proud of his country, thinking it big and powerful. Once a Han envoy visited Yelang. The ruler asked him: "Which is bigger, Han or Yelang?"	The conceited king of Yelang	Refers to those who are not very capable but are conceited	How did the person answer conceited king's question about the size of his country? What was the upshot of that answer?
自相矛盾 zì xiāng máodùn Long ago, there was a man who sold spears and shields. He used to boast, "My spears are the sharpest things in the world. They can penetrate anything." A moment later he would boast, "My shields are the toughest things in the world. Nothing can penetrate them." One day, a passer-by asked him: "What would happen if you threw one of your spears at one of your shields?"	Contradicting oneself	Same as literal	Did the man throw his spear at his shield? Which was true: was man's shield the toughest or was his spear the sharpest?

less with more punch. Taiwanese narrative conversations were shorter than American ones. Miller, Wiley, Fung, and Liang (1997) observed that Taiwanese mothers, unlike American mothers, had a tendency to emphasize social rules and moral standards when reminiscing with their children. But perhaps of greatest relevance was that Miller found that Chinese, unlike American, parents often ended narrative conversations with a didactic coda (e.g., "You can get it only if you go to the class," "Saying dirty words is not good," or "Oh now you don't cry at all, ya."). Koh and Wang (2013) also noted Chinese parents' tendency to focus on children's misbehavior and moral and social rules, which fits with their overall value in promoting social harmony. Such a focus is very much a contrast to what Wang (2013) called a Western preoccupation with encouraging children's self-esteem during parent-child reminiscences.

In addition to exchanging personal narratives, parents communicate cultural values when they read books with their children (Luo, Snow, and Chang 2011, 508). In their comparison of Taiwanese and American mothers reading books with their three-year-old children, Luo and colleagues found that Taiwanese mothers reflected Confucian notions of filial piety; that is, parents see a need to discipline, guide, and teach children, whom, in turn, are supposed to obey and respect their elders. Of particular interest was the occurrence of what Fung and colleagues (2004) term "opportunity education" in Taiwanese mothers' (but never American mothers') book reading, namely concrete opportunities to guide children to acquire normative behavior, moral values, and cultural regulations. In Luo and colleagues' work, such opportunity education consisted of (1) the importance of politeness ("Say thank you Teacher" [for loaning us this book]), (2) maternal expectations of the child ("You shall be a kind person, too"), and (3) the importance of good eating habits ([The hungry caterpillar] "ate too much—that is not a good eating habit"). Taiwanese parents see teaching as a critical part of parenting and engaged in such instruction not only through episodes of opportunity education but also by producing more evaluations and tag questions than their American counterparts, who seemed to view book-reading as a kind of entertainment. Taiwanese mothers, unlike American mothers, also pointed directly to the text during the sessions, as a way of teaching their children about Chinese characters. In a different, related study that compared low-income with middle-income mothers' book-reading in Taiwan, over half of all mothers from both classes produced incidents of opportunity education involving children's misdeeds or behavioral regulations (Chang and Huang 2016, 400). Specifically, the mothers noted things like the importance of cleaning up after yourself and of not playing with the mothers' possessions.

Chinese caregivers' cultural preference for punchy endings has been noted in literary fiction written by, for example, Lan Samantha Chang (1998, 116–119). In one of her short stories (written in English), Chang depicts a grandmother (Waipuo) telling her Chinese American grandchildren stories "just to keep up your Chinese." She tells them a story that ends with a daughter who goes missing. One granddaughter asks what happened to the daughter, but is answered with a brusque, "Who knows?" and mention of a couple of possibilities. The narrator reflects that "We had gotten used to Waipuo's abruptness, her habit of creating a question and leaving without answering it."

In *The Downstairs Girl,* Stacey Lee, a Chinese American author noted similarly that her adoptive Chinese father told her an enigmatic story without an ending, which she questions:

"Is that the end?" Old Gin grunts, "For now." He cocks an ear toward me, waiting for me to dig out the hidden meanings (Lee 2019, 105).

IDIOMS IN EDUCATIONAL CONTEXT

Teaching and learning the stories and origins behind *cheng-yu* are part of the curriculum of Chinese language/culture/history courses in primary, middle, and high schools in Chinese societies such as Taiwan and Mainland China. The Compulsory Education Chinese Curriculum Standards[4] formulated by the Ministry of Education of the People's Republic of China contains four parts: (1) Preface, (2) Curriculum objectives and content, (3) Implementation suggestions, (4) Appendix (e.g., excellent poetry reciting, recommended articles, suggestions on extracurricular reading materials). In terms of grade-specific objectives and content, The Compulsory Education Chinese Curriculum Standards stipulates that from the first to second grade, students are expected to read and learn common idioms.

Regarding extracurricular reading materials, the Compulsory Education Chinese Curriculum Standards requires students to read millions of extracurricular readings in 9 years. The reading materials include all kinds of books and newspapers. In addition to fairy tales, fables, poetry, prose, and literary classics, students are advised to read various stories, such as idiom stories, mythological stories, Chinese and foreign historical stories, and folk tales of other nationalities.

Based on those Curriculum standards, teaching of idioms in Mainland China is usually integrated into daily Chinese teaching to improve students' literary quality. In the lower grades (Grade 1–3) students are mainly asked to read idiom stories and understand their meaning, while in the middle and upper grades (Grade 4–6, and Grade 7–9) students are encouraged to use idioms in their writing. Prior to 2019, when the curriculum was changed, this was the common practice of teaching idioms in both public and private schools in China despite some variation in the then not-standardized textbooks.

In Chinese textbooks, some versions offer a unit that give students idioms around a theme, such as about winter, or about the quality of people. Other versions are centered on a specific word. For example, students may be asked to learn sets of idioms that include this word in various positions among the four characters, such as idioms that include the character "手(hand)."

Idiom exercises can be oral and/or written. Oral exercises include sharing idiom stories, performing idiom stories, or speaking a passage with one or more idioms. Written exercises may include what is known as an "idiom string-up puzzle." Students are given a specific idiom and first asked to write out another idiom beginning with the fourth character of the given idiom. Next they need to write out another idiom beginning with the fourth character of that last produced idiom. This may go on until they have written out four or five idioms in all. [一心一意yī xīn yī yì -意味深长yì wèi shēn cháng -长年累月cháng nián lěi yuè -月白风清yuè bái fēng qīng]. Families or friends may also play an idiom string-up puzzle as a game. In theory, these string-up puzzles could go on forever. There really is no equivalent to this puzzle in form or meaning in English. A hypothetical English version of the game would be something like, "In bad," followed by "a bad apple," followed by "An apple a day keeps the doctor away." Another could be "Give someone the slip," followed by "Slip one's mind," followed by "Mind one's ps and qs." In English, as in Mandarin, this game can go on for a while: "Give me a break," "Break a leg!" "A leg up," Up to no good," "Good for nothing," "Nothing ventured, nothing gained."

At other times, students are asked to do idiom categorical exercises, such as writing out idioms with antonyms, idioms with animals, idioms with numbers, etc. [东张西望dōng zhāng xī wàng (Look to the east and look to the west. "东"dōng east and "西"xī west are antonyms.), 叶公好龙yègōnghàolóng (A man called Yegong is fond of dragons. "龙" lóng means dragon.), 首屈一指 shǒu qū yī zhǐ (Second to none. "一" yī means one, namely the best, the first.)] What's more, students are sometimes asked to judge whether the use of idioms in a given text is appropriate or not.

Since September 2019, the Ministry of Education has stipulated that all private and public schools in China are going to use the unified, standard Chinese textbooks compiled by Renmin Education Publishing House. The new textbook has added more content of classical poetry and other Chinese classics, which also usually convey moral lessons. In general, there is an overarching emphasis on moral education in China; for example, in assessing honors students in any grade (first through twelfth), moral virtue comes first—before academic and physical accomplishment.

IDIOMS IN MASS MEDIA

Cheng-yu are not only used in textbooks for children; they are also found in talk shows, news stories, even advertisements for adults. In one advertisement, the idiom "事半功倍" (shìbàngōngbèi) in a poster means "Do more with less; less effort, much prosperity." This is an advertisement for a training class at an industrial design center. Idioms abound in both adults' and children's literature. Simplified versions of Chinese idiom storybooks are available in bookstores and libraries for young children to read and there are some related TV programs for them to watch. "Chinese Idiom Conference" is a major influential large-scale TV cultural program that landed on CCTV (China Central Television) on April 18, 2014. CCTV is one of the national television networks and has the largest number of viewers in Mainland China. Every Friday night, 20:00 CCTV-10 is broadcast during prime time. The program uses new media means to innovate cultural communication and launches a series of new media interactive products such as idiom memory competition, idiom filling in the blank, and so on. During the broadcast of the program, the audience could scan through the "CCTV Yuedong" client or QR code to get involved in real-time interactions. Such participation greatly mobilized the viewers' enthusiasm. A total of 12.95 million people participated in such interaction. The maximum number of interactions in a single-stage program reached 2.678 million, which caused a wave of "idioms" in the society. Children hence have many chances to hear and read idiom stories that have no resolution.

In sum, *cheng-yu* are ubiquitous in Chinese and Taiwanese culture and are valued. We argue that they exemplify what amounts to an alternative to resolved stories and narratives. Stories that end at a climax with a moral, perhaps, instead of a resolution are as valued as those that go on to resolve whatever problem or situation was narrated. Note also that this does not conform to the requirement of resolution proposed by Propp in his famous analysis of Russian folktales, an approach that we noted inspired several versions of what is known as story grammar in the United States. Specifically, Propp (1958/2015, 86–92) argued that folktales proper should end either with victory over a villain or a difficult task and its resolution and that a tale that ended instead with two brothers parting ways "should be excluded from the category of complete folktales." A consequence (i.e., resolution) of planned activity in a story is obligatory in order to call that story a complete episode (Stein and Glenn 1979). Mandler and colleagues (1980, 21) argued that this episodic "organization of simple stories is a cultural universal." This chapter argues that consequences or resolutions are *not* obligatory for Mandarin speakers, that stories that end without such are also valued.

In conclusion, in both Mainland China and Taiwan, Mandarin-speaking children end many of their personal narratives with no resolution, unlike their English-speaking counterparts. We argue that this reflects many aspects of the children's socialization that involve *Cheng-yu*. Such Chinese idioms abound in adults' and children's literature, educational practices, and mass media. In particular, Chinese parents emphasize social rules and moral standards in talking with their children about past personal experiences. Chinese parents also enjoy telling and reading various idiom stories to their children because these stories transmit cultural values and morals. In short, morals trump resolutions in Chinese narration.

NOTES

1. EXP refers to the experimenter; CHI refers to child being interviewed.
2. Here dripping refers to IV drip.
3. A Google search for the source of advice not to use idioms in formal English writing turns up almost five million results.
4. The Compulsory Education Chinese Curriculum Standards refers to the 2011 edition formulated by Ministry of Education of the People's Republic of China. edu.qq.com/a/20120202/000086.htm.

REFERENCES

Almerico, Gina M. 2014. "Building character through literacy with children's literature." *Research in Higher Education Journal* 26 (October): 1–13.

Bai, Yunfei. 2010. "Xiandaj Hanyu Cidian Lei Chengyu Yanjiu" [A Study on idioms in modern Chinese Dictionary]. M.A. thesis, Heilongjiang University. www.docin.com/p-178158990.html#documentinfo.

Chang, Lan Samantha. 1998. *Hunger: A novella and stories.* New York: Penguin.

Chang, Chien-ju. 2009. *Narrative development in Mandarin-speaking children: Personal narratives, fantasy narratives, and scripts.* Technical Report. Ministry of Science and Technology, Taipei, Taiwan.

Chang, Chien-ju, and Huang, Cho-chi. 2016. "Mother-child talk during joint book reading in two social classes in Taiwan: Interaction strategies and information types." *Applied Psycholinguistics* 37 (2): 387–410.

Cristofaro, Tonia N., and Tamis-Lemonda, Catherine S. 2008. "Lessons in mother-child and father-child personal narratives in Latino families." In *Spanish-language narration and literacy: Culture, cognition, and emotion*, edited by Allyssa McCabe, Alison L. Bailey, and Gigliana Melzi, 54–91. New York: Cambridge University Press.

Fernandez, Camila, and Melzi, Gigliana. 2008. "Evaluation in Spanish-speaking mother-child narratives: The social and sense-making function of internal-state references." In *Spanish-language narration and literacy: Culture, cognition, and emotion*, edited by Allyssa McCabe, Alison L. Bailey, and Gigliana Melzi, 92–118. New York: Cambridge University Press.

Fivush, Robyn. 1991. "The social construction of personal narratives." *Merrill-Palmer Quarterly* 37 (1): 57–81.

Fivush, Robyn, and Fromhoff, Fayne A. 1988. "Style and structure in mother-child conversations about the past." *Discourse Processes* 11 (3): 337–355.

Fung, Heidi, Miller, Peggy J., and Lin, Lu-Chun. 2004. "Listening is active: Lessons from the narrative practices of Taiwanese families." In *Family stories and the life course: Across time and generations*, edited by Michael W. Pratt and Barbara H. Fiese, 303–323. London: Routledge.

Jiao, Liwei, Kubler, Cornelius C., and Zhang, Weiguo. 2011. *500 common Chinese idioms: An annotated frequency dictionary.* London: Routledge.

Koh, Jessie Bee Kim, and Wang, Qi. 2013. "Narrative self-making during dinnertime conversations in Chinese immigrant families." In *Chinese language narration: Culture, cognition, and emotion*, Vol. 19, edited by Allyssa McCabe, and Chien-ju, Chang, 7–32. Amsterdam: John Benjamins Publishing.

Labov, William. 1972. *Language in the inner city: Studies in the Black English vernacular.* Philadelphia: University of Pennsylvania Press.

Lee, Stacey. 2019. *The downstairs girl.* New York: Putnam.

Louie, BelindaYun-Ying. 1996. "Children's literature in the People's Republic of China." *The Reading Teacher* 49 (6): 494–496.

Luo, Ya-hui, Snow, Catherine E., and Chang, Chien-ju. 2012. "Mother-child talk during joint book reading in low-income American and Taiwanese families." *First Language* 32 (4): 494–511.

Mandler, Jean M., Scribner, Sylvia, Cole, Michael, and DeForest, Marsha. 1980. "Cross-cultural invariance in story recall." *Child Development* 51: 19–26.

McCabe, Allyssa, and Peterson, Carole. 1991. "Getting the story: A longitudinal study of parental styles in eliciting narratives and developing narrative skills." In *Developing narrative structure*, edited by Allyssa McCabe and Carole Peterson, 217–253. Hillsdale, NJ: Lawrence Erlbaum Associates.

McCabe, Allyssa, and Rollins, Pamela Rosenthal. 1994. "Assessment of preschool narrative skills." *American Journal of Speech-language Pathology* 3: 45–56. doi .org/10.1044/1058-0360.0301.45.

Miller, Peggy J., Wiley, Angela R., Fung, Heidi, and Liang, Chung-hui. 1997. "Personal storytelling a medium of socialization in Chinese and American families." *Child Development* 68 (3): 557–568.

Minami, Masahiko, and McCabe, Allyssa. 1991. "Haiku as a discourse regulation device: A stanza analysis of Japanese children's personal narratives." *Language in Society* 20 (4): 577–599. doi.org/10.1017/S0047404500016730.

Peterson, Carole, and McCabe, Allyssa. 1983. *Developmental psycholinguistics: Three ways of looking at a child's narrative.* New York, NY: Plenum.

Propp, Vladimir. 2015/1958. *Morphology of the folktale.* Martino Publishing.

Reese, Elaine, and Fivush, Robyn. 1993. "Parental styles of talking about the past." *Developmental Psychology* 29 (3): 596–606.

Shi, Shi. 1979. *Hanyu Chengyu Yanjiu*. Sichuan: Sichuan People Publishers.

Stein, Nancy L., and Glenn, Christine G. 1979. "An analysis of story comprehension in elementary school children." In *New directions in discourse processing*, edited by Roy O. Freedle, 53–120. Hillsdale, NJ: Ablex.

Stellard, Lisa. 2011. "Chinese idioms *(Cheng-yu)* for second-language learners: Toward a pedagogical approach." M.A. thesis, University of Oregon.

Su, Lichang. 2004. "Cultural Effects As Seen in Chinese Metaphors." *Intercultural CommunicationStudies XIII* 3: 61–66.

Wang, Qi. 2013. *The autobiographical self in time and culture*. Oxford: Oxford University Press.

Wishard Guerra, A. 2008. "The intersection of language and culture among Mexican-heritage children 3 to 7 years old." In *Spanish-language narration and literacy: Culture, cognition, and emotion*, edited by Allyssa McCabe, Alison L. Bailey, and Gigliana Melzi, 146–174. New York: Cambridge University Press.

Wu, Chu-hsia. 1995. "On the cultural traits of Chinese idioms." *Intercultural Communication Studies* 5 (1): 61–84.

Yong, Yin Bin. 2003. *100 Chinese idioms and set phrases*. Taiwan: Sinolinguia Press.

Zhang, Xin. 2012. "*Chengyu* as cultural performances: Insights into designing pedagogical materials for four-character Chinese idioms." M.A. thesis, The Ohio State University.

Zhang, Xin. 2009. "Jiyu Yuliaoku de Hanying Chenyu Shiyongpinlv Yanjiu" [A corpus-based study of using frequencies of Chinese and English idioms]. M.A. thesis, China Ocean University.

Zhang, Fangfang, McCabe, Allyssa, Ye, Jiaqi, Wang, Yan and Li, Xiaoyan. 2019. "A developmental study of the narrative components and patterns of Chinese children aged 3–6 years." *Journal of Psycholinguistic Research* 48 (2): 477–500.

Zipes, Jack. 1983. *Fairy tales and the art of subversion*. London: Blackwell.

Chapter 4

Collectivism in Asian versus Western Folktales of (Extra) ordinary Companions

Juwen Zhang, Allyssa McCabe,
MinJeong Kim, and Charlotte L. Wilinsky

Changkes mouy bach kach min bat
A bunch of sticks cannot be broken.[1]

—Cambodian Proverb

Collectivism is a broad concept that refers to a culture that fosters a strong sense of collective interest among its participants (e.g., Zhang and Lauer 2015). It is usually contrasted to individualism, which emphasizes a strong sense of individual identity. Typically, collectivism is common in Asian cultures, while individualism is common in European and North American cultures, though there is considerable individual variation within cultures in both of these respects. Zhang and Lauer (2015) had Chinese and German twelve-year-olds read either a Chinese or a German fairy tale and answer a number of questions about it. Participants read the folktales from the country not their own in translation. Zhang and Lauer found cultural differences in story comprehension, specifically character evaluation, plot development, and time/space imagination. This work builds upon a line of research begun by Bartlett (1932), who examined the ways that British people (mis) remembered stories from a very different (Native American Indian) culture. In this chapter, we seek to build on such work by complicating the notion of collectivism, looking at it in a more fine-grained way than is often the case. And while Zhang and Lauer looked at collectivist versus individualist reader responses to fairy tales, we will look at detailed aspects and layers of collectivism in folktales from three Asian countries: Cambodia, Korea, and China.

A CAMBODIAN FOLKTALE ABOUT THE POWER
OF ORDINARY SNAILS ACTING COLLECTIVELY

One Cambodian folktale told in our focus group (Kim, McCabe, and Uy) with elders of that Lowell, Massachusetts, community went as follows: "Why the Rabbit Doesn't Drink from the Pond" describes a race around a pond between a snail and a rabbit to see who had the right to drink from that pond. The snail said that the rabbit could not come and drink the water from [his] pond. The rabbit then insulted the snail, "You crawling snail-ey, slowly, slowly [moving] animal. You cannot one day crawl the lengths . . . [that] I hop." The snail hear[d] this [and got] so mad at the rabbit. "If you say that you insulted me, that I could not crawl in one day to the length of your hop, so now we compete. We are running a race." The snail said that if he lost he would agree not to live in the pond any more. In turn, the rabbit pledged that he would not come and drink the water from the pond if he lost the race. Faced with this seemingly impossible challenge, the snails organized. They dispersed themselves around the pond. The rabbit mockingly called out to see where the snail was, "Where are you the slowey, slowey snail?" A snail replied, "Coo, I am here"—ahead of the rabbit. This continued until the rabbit conceded that he had been beaten when a snail—the rabbit assumes *the* snail—called out from the finish line ahead of him. The snails won the race and stayed in the pond, whereas the rabbit no longer came to visit or drink the water from the pond.

The elder explained to us, "The moral of the story is to not judge other people. Because when you judge other people, like the rabbit is judging the snail, like he's so slow he can't win. But he was able to win together, team up. . . . This story is talking about compare (comparing) about the idea and the power body. The rabbit use[s] the power body, run, run. And then the snail use[s] the brain."

As has been noted, what is now known as the Aarne-Thompson-Uther (ATU) Classification System is an index of types of folktales told in Europe and Western Asia used by folklorists since the early twentieth century. The rabbit and snails folktale is a variant of the ATU type 513, "The Extraordinary Companions" (Zipes 2015, xiv). This is a type of tale told in many countries around the documented folklore world (Zipes 2015). In the Grimm brothers' German tale, "How Six Made Their Way in the World (or 'Six Soldiers of Fortune')," a penniless soldier gathers a strong man who can rip up trees, a sharpshooter who can hit targets miles away, a blower who can rotate windmills miles away, a very fast runner, and a man who can make the air freeze if he takes off his hat. The soldier determines to make his fortune by marrying a princess, whose father proposes that whoever wants to marry his daughter must win a race against her. Whoever tries but loses to her also loses his head. The fast runner starts off, quickly reaches a brook, and fills a pitcher full of water. But on the way home, he gets sleepy and takes a nap, lying on a horse's skull so that he will not sleep too much. The princess catches him asleep and dumps out the water that will prove he made it all the way to the brook. The sharpshooter sees this from afar and shoots out the horse's skull, waking the runner up. The runner goes back and refills his pitcher and still wins the race. Neither the king nor his daughter is pleased. He invites them to a feast, locks them into the room where the feast is, and orders the cook to light a fire and burn them up. This time they are saved by the man with the hat, who cools the room down. The king then tries to get out of the marriage by offering gold to the soldier instead of his daughter. The strong man takes off with a huge amount of gold. At the prospect of losing all his wealth, the king sends two regiments after the six. The man who could blow enormous distances, blows away the soldiers except for one brave fellow who goes back to the king and informs him that any further efforts to have soldiers take back the gold will meet with the same fate. At this, the king resigns himself to the loss of his riches and the six companions divide the treasure and live well the rest of their lives. Together, then, the six outwitted and defeated the king because *each individual deployed their unique skill to collectively accomplish this.*

Most of the ATU type 513 tales involve a similar set of individuals whose individual special talents combine to collectively defeat an evil enemy. Below is a comparison of several tales from Europe in terms of extraordinary powers. As is clear from table 4.1, there are both similarities and differences in the gifts the individuals display.

Zipes (2015) notes that such collective action in the interests of promoting social justice has perhaps found its contemporary zenith in the wildly popular

Table 4.1 Gifts of Companions in Several Tales, ATU 513, Collected by Multilingual Folktale Database

Gifts:	Hearing	Blowing	Strength	Running	Cooling	Sight
The Flea (Italy)	Hearing	(Soap suds)	(Razors)	(Tangled wood)	Water Level	Sight
The Booby (Italy)	Quick ear	Blower	Strong	Back	Running	Archer
Six Men Travel the World (Grimm, Germany)	(man)	Blower	Strong	Running	Cooling	Sight
Six Servants (Grimm, Germany)	Hearing	(Obese)	(Tall)	(long neck)	Temp reg	Sight

superhero comic books and movies in American culture. While many super-hero comics and films focus on a single character with distinctive power(s), series such as Marvel's Avengers are back to the original (collectivist) extraordinary friends model, with multiple characters with distinctive powers working together to achieve justice.

Our Cambodian snails, however, differ from the extraordinary German companions by virtue of the fact that they are simply ordinary snails, each so much like the others that the rabbit is satisfied they are simply one snail. None has a superpower. Like a collection of identical sticks, as in the Cambodian proverb at the outset of this chapter, the identical snails prevail as a group. Despite some commonalities between East and West, then, regarding the potential power of collective action, there are very real differences in *preferences* for collectivism and individualism in Eastern versus Western countries.

Note that the Cambodian snails copied each other so as to be perceived as interchangeable; such copying is not possible when each member of the team has a distinctive skill. As it turns out, copying in a variety of arenas is a corol-lary of the distinct types of collective action in the two contrastive types of tales noted above. Gish Jen (2017) explores at length this differential preference for versus against copying in Eastern versus Western culture. That is, some West-ern readers of our snail and rabbit story might see the snails as cheaters, might see collaboration as violating the (Western) rules of racing that imply one indi-vidual competes against another specific individual; Jen, however, elaborates why that notion represents an incomplete understanding of collectivist cultures, which highly value collaboration in solving problems. At times, such collabo-ration takes the form of copying what others do, the way all the snails copied the first snail's behavior. Jen notes that copying is not always—or maybe even often—the passive, unskillful activity Western societies (and education sys-tems) deem it. After all, memorizing poetry is a form of copying that requires considerable skill. So is copying master paintings (e.g., van Gogh, Klimt), an industry in Dafen Oil Painting Village in southern China. So is the kind of reproduction of musical patterns (e.g., Twinkle, Twinkle, Little Star) fostered by the well-known and highly successful Suzuki method of violin instruction.

One motif related to collectivism is this: Little creatures can together achieve great power. That cooperation can triumph over a single individual who has an enormous competitive advantage is a value of many Asian cultures.

KONGJWI AND PATJWI: A KOREAN CINDERELLA STORY

Another Asian folktale where little creatures' collectivistic acts resolve the protagonist's problem is Kongjwi and Patjwi, a Korean Cinderella tale.

Kongjwi and Patjwi is one of the most well-known Korean folktales from the Joseon dynasty (1392–1897). The story of Kongjwi and Patjwi has been popular for young children in Korea due to moral lessons embedded in the plot. In addition, this tale is viewed as one of the most typical folktales that teach not only moral lessons of good and evil but also about the Confucian culture of traditional Korea (Grayson 2002) that heavily influences traditional Koreans' values, beliefs, and behaviors related to collectivism. This tale has been loved much, as Koreans use it in a textbook for moral education.

There are many variations of the tale of Konjwi and Patjwi, Tale Type 450 in *A Type Index of Korean Folk Tales* by Choi In-hak (1979), though note that in the Western ATU index, it is considered type 510A. Choi In-hak who is the author of the Korean type index recorded this tale in Kyongsang Province in South Korea in around 1944. This version recorded by Choi was translated into English by James Grayson (2001) in his book "Myths and Legends from Korea: An Annotated Compendium of Ancient and Modern Materials." We use this translated version of Kongjwi and Patjwi in this chapter to refer to specific parts of the tale to explore how the nature of cultural collectivism is reflected in the tale.

As in most folktales across the globe there are many variations of this tale. Different versions of this tale include variations in the characters' names, supporting animal characters, and endings. For example, the first written version of *Kongjwi and Patjwi* for children published in 1926 by Sim Uirin does not include a marriage episode. In some versions, the stepmother's vicious behavior continues on after Kongjwi's marriage to the magistrate. All available versions of this tale, though, contain the lost shoe motif of traditional Cinderella tales and the moral lesson of good and evil. Across different versions of the tale, the following main themes are central:

1. The good-natured girl, Kongjwi, lost her mother at an early age. Kongjwi's father was married to an evil-minded woman with a daughter, Patjwi, who was younger than Kongjwi.
2. Animals helped when Kongjwi was tormented by her stepmother and Patjwi.
3. The lost shoe motif and Kongjwi's marriage to the magistrate as a reward for her virtue are present.

As we have noted, collectivism is the tendency for a group of people to emphasize the views, values, goals, and social norms of the ingroup rather than of oneself (Triandis 2018; Cha 1994). Cha (1994) examined the collectivistic nature of traditional Korean culture and identified values, attitudes, and behaviors specific to traditional Korea. The collectivistic values revealed include dependence (e.g., preference for collective actions, fear of

independent decisions), obedience and courtesy to hierarchy, heartfulness/
fraternity, filial piety/loyalty, and sacrifice of women (Cha 1994, 165). These
collectivistic values are consistently reflected in the tale of Kongjwi and
Patjwi (See table 4.2) in both explicit and implicit ways.

The following part from Grayson's translation of Kongjwi and Patjwi
illustrates collective actions of animals to relieve Kongjwi from the hardship
caused by her stepmother (Grayson 2001, 347–350):

> One day, in a neighboring village a banquet was to be held at a relative's
> house. The stepmother wanted only to take P'atjwi along to the banquet. How-
> ever, K'ongjwi asked for permission to go along too. The step-mother gave
> her a list of chores which had to be done. First, the stepmother produced five
> sheaves of flax and five sheaves of Chinese silk plants and said to her, "First
> weave these. After that, clean each of the nine rooms in the house. Then, take
> out the ashes from the firepits for each room, and set a new fire in each firepit.
> Then, fill the (leaking) jar to the top with water. Then, mill the five large
> containers of rice which are spread out in the garden to dry. Then, prepare the
> evening meal. Only after you have completed all these tasks, can you come
> to the banquet."

Table 4.2 Specific Features of Collectivism in *Kongjwi and Patjwi* Modified from Cha (1994)

Collectivism Values	Characters' Behaviors	Character's Beliefs
Dependence	Kongjwi depended on the animals to resolve life challenges. The supporting animals helped Kongjwi based on group efforts.	Lack of Kongjwi's right as an individual. Group efforts are required to resolve challenges.
Hierarchy/Courtesy	Kongjwi was rewarded and Patwji was punished by the authorities.	Obedience to authorities and elderly family members.
Heartfulness/fraternity	Animals are willing to help. Kongjwi did not complain about hardship.	One is rewarded for his or her friendly and loyal behaviors.
Filial piety/loyalty	Kongjwi obeyed her evil-minded stepmother, suppressing her own emotions and keeping her thoughts to herself.	Loyalty, obedience, and deference to parents and ancestors is highly valued.
Sacrifice of women	Kongjwi's sacrifice for her father's new family.	Women's self-effacing work for male family members.

K'ongjwi immediately began the chores, but as each chore was more difficult than the last, she soon grew exhausted. On top of that she grew despondent and began to weep. With that, a surprising thing happened. Out of nowhere a large flock of sparrows came. With their beaks, they pecked and pecked at the rice in the garden, removing the husks. Before long, the rice was as white as if it had been threshed properly. Next, a bee[2] came and said to K'ongjwi, "I will block the hole in the water jar while you fill it up." K'ongjwi did exactly as she was told. Before she knew it, all of the chores had been completed. But when she thought about going to the banquet, she realized that she had no clothes. Once again, she began to weep. Then the ox flew down from the sky and gave her a beautiful dress and slippers. K'ongjwi felt as if her dream had come true and off she went to the banquet. When all of the guests saw the beautiful Kongjwi, they complimented her highly. However, her stepmother and P'atjwi were not too pleased. They were so jealous that they beat her away from the banquet. K'ongjwi ran as fast as her legs could carry her. She was so flustered that when she was running she lost one of her slippers. Just then, the magistrate happened to pass by. He picked up the slipper and looked around for its owner

The main themes of this tale described above clearly reflect values and beliefs associated with collectivism. The scenes where the sparrows and the ox help Kongjwi complete the difficult tasks might be viewed as cheating by Western readers as in the interpretations of the Cambodian snail and hare tale. However, these values function as motifs and a coping mechanism for the characters in the tale of Kongjwi and Patjwi as they are part of the broader Korean familial and societal values.

The supporting animals' behaviors are an explicit behavior pattern of collectivism. There are less obvious yet important patterns of behaviors representative of Korean collectivistic culture. For example, the motif of the animals' collective behaviors stems from Buddhism/Confucian culture that a good-hearted person will be rewarded for her virtue.

Another behavior pattern of collectivism is that Kongjwi suppressed her emotions and tolerated hardships to obey her stepmother. This behavioral pattern was viewed as a virtuous one in collectivistic Korean society with Confucian culture. As a result, Kongjwi's role in resolving the challenges is minimized. She did not challenge the status quo and did not complain, very much following the tradition of obeying parents. Rather, Kongjwi relied on collective help from the animals to tackle life challenges. In addition, the animals' unusual and extraordinary behaviors such as recognizing, talking to, and helping a good-hearted person are examples of traditional Korea's animism, which is prevalent in many Korean folktales. These traditional values in this tale associated with collectivism permeated the mind of the people of traditional Korea; they were not "extraordinary" to the native audience. This tale of Kongjwi and Patjwi is classified under "ordinary tales" in A Type Index of Korean Folktales by Choi In-hak, which is a more localized index than ATU, while the tale is classified as an "adventurous" tale according to Grayson's classification (2001).

Grayson (2002) defined this type of good and evil tale using two parallel events as a double contrastive narrative structure. On a surface level, this double contrastive tale seems to be a story of good and evil. However, what distinguishes the Kongjwi and Patjwi tale from other similar good and evil tales is that it goes beyond the simple notion of rewarding good and punishing evil. Some variants of this tale emphasize the importance of moral responsibilities of older people using a happy ending for both Kongjwi and Patjwi as Kongjwi, Patjwi's older sister, forgave Patjwi for her evil behaviors in the end.

This Confucian value emphasizes moral responsibilities of an older sibling, which is one of the Five Relationships, a key concept taught by Confucius (551–497 BC). According to the Confucian ethical principle, family is a foundational unit of society. In Confucian society, the elder brother is expected to be morally superior to his younger brother and is meant to cultivate moral values in his younger brother. As Patjwi's elder sister Kongjwi forgave Patjwi, and as a result of Kongjwi's moral behaviors, Patjwi realized her evil behaviors and was reformed. This kind of Confucianistic ending demonstrates the power of moral education by example. Thus, this Korean double contrastive narrative structure can be considered as "an illustration of the Confucian concept of moral suasion and not simply about rewards and punishments" (Grayson 2002, 53). In fact, there is a variant of this tale among the Korean community in Northeast China, in which, as told by a Korean Chinese woman in her eighties and recorded in Chinese, the two sisters are "Kongji and Paji" (Jin 1994, 485–488; see also English translation, Zhang 2021, 39–42). In sum, the collectivistic values embedded in this folktale are a means to reflect educational, social, and cultural dimensions of traditional Korea rather than serving as mere rhetorical devices of folktale.

WEIRD BROTHERS: A CHINESE FOLKTALE

While the Cambodian Snails and Rabbit tale and the animals in the Korean Cinderella tale exemplify what we might call tales of Ordinary Companions, we do encounter tales of Extraordinary Companions in Asian folktales. Consider the tale of the Weird Brothers, translated into English here for the first time by the first author (see also, Zhang 2022, 157–159).

Source of this translation is from Lin (1930, 1–6).

Tale Type ATU 513

Once there was a woman who had ten sons. From the first to the tenth, they were named Long Spirit, Flying Legs, Iron Neck, Loose Skin, Thick Legs, Big Head, Long Legs, Big Nose, Water Eyes, and Pout Lips.

At that time, there was an emperor who wanted to build a Five-Phoenix Building, but three years passed, and he could not get it done. Then Long Spirit went to the emperor, and he finished the job in three days. He built it high up to the sky with five phoenixes on the roof as if flying. The emperor said, "How capable he is! If I don't kill him, he will eventually rebel." So, Long Spirit was bound and sent to the execution site.

Meanwhile, Flying Legs carried Iron Neck on his back to the site, and he ran ten miles in one breath. Iron Neck said, "Kill me, please! I am so skinny and can't do anything, but my big brother has strength and can beg food for our mother." Thanks to Iron Neck's pleas, Long Spirit was released. When the two executioners chopped on his neck, there were only sparks. So the emperor cried out, "Since the blade can't kill him, he will be replaced by Loose Skin!"

Flying Legs heard they would execute Loose Skin instead of Iron Neck. So, he hurried back and carried Loose Skin on his back to the site. When he arrived, Loose Skin shouted, "Pull me! I am a useless person and have skins all over my body."

So Iron Neck was released. Now Loose Skin had one cow tied to his head, one cow to his left hand, one cow to his right hand, one cow to his left foot, and one cow to his right foot. There were five whips for the five cows, and they were all whipped at the same time. Loose Skin's head skin was pulled a few miles long. However, he did not die at all.

The emperor was angry and cried out: "Since we can't kill Loose Skin, bring their entire family here and kill them all!" When Flying Legs heard that his whole family would be killed, he carried Loose Skin back home on his back, shouting from far away, "The Emperor wants to kill the whole family! Everyone run away quickly!"

Well before the Emperor's guards arrived, the family had run away. They came to a big river. Long Legs said, "Let me walk in and see how deep it is." So he walked into the river. It was several dozen yards deep, but it was only up to his leg calf. He then carried the whole family across the river.

Now they were hungry. What to do? Long Legs said, "Let me catch a few fish in the river." Within seconds, he caught two big fish. Then he asked his mother to cut open the fish's stomach. When she cut open one fish, out came a boat with thirteen sails. She cut open the other fish, and out came another boat with thirteen sails. There were also many people on the boats. They thanked her and said, "If you hadn't cut open the fish, we would have never seen the sky again."

The two boats sailed downstream, and the people on the boats gave two rolls of red silk to her to make clothes. The two fish were put in a pot, but there was no firewood. Now Thick Legs said, "There are still two splinters in my legs. Pull them out, and there should be enough wood." They pulled out two thick logs and cut them into two bundles.

Big Nose was blowing the fire. Soon, the smell of the cooked fish reached his nose and caused him to drool. He lifted the pot cover and smelled with his nose. The two fish were sucked into his stomach by his nose. Big Head frowned and wanted to hit Big Nose. However, their mother said, "Don't be upset. I will not make clothes with the red silk. I'll make a hat for you."

She quickly made a hat with the two rolls of silk, but it could not even cover his head top. He was upset and threw it on the ground. Water Eyes was sleeping. The hat touched his eyes, and water flowed out of his eyes. It formed a flood that covered only nine counties and twelve districts. The tenth brother Pout Lips looked around, and said, "This is really going too far! Wow!" He pouted his lips and blew open the South Heaven Gate!

This tale (ATU513) is told across China with many variants, and also in East Asian and some Southeast Asian countries. In his *A Type Index of Chinese Folktales,* Nai-Tung Ting collected nearly 70 variants from collections published from the late nineteenth century till the mid-twentieth century (1978). Although similar tales like Brothers Grimm's "Thumbling" are classified as ATU 700, Chinese and Asian scholars prefer to consider tales like "The Weird Brothers" as a different tale type because they have different cultural meanings as discussed below. The same case is seen in the above-mentioned tale of Kongjwi and Patjwi, which is considered by Korean scholars as ATU 450, but ATU 510A by others. The central plot is that the hero, with several brothers, solves the problem or overcomes a difficulty but is then persecuted by the king or emperor. With collective talents from his brothers or team-mates, he destroys the king's plan. For example, among the Chinese variants, one variant emphasizes that the hero died when he was separated from his brothers. Another variant tells that he killed the cruel king. Still another variant relates to the building of the Great Wall in China when the hero eventually destroyed the wall with a flood.

Collective effort seems to be the most striking theme in this tale. Besides its social and political implications, the tale reveals a distinctive characteristic in the Confucian culture circle, that is, the cultures in East and Southeast Asian countries surrounding China.

While there is a general conceptualization that Western culture is oriented toward individualism and that Eastern culture is oriented toward collectivism, as noted above, we must keep in mind that even the concepts of individualism and collectivism have a short history of one century or so in their philosophical or academic articulation. Therefore, in understanding collectivism in East/Southeast Asian cultures, we need to first differentiate the layers of meaning in context, and, second, to have an understanding of the origin of this cultural value.

Collectivism is based on the concept of "group" with which an individual identifies or belongs and prioritizes over himself. Yet, the connotation of *group* changes as it may be based on a family or family clan, or a village, a region, and even a state or country. As a result, the sense of "collective" implies different levels of priority for individuals and their groups. It is difficult to draw the line between those priorities, but it is even more problematic to judge individuals and their groups through this binary lens.

This leads us to explore how the values of self-priority and group-priority have played their role in the development of a culture. In Chinese culture, for example, when Confucian ethics became dominant in social and political systems as an ethical norm in everyday life about two thousand years ago, family played a pivotal role in individual and social life. Confucian ethics is centered on family, which is a medium between individuals and the state or society, and between the human and the supernatural. In contrast, at about the same time, Aristotelian ethics focuses on the relations between individuals and state or society, and between humans and gods, without the intermediate role of family.

Indeed, collectivism in East/Southeast Asia has much to do with Confucian ethics as its origin. In everyday life, we can see many family-centered examples in which "family," or elders/parents, has priority over individuals, which is known as the virtue of *xiao* (孝; filiality, or filial piety), essentially, respect. As seen in the tale of Weird Brothers, no brothers would disobey their mother, but would collectively hold it as their duty to serve their mother by all means.

Yet, this collectivism could be transformed to a different level. For example, the story of *Mulan*, in which a daughter took over the role of a son in fulfilling both the virtue of *xiao* to parents and the virtue of *zhong* (忠; loyalty) to the country, transforms the "collectivism" at the family level to the state level as patriotism. At the level of patriotism to a state or country, it becomes universal in modern history, and thus this kind of collectivism is not unique to Chinese or Asian cultures. The modern Olympic Games is an example of the priority of the state (or nation, country) over individuals at the international level.

Another example to illustrate the relationship between individualism and collectivism in Chinese culture can be the Civil Service Examination. This examination system began in the sixth century and continues today. It is also deeply rooted in Confucian ideas about education. As the greatest teacher in Chinese history and culture, Confucius encouraged individuals to study regardless of their family background, and his students were from both rich and poor families. Through education, individuals would elevate their personal status and then serve their family and society as a useful individual. As a result, the Civil Service Examination essentially promotes individual efforts, or the idea of self-priority in seeking improvement of social status. Of course, along the way, family, family clan, village, even hometown region or state gain pride about the successful individuals in their groups at these different levels.

Similarly, court music throughout Chinese history emphasizes collectivism. In fact, among those musical instruments used in the orthodox court music (known as "eight-sounds," *bayin*, referring to the instruments made of eight types of material) until the end of nineteenth century, there was not any single instrument for "solo" performance. All the instruments played together at the same time, while each had its role to make the entire orchestra possible, or a harmony with differences. It was only by the twentieth century that some of those instruments were developed for solo performances, like the bamboo flute, *dizi*. Yet, parallel to this history of more than two thousand years, there was one individual instrument that was widely used for individual entertainment or self-cultivation, that is, the *qin* (or *guqin*, the seven-string zither). It was not used in the orthodox court music system, but rather was only encouraged for individual use.

CONCLUSION

Collectivism has to be understood in context. In the Cambodian tale of the Snail and Rabbit, the Korean tale of Kongjwi and Patjwi, and the Chinese tale of the Weird Brothers, we have seen collectivism practiced at different levels. The snails demonstrate that their collective wisdom is the source of their strength to win a competition and gain status and respect among all others in their world. In the Korean tale *of* Kongjwi and Patjwi collectivism is reflected both explicitly and implicitly in the motifs of the tale, behaviors and beliefs of the characters with an emphasis on co-dependence to resolve life challenges (e.g., explicit collectivistic actions of animals) and group harmony (e.g. filial piety and sacrifice of women for family), heavily influenced by a Confucian worldview. Collectivistic values embedded in this tale are not just used as rhetorical devices to substantiate a good and evil motif. Rather, such values can be considered as a means to illustrate educational, political, social, and cultural dimensions of the highly Confucianised society of traditional Korea.

In the Chinese tale of the ten weird brothers, however, the brothers' efforts are centered on their mother, further exhibiting Confucian values of filial piety. The ending of this particular version also indicates their potential power in engaging in social affairs. It is one expression of the fundamental values in Chinese culture: *he'erbutong* (和而不同; to reach harmony while keeping differences). Given that this particular version was told and collected in the 1920s in China, when China had just experienced a transition from the previous Qing Dynasty (1644–1911) ruled by the Manchu to the Republic of China newly founded in 1912, it certainly implied that there was the need of a collective effort of the whole nation to overcome difficulties and enter a new stage as an independent modern nation in Chinese history (Zhang 2022). As a result, there appeared the "Grimms of China," known as Lin Lan, to call attention, by collecting oral tales, to the oral traditions that reflected the "Chinese national spirit" (*minzu jingshen*), that is, maintaining the unity of state/country (*guo*) and family (*jia*)—the Chinese concept of "country" (*guo jia*) (Zhang 2020).

Therefore, collectivism in Chinese/Asian practices is not to be interpreted with a fixed binary system in contrast to individualism in the European ideology. Individualism or collectivism is sometimes a virtue in Eastern cultures, but not a personal right as it is in the West. At times, individualism (e.g., Civil Service Examination performance) is a way to pursue harmony at family, village, and greater community levels. Collectivism in Asian and Southeast Asian folktales is a very complicated, layered concept.

NOTES

1. Note that Aesop's fable about the bundle of sticks is quite similar to this one; perhaps there was an exchange between East and West in this regard, though determination of direction is beyond the scope of this chapter.

2. In other versions of Kongjwi and Patgjwi, a toad helps Kongjwi to mend the hole in the pot and an ox weeded rice paddies for her.

REFERENCES

Bartlett, Frederic Charles. 1932. *Remembering*. Cambridge: Cambridge University Press.

Cha, Jae-Ho. 1994. "Aspects of Individualism and Collectivism in Korea," In *Individualism and Collectivism: Theory, Method, and Applications*, edited by Uichol Kim, Harry Triandis, Kâğitçibaşi Çiğdem, Sang-Chin Choi, and Gene Yoon, 157–174. Thousand Oaks, CA: Sage.

Choi, In-hak. 1973. *A Type Index of Korean Folktales*. Seoul: Myung Ji University Press.

Grayson, James. 2001. *Myths and Legends from Korea: An Annotated Compendium of Ancient and Modern Materials*. New York: Routledge, 347–350. Kindle.

Grayson, James. 2002. "The The Hǔngbu and Nolbu Tale Type: A Korean Double Contrastive Narrative Structure." *Folklore,* 113(1): 51–69. DOI: 10.1080/00155870220125444

Jen, Gish. 2017. *The Girl at the Baggage Claim: Explaining the East-West Culture Gap*. New York: Knopf.

Jin, Deshun. 1994. Kongji and Paji (孔姬和葩姬). In *Zhongguo min jian gu shi ji cheng: Liaoning juan* (*The Grand Collection of Folktales in China: Liaoning Volume*), 485–488. Beijing: China ISBN Press.

Kim, Minjeong, Allyssa McCabe, and Phitsamay Uy. 2016. *Focus Groups for Gathering Southeast Asian Folktales*. Lowell, MA. Unpublished grant proposal to President of University of Massachusetts' office.

Lin, Lan. ed. 1930. *Weird Brothers* (*Guai xiong di* 怪兄弟). Shanghai: Beixin shuju, pp. 1–6.

Markus, Hazel Rose, and Allana Conner. 2013. *Clash! 8 Cultural Conflicts That Make Us Who We Are*. New York: Hudson Street Press.

Multilingual Folk Tale Database. Aarne-Thompson-Uther Classification of Folk Tales. www.mftd.org/index.php?action=atu

Ting, Nai-Tung. 1978. *A Type Index of Chinese Folktales*. FF Communications No. 223, Helsinki: Finnish Academy of Science and Letters.

Triandis, Harris. 2018. *Individualism and Collectivism*. New York, NY: Routledge.

Uther, Hans-Jörg. 2004. *The Types of International Folktales: A Classification and Bibliography. Based on the system of Antti Aarne and Stith Thompson*. FF Communications no. 284–286. Helsinki: Suomalainen Tiedeakatemia.

Zhang, Juwen. 2020. "Rediscovering the Brothers Grimm of China: Lin Lan." *Journal of American Folklore*, 133(529): 285–306.

Zhang, Juwen. 2021. *The Magic Love: Fairy Tales from Twenty-First Century China*. With a Preface by Jack Zipes. New York: Peter Lang.

Zhang, Juwen. 2022. *The Dragon Daughter and Other Lin Lan Fairy Tales*. With a Preface by Jack Zipes. Princeton University Press.

Zhang, Yehong, and Gerhard Lauer. 2015. "How Culture Shapes the Reading of Fairy Tales: A Cross-Cultural Approach." *Comparative Literature Studies,* 52(4): 663–681.

Zipes, Jack. 2015. *Grimm Legacies: The Magic Spell of the Grimms' Folk and Fairy Tales*. Princeton University Press.

PSYCHOLOGICAL PERSPECTIVE

Chapter 5

A Developmental Perspective on Violence in Southeast Asian Folktales

Charlotte L. Wilinsky and Allyssa McCabe

Anyone familiar with folktales will not be surprised to learn that violence appeared in some of the tales we collected from elders from four Southeast Asian communities. This chapter will document and describe those folktales containing violence. We will then present the perspective on those tales by the elders themselves (emic perspective), along with two sorts of etic perspectives: (1) developmental psychological research on the effects of violence in various formats (screen, story), and (2) determination as to whether or not the folktales we collected may be aptly described by the Aarne-Thompson-Uther (ATU) Classification of folktales, a well-known, largely Eurocentric system (Dundes 1997) developed primarily to classify German and English folktale themes ever since 1910. It has since been applied to folktales from a number of different countries (including some from West Asia), but, so far as we have been able to determine, not to folktales from Southeast Asia. "A tale type is a composite plot synopsis corresponding in exact verbatim detail to no one individual version but at the same time encompassing to some extent all of the extant versions of that folktale" (Dundes 1997, 196, emphases this).

DEVELOPMENTAL PSYCHOLOGY RESEARCH ON VIOLENCE

Violence in the media has been a source of concern for quite some time for those invested in healthy child development. The debate surrounding the possibility that violent media, such as television and video games, increases aggression and violence in children has evidence both that such aggression and violence increases and that it decreases such behavior, making it an ongoing controversial issue (e.g., Boudinot 2005; Ferguson and Beresin 2017;

Ferguson et al. 2013; Greitemeyer and Mügge 2014). Despite this conflicting evidence, and the fact that children may utilize violent media such as video games in positive ways, for example, to deal with stress, develop the ability to work toward a goal, increase creativity, make social connections, and even to practice hand-eye coordination (Kutner et al. 2008), researchers, parents, and pediatricians appear to agree that children who consume violent media can act more aggressively (Bushman, Gollwitzer, and Cruz 2015). Furthermore, many people feel that violent media causes aggression. Specifically, the most agreed-upon dangerous forms of media in Bushman et al.'s (2015) study with researchers, parents, and pediatricians were violent video games and movies, while the least agreed-upon forms of media were written media, including violent comic books and literature. The groups did not believe that consuming violent literature was a factor in increased aggression. However, other studies disagree with this notion and have found effects of reading violent or aggressive literature.

Compared to other forms of media, there are far fewer studies that examine the effect of reading violent or aggressive content in literature (e.g., Bushman et al. 2007; Coyne et al. 2012), and fewer still that examine the effect of this literature on children (e.g., Stockdale et al. 2013). One study that did examine this topic looked at the influence of reading physically or relationally aggressive literature on undergraduate students (Coyne et al. 2012). Findings showed that, compared to participants who read the story that included relational aggression, after reading the story with physical aggression, participants acted more physically aggressive as measured by a task that had participants choose noise levels to which to expose an opponent. Additionally, after reading the story with relational aggression, participants showed more of this type of aggression as measured by a task that examined exclusion and ostracism against an opponent via a computer program. While these findings are important, demonstrating aggression in such a laboratory study does not necessarily equate to violence acted out in the real world (Ferguson and Beresin 2017). Some more recent studies in fact do not support the link between violent media and societal violence (e.g., Ferguson 2015; Markey, Markey, and French 2015).

Another study (Stockdale et al. 2013) examined the impact of aggression in books on middle-school students. The students completed a questionnaire that asked about physical and relational aggression, prosocial behavior, preference for aggression in media, prosocial behavior in books, and time spent on media, including reading. Regarding aggression in books, Stockdale et al. (2013) found that reading such books was positively related to self-reported aggression, controlling for consuming other aggressive media. More specifically, their model demonstrated that reading books that included physical aggression was a predictor of physical aggression and reading books with relational aggression was a predictor of relational aggression, aligning with Coyne et al.'s (2012) findings. However, self-reported aggression was not a predictor of reading books with aggression; that is, rather than two-way influences, Stockdale et al. (2013) claim their model, instead, was most consistent with the idea that being exposed to aggressive media over and over can affect aggression, though they note that causality cannot be determined from their study.

As these studies on aggression in literature suggest, the question of how young readers are impacted is a valid one, but one that needs further ecologically valid inquiry before a consistent conclusion can be reached. Folktales are a form of literature passed down through time that include descriptions of aggression and violence that are just as gory as, if not more so than, other forms of media that children are consuming. Therefore, it is warranted to question how violence in folktales may influence children. Stockdale et al. (2013) suggest that reading violent content is a more active and involved process than watching violent television or playing violent video games as the child has to construct and picture the violence in their own mind. This idea could be applied to reading folktales, further validating the concern regarding violence in these tales.

VIOLENCE IN FOLKTALES IN GENERAL

Folktales are one specific form of written, oral, or cinematic entertainment in which violence may be present, triggering concerns regarding the impact of such violence on children. Such concerns have caused some violent tales to be edited and censored (Bengtsson 2009; Quinn and Sonu 2017), though this has not eliminated violence in folktales and many stories remain generally preserved or have even had the violence restored (Quinn and Sonu 2017). For example, violence directed toward and abuse of children is not uncommon in folktales (e.g., Shannon 1981). Even after editing, the Grimm brothers' folktales included some uncensored incidents of child abuse, including starvation and harsh punishments (Bengtsson 2009; Zipes 1988). Isaacs (2013, 988) notes that, "fairy tales described child sexual abuse long before paediatricians acknowledged its existence." Other portrayals of violence, in addition to child abuse, also remain in folktales. This chapter henceforth examines the manifestations and uses of violence in Southeast Asian folktales, a largely understudied avenue of inquiry, and implications for the development of children who read the tales.

VIOLENCE IN SOUTHEAST ASIAN FOLKTALES

The present chapter discusses violence in Southeast Asian folktales that come from a project that collected folktales from community organizations (see Introduction for more details concerning this project). Instances of violence in these tales were documented through a close reading of the tales. In doing so, we followed Allen and Anderson's (2017) definition of violence as a severe type of aggression with the aim of inflicting serious physical harm on others (Anderson and Bushman 2002; Bushman and Huesmann 2010; Huesmann and Taylor 2006). It is not necessary, however, that an action results in actual harm to be described as violent; for example, attempting to kill someone is still considered violent (Allen and Anderson 2017). Threats, though apparent in some of the collected folktales, were not considered violence, as Allen and Anderson (2017) define threats specifically as coercion and separate from violence.

Violence in this sample of folktales includes instances of murder, suicide, and fighting that often resulted in death. The violence is perpetrated not only by humans but also by anthropomorphized animals and deities. Despite the generally negative connotations of violence, the violence in these tales may have some positive functions and effects on development, though these remain understudied, especially in the context of Southeast Asian tales. Specifically, the functions of violence in the collected tales include using the stories as cautionary tales, presentation of a moral dilemma or opposing moral forces, and explanation of phenomena. These functions are discussed in more depth below with illustrative examples from the sample of folktales.

Cautionary Tales

Violence in folktales is often used, perhaps paradoxically, as a vehicle through which to protect children from harm, imminent or potential (e.g., Boudinot 2005). For example, a cautionary folktale (Boudinot 2005; Isaacs 2013) may use violence or tragedy to instill fear in children in order to warn them about some danger (Boudinot 2005; Isaacs 2013). An example of such a cautionary tale from our sample is the Burmese folktale "The Story of Cuckoo Bird," which warns children about the dangers of sleepovers, a fear that differentiates Asian culture from American culture (e.g., Yoon et al. 2017). In this story, a six-year-old girl wants to go sleep at her friend's house, but her parents never allowed her to have a sleepover because she sleeps very heavily and there are robbers in the village, and the girl might sleep through a robbery. Finally, one night, the girl was nagging her mother so much to have a sleepover that the mother let her go. That night the robbers came to the sleepover house, and the girl was left in the house and beaten badly by them. The robbers demanded that she give them money. They beheaded her when she did not have any and could not get any from her mother. The girl was reincarnated as a cuckoo bird. From that time, she was trying to call her mom, "Cuckoo, cuckoo," "Mom, Mom." The beating of the girl in this tale and her beheading are clearly violent acts that are meant to warn children about the dangers of sleeping over at someone's house, making this story a prime example of a cautionary tale. The fact that it is a young girl who is killed in this tale is especially powerful as the child hearing/reading the tale may more easily identify with her.

One elder explained the story this way: "The reason . . . is not to go and sleep in someone's house. You will be in trouble if you go and sleep in someone's house. . . .The thing is [parents] don't want their children to go sleep in someone's house. They want their people to stay in the family. If they are in trouble, they will solve it together. . . . Because they have to run all the time, they are on the run all the time. . . . In our Karen [Burmese] house, we have a very long obviously post [stilts]. At nighttime, you pull it up so that the people [robbers] cannot come into the house. [House] is very, very high. Under the house, they have something like a pig, cow. My grandfather raised chickens. . . . Sometimes you have to be afraid of the tigers and other animals. We live in the jungle."

When researchers inquired about how elders had encountered the folktales they had just told us, one answered that her mother "read/heard it from the Karen Storybook." But another explained: "Especially people in the village style, sometimes . . . the grandchildren, every night we go and sleep in our grandma['s house]. Listen to the story every night. The grandma might have something like ten, fourteen grandchildren. So every night we have to go and sleep there."

The ATU tale type index includes a section on Robbers and Murderers (950–969). The most famous such tale is The Robber Bridegroom (Tale Type 955), collected by the Brothers Grimm. In this tale, a bird in a cage cautions a young bride who is about to join her new husband, "Turn back, turn back thou bonnie bride. Nor in this house of death abide." She sees her husband and a band of other thieves kill and eat a young woman, whose finger they chopped off because it had a gold ring on it. Obviously, there is a difference between a child sleeping over at a friend's house and a bride joining her husband, but really the similarities of birds calling out and dangers of sleeping in houses other than one's parents are apparent.

Another cautionary tale from our sample is the Burmese folktale "Swine, Pig, and Lion,"[1] which uses animals as characters in the tale to warn readers about the dangers of listening to lying outsiders. In this story, the pig, lion, and swine are great friends. A fox, however, goes to the friends separately and says bad things about the others, specifically that they are going to kill each other. After the fox does this, the three friends no longer understand or trust each other. They begin to fight among themselves, and then the fox eats all three of them. The fighting between the former best friends, and even the fox eating them, interjects violence into the story. The violence occurs because the three friends believed what the fox said. This cautions children about the dangers of automatically believing what outsiders say. As one elder put it, "So that's why we cannot believe every people something like this. The people come and say the lies. . . . It can divide our family if you believe the [sly person]."

Western European literature is pervaded by trickster foxes. One famous set of stories concerns Reynard the Fox, who was the leading character in a book for adults that became a best-seller in the fifteenth century, popular for the next couple of centuries. Reynard was a scoundrel and tales about him included "violence, murder, adultery, rape and corruption in high places" (Varty 1999, 23; Parlevliet 2008). Tricksters, often foxes, appear in folktales around the world (Uther 2006) and the ATU tale types 1-299 deal with animals in general, and types 1-99 with Clever Foxes, so this tale would appear similar to many Western tales. However, closer examination of the types[2] reveals that none exactly involves deception of previously friendly animals who fight each other and are thus eaten by the fox. As the elder previously quoted pointed out, the unique feature here is the emphasis on the importance of maintaining a close family unit, to thwart outsiders. Others (e.g., Boss 2020) also note that while trickster foxes are found around the Eastern and Western world, subtle differences reflecting culture of origin are simultaneously evident; see also Minami (this volume) for more on the cultural embeddedness of one fox in a Japanese folktale.

Presentation of a Moral Dilemma or Opposing Moral Forces

Violence or evil in folktales can provide a counterpart to the peaceful or good aspect of the folktale (Bettelheim 1975). The elements of violence and good in a tale can also present opposing moral forces that can play off each other. In fact, Bengtsson (2009) states that for there to be an apparent good element to the story, there needs to be an evil element as well. The presence of a moral dilemma or opposing moral forces provides an opportunity for children to consider both sides of the storyline.

An example of a folktale from our sample that shows the opposition of good and bad was told in the Lao focus group. In this tale, a farmer's mother brings him lunch while he works, but one day his mother is late with his food. The son was too hungry and frustrated and he ended up hitting and killing her. The mother had saved the little bit of food they had for him, and she did not get to eat herself because it was the end of the harvest season. After he killed his mother, the son could no longer eat the food she brought him. The mother in this tale represents positive characteristics—selflessness, generosity—while the son represents negative characteristics—impatience, anger, violence—presenting the reader with clearly oppositional forces. The fact that these forces are embodied by mother and son adds an additional complexity to the story. This is especially true in light of the fact that, according to Wilhelm Grimm, children have a more difficult time with an evil mother than an evil stepmother (Bengtsson 2009), and evil stepmothers are common in folktales (Shannon 1981). By extension it could be inferred that children may also have a more difficult time with a mother's death in a tale versus a stepmother's death. This notion is supported by the fact that children can be hesitant to label mothers in stories as evil (e.g., Quinn and Sonu 2017). At the end of this tale, however, the son does recognize his mistake and wishes he could apologize to his now deceased mother, providing a moral lesson to the reader/listener.

The elders explained the lessons of this story:

"So . . . this story is teaching about the anger of youth that in that moment when you're out of control, when you cannot hold yourself, and then you end up doing something really bad and you're going to regret it in life. . . . I went to a temple, probably like seven or eight years old and I always hear this story all the time. We tend to—when we're young, we don't know how to conserve . . . the food that we consume. A lot of times we're wasteful. So the monk and the elder—our father, mother always tell us, you know, don't be wasteful. . . . So the story begin when the mother [is] trying to get the food ready for the son and it's the end of the harvest, okay, where the food is still being harvested, so we don't have that much. So the mother only have one handful, not even handful, probably. One bite, and so he bring over and the mother [is] already scared that it's going to be late, okay? Because it's around noontime, because the son didn't get to eat breakfast. . . . Breakfast in our country is the big, big thing, you know? And the son skipped breakfast, so he's hungry after a long afternoon, hard work, you know, in the farm. Plowing and all that. So he's waiting for his mom. Finally, his mom show up. He said, 'Why'd it take you so long?' He's scolding his mom, you know, cursing and stuff like that. . . . What do we learn? We learn that he's disrespectful. We learn that he's very impatient. We learn that he's really mean, okay. And basically the elder, from what I learned from the monk that taught me is that you know, you're supposed to be the opposite.

"So the summary of the story is that he—instead of focus on what she brought him and the lunch, you know, only have salt and one bite. She didn't even get to eat. She saved that bite, you know, to give him. And when she brought that over and she was trying to explain . . . he didn't want to hear what she had to say, so . . . hit her, club her, and she died. After she died, now he's still hungry. He look at the bite he's about to eat, but he could not eat. He realized that, you know, his impatience got the best of him. And then . . . [he] killed his own mom, and he wanted to say 'Sorry' but he couldn't. He wanted to eat, but he couldn't. You know, so the moral of the story is that it's not what you want, it's what you have and make the best of it."

Of interest here is the lengthy explanation the elder gave, clarifying the several lessons to be conveyed to children and giving us information about the context and ubiquity of the story. This is clearly considered a very important educational tale for Laotian children. In addition, the elder possibly wanted his non-Laotian listeners to not get the wrong idea about his culture, to understand the pedagogical implications of the tale.

As we noted above, the ATU index refers to many kinds of violence, but not to matricide per se. Yest Bascom (1977, 2019) mentions its ubiquity in folklore in general. Perhaps this is a type of violence that was simply too offensive for the compilers of that index; Dundes (1997) notes that Thompson engaged in other kinds of censorship. Tales of matricide have been found in folklore from other countries. For example, Haney (2013) noted that folktales from the Far North of European Russia involve matricide. Deutsch (2017) describes a myth collected among the Inuit in the late nineteenth and early twentieth centuries in which a mother with long, plaited hair deceives her blind son—starving him despite having plenty; the son, in revenge lashes her to a white whale that drowns her, turning her into a narwhal. Ashliman's online collection contains tales from many European countries many of which involve people planning to kill parents/stepparents (ATU type 981), some of which begin, "In ancient times people did not die their own deaths." The ATU also includes infanticide; Grimms' The Juniper Tree[3] involves a stepmother who kills her stepson, makes a stew of him. And serves him to his father. The son's half-sister gathers his bones and places them under a Juniper tree. A bird begins to sing, "My mother, she killed me. My father, he ate me." Versions of this tale have been collected from many European countries. In short, once again, we do not find evidence that even the particular violence encountered in Southeast Asian folktales departs much from that of Western tales.

Another folktale from our sample, specifically from a Burmese individual interview, also presents the forces of good and evil as embodied by a dove and python, respectively, with a type of violence resulting from the python's evil doings. In this tale, the python wants to marry someone's wife. Her husband knows this and protects her with a knife. One day when he has to go out of town for business, the python is able to lure the wife and take her to his den. A dove tries to alert the husband to what has happened, and the wife puts a necklace on the dove so that the husband will know what had happened to her. When the husband returns, the python tells him he has to cut his own throat to prove his love for his wife. After trying to outwit the python with chicken blood and blood from his finger, the husband ultimately does cut his throat. When the wife finds this out, she burns her husband's body and goes into the fire herself.

In addition to presenting opposing moral forces in the form of the python and the dove, this tale also presents the suicide of the husband and wife. This is reminiscent of the former practice in India called sati, which is when "widows commit suicide by burning themselves (or being burned) on their husband's funeral pyres" (Oberhauser, Fluri, Whitson, and Mollett 2018).[4] These suicides would not be considered aggression according to Allen and Anderson (2017) because with suicide the person who is being harmed is not trying to avoid being harmed. However, in this tale, the husband tried to avoid slitting his own throat before ultimately doing so. Additionally, from the point of view of a child consuming the tale, the suicides exhibited in this tale would very likely seem violent.

We asked one of the Burmese elders to explain why s(he—Kuku Lee) felt that this love story represented the Burmese culture. S/he replied:

[Story represents] the way, how we live, . . . how we need to be honest, something like, you know, to love each other because for our culture we think that love and honesty, this is the value of our people. If we say if you are Karen, you have to be honest, you have to love each other. So if you don't have this, people, they say you are not Karen anymore or something like. So since we were young, we were taught that we have to be honest with each other.

The wife expresses love for her husband and is honest with him about her lapse with the python/devil, and the husband expresses his love for his wife by eventually making the ultimate sacrifice with his suicide, which his wife reciprocates.

While suicide per se is not listed as its own category in the ATU index, a group of stories (ATU 332) that D. L. Ashliman calls "Godfather Death"[5] does involve a man whose godfather—Death—makes him a successful doctor by joining him and predicting which patients will live and which will die. Death gives the man a flask to cure those who will live. All is well until the man tries to deceive Death by reviving the king (whom Death said would die). The king is revived but the man's deception costs him his own life. This is similar to the Burmese story in that the man brings about his own death albeit not willingly.

Explanation of phenomena

In one tale told in our Vietnamese Focus Group, an explanation for tsunamis and flooding is offered through the depiction of violence. King Honban the 18th is looking for a suitable husband for his daughter, the princess. The God of the Mountain and the God of the Sea were both eager suitors, but the God of the Mountain was the first to come back with an offering and so married the princess. When the God of the Sea found this out, he was very upset and became aggressive, raising the sea level up and making wind and rain. In response to the God of the Sea's aggression, the God of the Mountain also raised the mountain, and the two continued fighting for several days. People died as a result of this fighting. Eventually, the God of the Sea settled down and the fighting stopped. However, sometimes he still gets upset about the princess and shows this aggression again, causing tsunamis, though he always loses to the God of the Mountain. The reason for tsunamis and flooding that becomes apparent in this story through the depicted violence, that is, the aggression and fighting between the Gods contributes a unique explanatory aspect to this tale. As the elder who told the tale said, "Almost every year they have either flooding or a rematch. . . . But every time they fight, the Sea God lost."

This is a classic example of a Porquoi Tale—an account of why something happens in nature, the origins of many phenomena (Foster et al. 2008). Long before the scientific method was perfected and employed to explain those phenomena, people sought to ask why such things occurred, and the pouquoi tale served this purpose. This type of tale crosses the categories of the ATU index, and examples have been documented from all over the world.

IMPACT OF VIOLENCE IN FOLKTALES
ON CHILD DEVELOPMENT

Children's individual differences, including age and sex, can influence their interest in and the ways in which they respond to frightening folktales involving violence (Cargill 2004; Collins-Standley and Gan 1996). Additionally, children's development of fear as an emotion, such as fear in response to the violence depicted in the tale, is impacted by their individual temperament (Braungart-Rieker, Hill-Soderlund, and Karrass 2010). When reading folktales, children bring their own socialization, families, experiences, and perspective to them, which impact the interpretation of violence in the tales (e.g., Quinn and Sonu 2017). Furthermore, the environment in which folktales are relayed to children influences how they understand them (Boudinot 2005). The remaining portion of this chapter considers the impact of violent folktales on children's development, specifically children's moral, social, emotional, and cognitive development. This is not meant to be an exhaustive examination of these areas of development, but rather a broad exploration of the potential role of violent folktales.

Moral Development

As previously discussed, violence or evil in folktales can provide a counterpart to the peaceful or good aspect of the folktale (Bettelheim 1975) or can present oppositional moral forces. This can create a moral dilemma in the story (Bettelheim 1975), which can then encourage children to develop independent judgment (Boudinot 2005) and advance their moral thinking.

Children's progress in the development of morality may impact their interpretation of violence in stories. This was evident in Quinn and Sonu's (2017) study that examined elementary school students' reaction to the tale of Hansel and Gretel. The students revered Gretel and her courage in rescuing her brother from being eaten by the witch by outwitting the witch and pushing her into the oven (Quinn and Sonu 2017). Gretel seemed to act as a positive model of empowerment and family loyalty to the students. Despite the violence inherent in Gretel pushing the witch into the oven and killing her, the students did not seem bothered by this, but rather seemed to think this act was fair. Quinn and Sonu (2017) note that this sense of fairness is in line with Kohlberg's (Kohlberg 1976) first two stages of moral development: the pre-conventional stage and the conventional stage. In these stages, the concrete results of an action are used to determine how moral the action was, so with this perspective, Gretel's freeing of her brother through getting rid of the witch is judged as a completely moral and good action (Quinn and Sonu 2017).

In contrast to Gretel, Quinn and Sonu's students perceive the witch as bad, though some of the older students discuss potential reasons behind her evil actions. Such attempts to explain her behavior demonstrates a higher level of critical thinking surrounding opposing forces of good and evil. Perhaps teachers could use folktales like Hansel and Gretel to ask questions to encourage this type of critical thinking, thereby helping children to develop a more complex moral understanding.

Quinn and Sonu (2017) also note that all of their participants considered intentions and emotions as well when judging a character as good or bad. For example, when judging the actions of Hansel and Gretel's father. Students tried to explain what their father must have felt to make him go along with the mother's idea of leaving their children in the woods. This is evidence of Kohlberg's conventional morality stage where intentions and other peoples' points of view are considered, as well as Piaget's morality of cooperation stage (Piaget 1965), where actions are judged on both outcomes and intentions. Additional guided discussion could assist children in further understanding the nuances of good and evil through discussion of folktales like Hansel and Gretel.

Social Development

Violence in folktales may impact social development through modeling aspects of friendship and betrayal. For example, the cautionary Burmese tale of "Swine, Pig, and Lion," recounted earlier in this chapter initially models friendship between different animals. As told by one of the participants of our study, this tale portrays the friends as mutually trusting and understanding of each other, two characteristics that define the later stages of friendship development, that is, the mutual trust and assistance stage and the intimacy, mutual understanding, and loyalty stage (Damon 1977, 1983). The fox, however, in talking to the friends separately, succeeds in causing a fight between them which ultimately results in their demise. This violence teaches children to be cautious of listening to those who try to drive friends apart and to value strong friendships despite what others say.

Violent folktales may also socialize children through portrayal of gender roles and victimhood. In many of the folktales in our sample, the female is the victim of violence, for example, the little girl who wanted to have a sleepover in the Burmese folktale "The Story of Cuckoo Bird"; the mother killed by her son in the tale told in Lao focus group; and the wife taken by the python in the tale from a Burmese individual interview. The first two of these stories show the female character as unable to overcome the violence enacted against her and dying as a result of this violence. This clearly depicts to readers/listeners the vulnerability of being female. In the Burmese individual interview folktale when the wife finds out that her husband slit his own throat, she burns her husband's body and goes into the fire herself. This may, on the one hand, suggest the depth of their true love. On the other hand, it depicts the female character as not wanting to or unable to live without the male character by her side.

Emotional and Cognitive Development

Emotions and cognitions influence each other in a bidirectional manner, and there is a cognitive aspect to emotions (Gray 2004). Children's still-developing emotions and cognitive skills may mean that violence in cautionary folktales is sufficient to keep children away from certain dangers or to convince them of the dangers of something, such as a sleepover; as Boudinot (2005, 2) states, "either the child's gullibility or impressionable mind (or both) makes the fantasies of folktales into a pseudo-reality." As children mature emotionally and cognitively, however, these cautionary tales may not be enough to keep them away from certain dangers.

Broadly, folktales show children a range of good and bad emotions displayed in both appropriate and inappropriate ways, with violence usually, though not always, accompanied by inappropriate and harmful displays of emotion. In terms of negative emotions and development, children usually first exhibit anger between four and six months, and displays of anger tend to increase with age (Braungart-Rieker et al. 2010), for example, as children become more eager to exercise their own autonomy. As children develop anger, and other negative emotions such as fear, which is first seen between six and twelve months (Braungart-Rieker et al. 2010), violence in folktales may provide a way for them to discuss and deal with these aggressive and darker thoughts and emotions in a way that can feel safer for them (Bettelheim 1975; Boudinot 2005; Cargill 2004; Isaacs 2013). In relation to this, folktales can be tools to help children learn to cope with frightening and violent aspects of the real world (Boudinot 2005). This, of course, would require that adults engage in and help to guide the child in learning these coping skills, with folktales offering an appealing platform from which to do this.

CONCLUSION

As we have noted, violence in various forms of media has long been a controversial issue (e.g., Boudinot 2005; Ferguson and Beresin 2017), triggering concerns about the effect of violence on childhood aggression and violence. Currently, there is no clear consensus on whether violence in media produces aggression in children (e.g., Boudinot 2005; Ferguson and Beresin 2017), though many pediatricians, parents, and researchers continue to believe that it does (e.g., Bushman et al. 2015). Compared to violence in television, movies, and video games, there have been far fewer studies on the effects of violence in literature. Folktales is a genre of literature where violence is present, and this chapter considers violence in Southeast Asian folktales and potential ways it may impact child development in multiple domains. While concerns regarding violence in folktales are worthy of consideration, we have discussed several positive ways in which violent folktales may influence moral, social, emotional, and cognitive development. We believe this is a more productive avenue of inquiry as violent folktales have remained around the world for centuries despite editing and censoring (Bengtsson 2009; Quinn and Sonu 2017), at times. Furthermore, as many Southeast Asian children hear these folktales orally from their elders, as we noted above, the opportunity for elders to discuss the violence, along with intended messages, is clear.

We also determined that the ATU index applies to these Southeast Asian folktales as well as the many other folktales from other parts of the world, so the ATU is less Eurocentric than some have claimed (Dundes 1997). Both emic (elders) and etic (ATU, psychological research) concur in finding violence in Southeast Asian folktales to be of value rather than harm. Violence in folktales simply echoes the fact that the world children live in never seems to become less violent. This inclusion gives children the opportunity to confront this unpleasant fact of life in a safe, pretend situation in order to prepare them for future encounters.

NOTES

1. Note that *swine* is often a synonym for *pig*, but these are the words our elder used, so we honor them here.
2. libraryguides.missouri.edu/c.php?g=1039894&p=7609090#s-lg-box-wrapper-28359391.
3. Retrieved from https://www.pitt.edu/~dash/type0720.html.
4. Note that Burma was part of British India from 1824 to 1937.
5. www.pitt.edu/~dash/type0332.html.

REFERENCES

Allen, Johnie J., and Anderson, Craig A. 2017. Aggression and Violence: Definitions and Distinctions. In *The Wiley Handbook of Violence and Aggression*. New York, NY: John Wiley and Sons, pp. 1–14. doi:10.1002/9781119057574.

Ashliman, Dee L. (online archive of folktales, University of Pittsburgh). https://sites.pitt.edu/~dash/ashliman.html.

Bascom, William R. 1977 (reissued 2019). Frontiers of Folklore: An Introduction. In *The Frontiers of Folklore*, 1–16. Edited by William R. Bascom. Boulder: Westview Press.

Bengtsson, Niklas. 2009. Sex and Violence in Fairy Tales for Children. *Bookbird: A Journal of International Children's Literature*, 47(3), 15–21. doi:10.1353/bkb.0.0181.

Bettelheim, Bruno. 1975. *The Uses of Enchantment*. New York: Vintage.

Boss, Aaron. 2020 An Analytical Comparison of Foxes within European and Japanese Beast Tales. Unpublished master's thesis, University of British Columbia.

Boudinot, David. 2005. Violence and Fear in Folktales. *Looking Glass: New Perspectives on Children's Literature*, 9(3). Available at http://www.the-looking- glass.net/index.php/tlg/article/view/31/35.

Braungart-Rieker, Julia M., Ashley L. Hill-Soderlund, and Jan Karrass. 2010. Fear and Anger Reactivity Trajectories from 4 to 16 Months: The Roles of Temperament, Regulation, and Maternal Sensitivity. *Developmental Psychology*, 46(4), 791–804. doi:10.1037/a0019673.

Bushman, Brad J., Mario Gollwitzer, and Carlos Cruz. 2015. There is Broad Consensus: Media Researchers Agree that Violent Media Increase Aggression in Children, and Pediatricians and Parents Concur. *Psychology of Popular Media Culture*, 4(3), 200–214. doi:2160-4134/15/$12.00.

Bushman, Brad J., Robert D. Ridge, Enny Das, Colin W. Key, and Gregory L. Busath. 2007. When God Sanctions Killing: Effect of Scriptural Violence on Aggression. *Psychological Science* (0956-7976), 18(3), 204–207. doi:10.1111/j.1467-9280.2007.01873.x.

Cargill, Jenni. 2004. Frightful Witches and Kissable Toads: Why Folktales? *Orana*, 40(2), 16–19.

Collins-Standley, Traci, and Su-lin Gan. 1996. Choice of Romantic, Violent, and Scary Fairy-tale Books by Preschool Girls and Boys. *Child Study Journal*, 26(4), 279–303.

Coyne, Sarah M., Robert Ridge, McKay Stevens, Mark Callister, and Laura Stockdale. 2012. Backbiting and Bloodshed in Books: Short-term Effects of Reading Physical and Relational Aggression in Literature. *British Journal of Social Psychology*, 51(1), 188–196. doi:10.1111/j.2044-8309.2011.02053.x.

Damon, William. 1977. *The Social World of the Child*. San Francisco: Jossey Bass.

Damon, William. 1983. *Social and Personality Development: Infancy Through Adolescence*. New York: W. W. Norton.

Deutsch, James. 2017. How the Narwhal Got its Tusk. *Smithsonian Magazine*. www.smithsonianmag.com/smithsonian-institution/how-narwhal-got-its-tusk-180964331.

Dundes, Alan. 1997. The Motif-Index and the Tale Type Index: A Critique. *Journal of Folklore Research*, 34(3), 195–202.

Ferguson, Christopher J. 2015. Does Media Violence Predict Societal Violence? It Depends on What you Look at and When. *Journal of Communication*, 65(1), E1–E22. doi:10.1111/jcom.12129.

Ferguson, Christopher J., and Eugene Beresin. 2017. Social Science's Curious War with Pop Culture and How it was Lost: The Media Violence Debate and the Risks it Holds for Social Science. *Preventive Medicine*, 99, 69–76. doi:10.1016/j.ypmed.2017.02.009.

Ferguson, Christopher J., Adolfo Garza, Jessica Jerabeck, Raul Ramos, and Mariza Galindo. 2013. Not Worth the Fuss after All? Cross-sectional and Prospective Data on Violent Video Game Influences on Aggression, Visuospatial Cognition and Mathematics Ability in a Sample of Youth. *Journal of Youth and Adolescence*, 42(1), 109–122. doi:10.1007/s10964-012-9803-6.

Foster, Karen K., Deb Theiss, and Dawna Lisa Buchanan-Butterfield. 2008. Pourquoi Tales on the Literacy Stage. *The Reading Teacher*, 61(8), 663–667. doi:10.1589/RT.61.8.9

Gray, Jeremy R. 2004. Integration of Emotion and Cognitive Control. *Current Directions in Psychological Science*, 13(2), 46–48. doi:10.1111/j.0963-7214.2004.00272.x.

Greitemeyer, Tobias, and Dirk O. Mugge. 2014. Video Games Do Affect Social Outcomes: A Meta-analytic Review of the Effects of Violent and Prosocial Video Game Play. *Personality & Social Psychology Bulletin*, 40(5), 578–589. doi:10.1177/0146167213520459.

Haney, Jack V. 2013. *Long, Long Tales from the Russian North*. Jackson, Mississippi: University Press of Missippi.

Isaacs, David. 2013. Sex and Violence in Fairy Tales. *Journal of Paediatrics and Child Health*, 49(12), 987–988.

Kohlberg, Lawrence. "Moral Stages and Moralization: The Cognitive-Developmental Approach." *In Moral Development and Behavior: Theory, Research and Social Issues*, ed. Thomas Lickona (New York, NY: Holt, Rinehart and Winston, 1976), 31–53.

Kutner, Lawrence A., Cheryl K. Olson, Dorothy E. Warner, and Sarah M. Hertzog. 2008. Parents' and Sons' Perspectives on Video Game Play: A Qualitative Study. *Journal of Adolescent Research*, 23(1), 76–96. doi:10.1177/0743558407310721.

Markey, Patrick M., Charlotte N. Markey, and Juliana E. French. 2015. Violent Video Games and Real-world Violence: Rhetoric Versus Data. *Psychology of Popular Media Culture*, 4(4), 277–295. doi:10.1037/ppm0000030.

Oberhauser, Ann, Jennifer Fluri, Risa Whitson, and Sharlene Mollett. 2018. *Feminist Spaces: Gender and Geography in a Global Context*. Abingdon, Oxon: Routledge.

Parlevliet, Sanne. 2008. Hunting Reynard: How Reynard the Fox Tricked his Way into English and Dutch Children's Literature. *Children's Literature in Education* 39(l), 107–120. doi:10.1007/s10583-008-9062-z.

Piaget, Jean. 1965. *The Moral Judgment of the Child*. New York: The Free Press.

Quinn, Molly, and Debbie Sonu. 2017. Following Pebbles by Moonlight: Elementary Students Shed Light on Power, Peace, and Violence in Response to the Classic Tale Hansel and Gretel. *Taboo: The Journal of Culture & Education*, 16(1), 55–72. doi:10.31390/taboo.16.1.07.

Shannon, George. 1981. The Survival of the Child: Abuse in Folktales. *Children's Literature in Education: An International Quarterly*, 12(1), 34–38. doi:10.1007/BF01147415.

Stockdale, Laura A., Sarah M. Coyne, David A. Nelson, and Laura M. Padilla-Walker. 2013. Read Anything Mean Lately? Associations Between Reading Aggression in books and Aggressive Behavior in Adolescents. *Aggressive Behavior*, 39(6), 493–502. doi:10.1002/ab.21492.

Uther, Hans-Jorg. 2004. The Types of International Folktales: A Classification and Bibliography, Based on the System of Antti Aarne and Stith Thompson. Suomalainen Tiedeakatemia, Academia Scientiarum Funnica (FF Communications), Helsinki.

Uther, Hans-Jorg. 2006. The Fox in World Literature: Reflections on a 'Fictional Animal. *Asian Folklore Studies*, 65(2), 133–160.

Varity, Kenneth. 1999. *Reynard, Reinhart and Other Foxes in Medieval Britain*. Amsterdam: Amsterdam University Press.

Yoon, Eunju, Kristen Adams, Angela Clawson, Hanna Chang, Shruti Surya, and Gihane Jérémie-Brink. 2017. East Asian Adolescents' Ethnic Identity Development and Cultural Integration: A Qualitative 4nvestigation. *Journal of Counseling Psychology*, 64(1), 65–79. doi:10.1037/cou0000181.

Zipes, Jack. 1988. *The Brothers Grimm: From Enchanted Forests to the Modern World*. New York: Routledge.

Chapter 6

What You Hate Becomes Your Fate

Researcher Reflexivity in Encounters with Southeast Asian Folktales

Allyssa McCabe and George Chigas

One of the most distinctive and profound folktales to emerge from our Southeast Asian Folktale project was told in our meeting with elders from the Cambodian community in Lowell, Massachusetts (see Introduction for details). One man told an elaborate story about a man who was afraid of lawsuits going off to farm in a tree. He slipped one day and was hanging by his hands, calling for help. Another man heard him, a man so afraid of poop that he rode an elephant so as not to encounter it more closely. He positioned himself under the man who was afraid of lawsuits and grabbed the man by the ankles. Unfortunately, he also startled the elephant who galloped off, leaving the man who was afraid of poop hanging on to the ankles of the man who was afraid of lawsuits. This frightened the man who was afraid of lawsuits so much that he pooped on the man below him. After they were rescued, the man who was afraid of poop sued the man who was afraid of lawsuits.

The narrator explained this tale as, "If you hate something, you will meet that kind of thing." Another member of the Cambodian community extended the conversation with an example from her own life:

> "[I used to say] I'll never marry [a tall person]—because I see people married: short person married to tall person, fat people marry skinny people. It's like, 'Why are you married to opposite all like that?' So I told myself as a kid. Guess what my husband was? Six foot nine."

A multivolume collection of folktales published by the Buddhist Institute (of Cambodia) includes two written versions of this tale, *The Man who Rode an Elephant out of Detesting Excrement and the Man who Climbed a Palm Tree out of Detesting Litigation.* And *The Four Bald Men.* In both of those versions, the focus shifts away from the original two (the man who hated lawsuits and the man who hated poop) to instead detail four bald men who saved those two by stretching out a cloth to catch them and wound up dying because they bumped their heads together when the two dropped from the palm tree—a very different version of the tale, one that verges on slapstick rather than the very interesting message that emerged from the version told in our focus group. We will return to this intriguing folktale later on in this chapter, but first we have to address a few issues that arise in ethnographic research, including first and foremost the issue of outside researcher responsibility.

REFLEXIVITY

The matter-of-fact reference to what has been a taboo subject of conversation and stories from the first author's American childhood days—poop— occasioned her self-reflection. While thinking about the profound implications of the folktale itself, I simultaneously squirmed. What is more, this was far from the only story about poop and pee that we collected in our project on tales from Southeast Asia. How were we going to deal with this issue, especially since one of the early goals of our project was to prepare illustrated versions of some of those tales for teachers to use in their classrooms? In fact, at a workshop for local teachers to introduce our illustrated folktales, a picture of a dog pooping on an alligator was met with shock by the teachers who read it, almost all of whom were from European North American backgrounds.

> Reflexivity may be defined as . . . "A researcher's background and position will affect what they choose to investigate, the angle of investigation, the methods judged most adequate for this purpose, the findings considered most appropriate, and the framing and communication of conclusions" (Malterud 2001, 483–484).

Unless we come to terms with this issue of how we Westerners avoid mention of poop, we will shy away from stories like the one that opens this chapter and other excellent tales. This means that an element of Cambodian culture is not only misunderstood, but perhaps censored because it is beyond our expectation and understanding. And censorship of any culture is not acceptable when you are seeking to understand it, as we were, and promote understanding of it.

As mentioned, the opening folktale is a version of one that is included in a large collection of Khmer folktales (Buddhist Institute 1968). We examined this collection (all folktales are presented in Khmer and English) to determine whether it was anomalous or not. We found numerous instances of diverse subjects that have long been and are considered taboo in Western folktales.

First, in the interests of aforementioned research reflexivity, we need full disclosure of our own relevant backgrounds. As noted, the first author was born and raised in the United States. The second author teaches Cambodian at a university in the Northeastern United States and has spent a great deal of time in Cambodia.

A BRIEF HISTORY OF CAMBODIA

Cambodia's cultural history is long. New archeological evidence traces the beginnings of Khmer civilization to before the first millennium BCE. From this evidence, we know that the Khmer lived in stilt houses, practiced wet-rice cultivation, raised livestock, and worshipped ancestral spirits associated with the land. These same ways of living still exist today (Chandler 1972). Subsequently, after eight hundred years of contact with Indian culture, new Cambodian cultural production flourished during a period referred to now as the Angkor Empire (802–1431), when world-renowned stone temples were constructed, most notably Angkor Wat. As the Angkor Empire declined for various reasons, a new period of Cambodian cultural production followed, inspired by Theravada Buddhism. It was during this period, referred to as the Middle Period (1431–1863), that Cambodia's classical literature was produced, including the folk stories discussed below (Jacob 1996).

During Cambodia's Middle Period, the increasingly powerful Thai (Siamese) and Vietnamese kingdoms to the west and east respectively turned Cambodia into a vassal state. The start of the French Protectorate in 1863 kept Cambodia from being absorbed by its neighbors and created the fixed borders that now define Cambodian territory. The primary interest of the French in Cambodia was the Angkor temples, but several French scholars also took a strong interest in the Cambodian literature that had been produced during the Middle Period and had been passed down orally over the generations. The French transcription and publication of Cambodian folk stories began in the late nineteenth century (Pavie 1903) and continued at the Buddhist Institute, created by the French in 1930, in the institute's periodical *Kambujsuriya* (Light of Cambodia). However, it was not until after Cambodia gained independence from the French in 1953 that an organized effort was made to collect and publish a large selection of folk stories (Dy and Mak 1989).

After ninety years of colonial rule under the French, Prince Norodom Sihanouk's Cambodia undertook a large-scale effort to define Cambodian national and cultural identity as a modern, independent state. In less than twenty years, Cambodian architects, musicians, dancers, writers and scholars produced an enormous quantity of high-quality work. A new style of architecture called "New Khmer Architecture" emerged that combined modern methods and materials with traditional elements; a repertoire of Cambodian folk dances were choreographed with new musical scores by teachers and students at the newly created Royal University of Fine Arts; hundreds of modern novels were written and nine volumes of folk stories were collected and published by the newly established Commission of Mores and Customs located at the Buddhist Institute. The nine volumes were published from 1959 until 1974 and organized into five main categories: (1) etiological tales; (2) tales of justice; (3) tales of hunting and fishing; (4) tales of customs; and (5) tales for edification. In the introduction to the first volume, the Commission states that a central purpose of transcribing and publishing the tales was to preserve the original character of the stories before they were changed, forgotten, or lost (Buddhist Institute 1968).

In 1975, a year after the final volume of folktales was published, the Khmer Rouge took power. In less than four years, nearly a quarter of the population died from overwork, starvation, disease and execution, along with most of the Cambodian artists who produced the buildings, dances, and literature from the Sihanouk era. Fortunately, copies of the nine volumes of folk stories were preserved and reprinted in refugee camps along the Thai-Cambodian border in the 1980s. Subsequently, in the early 2000s, the collection was reprinted, and with the advent of English as the new lingua franca in Cambodia, an enterprising scholar recently undertook the task of translating the stories into English. The written tales for this chapter are based on these English translations, as well as folktales told in Khmer and then translated into English in the meeting we held with members of the Cambodian community in Lowell.

In short, the collection, publication, and translation of Cambodian folktales have occurred in a relatively compressed time period—a little over one hundred years. Folktales are told in various ways in various places for various reasons, and such context affects the format of oral transmission. We know, for example, that the traditional wise Judge Rabbit Cambodian stories were often told to children sitting in the shade of a pagoda on a hot day. But relatively little is known about how, when, and by whom other tales were told (Bunly 2004). Bunly (2004) attempted to document settings for folktales in modern Cambodia and found that according to members of the rural, isolated village he examined, prior to Pol Pot, people tended to hear folktales in many places, but especially at home from older family members. Family wanted to keep children home at night by amusing them and also instructing them in moral values. However now elders in that same village refrain from telling folktales to young people, complaining that children do not ask them to tell these tales or that elders reserve that practice for tourists who pay to hear the tales. Television, books, and other mass media have also contributed to the decline in the transmission of oral folktales. Though Bunly (2004) notes that further study of transmission of oral folktales in Cambodia is warranted, such a task is beyond the scope of the current chapter.

As we noted, unless we come to terms with this issue of how we Western-ers avoid even mere mention of poop in folktales, we will shy away from sto-ries like the one that opens this chapter and other excellent tales. The present article aims to look at the variety of mentions of scatology in these stories, along with considerations about why it might be included in these tales and the role it plays in the narrative structure of the tales. Although our focus here is scatology, this symbolism occurs among other interesting topics (see table 6.1). A remarkable *thirty-four percent* (84 tales) of the collection of 244 sto-ries (Buddhist Institute 1968) mentioned issues that would surprise Western readers, including scatology in 6.6% (16 tales). We will focus on scatology because it is the second most common such topic (after adultery and other sexual practices). To explore all such topics would be too wide-ranging and

Table 6.1   Interesting Topics Included in Cambodian Print Collection (Number of Tales that Mentions Topic)

Sex outside conventional marriage	*35*
Adultery (25)	
Incest (4)	
Sex of humans with animals (4)	
Sex in public (1)	
Rape (1)	
Emissions	23
Scatology (16)	
Vomit (2, one from eating poop)	
Menstruation (2)	
Pus (1)	
Fart (1)	
Laughing soup out of nose (1)	
Nakedness or mention of body parts	21
Genitals (male or female) (12)	
General nakedness (2)	
Female breasts (2)	
Breastfeeding (3)	
Female thigh (1)	
Female pubic hair (1)	
Other topics	19
Corpses (6)	
Suicide (5)	
Abortions/miscarriages (4)	
Curses (2)	
Homosexuality (2)	

Note. Because some tales mentioned more than one such topic, total is greater than 83 (34% of 244 tales).

beyond the scope of this project. We mention the entirety of topics surprising to Western readers in order to provide a context of the frankness found in these folktales; Cambodian folktales sometimes mention other bodily emissions, body parts, and corpses, suicide, abortions and miscarriages, homosexuality, and obscenity (actual curses). We will make the argument that those topics are useful to listeners, that much is lost with censorship of tales told to inform listeners/readers about facts of real life, that sanitization of Western folktales also fundamentally changed those Western tales.

FUNCTIONS OF SCATOLOGY IN CAMBODIAN FOLKTALES

Scatological references serve a number of different functions in Cambodian folktales. Some of these are minor, but some are major, like the one at the outset of this chapter. Here are the functions served by scatological references in the published Cambodian folktales which are summarized in table 6.2:

Fact of Life; A Convenient (Minor) Plot Device

The Prasat Way Nokor Temple contains a folktale about a little boy who was set under a tree while his parents began to plow their land. A bird pooped on the baby and then a phneow fruit fell on his head, cutting him and making him bleed. The parents took their baby son to the river to wash all this mess off. But the baby slipped out of their hands into the river, where he was swallowed by a big fish. The fish swam to China, where a fisherman caught the fish, cut him open to reveal a live baby boy, and presented this boy to the Chinese emperor, who raised him to be a scholar. When he grew up, he wanted to return to Cambodia to find his parents, and the emperor granted him his wish. He returned to Cambodia and lodged with a widow. He fell in love with and married this woman. One day, however, his wife noticed a scar on his head. He told her the story of his unfortunate beginnings. His wife realized that she was also his mother. The two atoned for their unwitting sin. Scatology actually played a very minor role in this *Oedipal* story. Here poop served as the stimulus to get the boy to the river to be swallowed up by the fish.

In *The Man called Kong Hean*, a man soiled himself out of cowardly fear of a vicious tiger and alligator. He was supposed to kill those, but his two wives did so instead. The link of voiding oneself due to fear is also found, more prominently, in *What You Hate Becomes Your Fate*, the story at the outset of this article. This normalizes a very human reaction.

In *Neak Ta Chumteav Mao*, much information is provided about the ways in which one male guardian spirit, Neak Ta, is angered or appeased and the consequences of these reactions. One of the things that made this particular Neak Ta "very angry" happened in 1940 when the Japanese conquered Cambodia and put local people to work. Some of these locals "passed solid waste and urinated." Neak Ta made such men sick and die, leaving their widows behind. Similarly, in *Neak Ta Moen Kong* a man defied being forbidden to urinate into a hole and was punished by being struck with illness and made deaf and blind. Control of elimination processes is key to most civilizations.

In *The History of Neak Ta Khleang Moeung*, elephant dung recurs. The overall story is quite complicated, and involves the conflict between Cambodia and Siam. A Siamese prince was killed. His father retaliated by torturing and killing Cambodians, but one pregnant woman escaped this and gave birth to a healthy boy. In order to escape Siam and return to Cambodia, this boy, Uten, collected elephant dung and burned it to fertilize cabbages. The cabbages thrived and Uten presented them to the Siamese king, who was pleased and rewarded him by making him the controller of mahouts, which he was good at. Nonetheless, Uten wanted to leave Siam to return to Cambodia to succeed his father to the throne. To this end, Uten again collected elephant dung to create a false impression of huge elephants. The Siamese king ordered him to catch these. Uten announced his real identity, which the Siamese king heard about and sent an army to seek revenge. Cambodians ultimately defeated the Siamese. Poop serves both as fertilizer and manufactured "evidence" suggestive of enormous animals.

Sometimes the minor plot device played by mention of scatology is as a means of escape. *The Chek Chhvea Banana Tree and the Baymath Tree* is a story of a cholera outbreak in a district. A man who had been forced to work outside that district longed to return to his wife and children. When he arrived back home, he was greeted by his wife but noticed that she acted strangely. He also smelled dead bodies and found the dead bodies of his wife and children covered with maggots. Realizing that his "wife" was really a ghost, he excused himself to go outside to urinate, mimicking the sound of urination by poking a hole in a pot full of water. He fled to a pagoda where monks knew anti-ghost incantations.

Table 6.2 Functions of Scatology in Published Cambodian Folktales

Major plot device	2 (both are versions of story told at outset)
Facts of life, minor plot device	5
Explanation of real phenomena	3
Tricks	2
Symbolic of gold, wealth	1

Explanation of or Reference to Real Phenomena

Several stories in the published Cambodian collection involve mythical allusions to or explanations of actual occurrences, much like Pourquoi tales or the famous *Just-So Stories* of Rudyard Kipling. One such occurrence, all too frequent, is people's pretense of knowledge. This is a very minor part of *The Naïve Men*, a story in which a stranger tricked four men into uttering supposedly litigious phrases, one of which was "The dog shits where there is rubbish." The men repeated these phrases in ridiculous, nonsensical contexts. The other phrases were "When the stick goes, the fruit will come down," "The water flows where there is a canal," and "It is true just as people say." The moral of that story was given as, "Do not try to pretend to be knowledgeable." *The Four Bald Men* told an elaborate variation of this, combined with a variation of the tale that began this chapter. Those four were naïve and greedy and ashamed of being bald. They sought cures for their baldness, but none succeeded. They married the same widow, who worked them very hard. When they tried to escape, they came upon a basket-maker and a mahout dangling from a tree, attempted to rescue them by having them drop onto a cloth they all held. When the two men dropped, their weight made the four bald men bump their heads together and die.

The Traditions of the Dog undertakes to explain two phenomena: (1) Whenever dogs meet each other, they sniff each others' buttocks, and (2) When a male dog urinates, it always raises one of its hind legs. The story behind the first is that one day when monks fed dogs their scraps of food in a temple, one dog farted but no dog would admit it. As a result, a monk magically punished all the dogs by banishing them, which condemned them to miserable, hungry lives. To this day, dogs are trying to find out who was the guilty party by sniffing each others' buttocks. As for the second story, an old couple wanted to hold a religious festival for the sake of their next lives. This involved slaughter of dogs, along with gathered rice, served to monks. An abbot (higher than a monk) sought to reverse the deaths of the dogs and gathered all the pieces of meat from monks, except for one. The abbot recited incantations to bring the dogs back to life, but those only had three legs. Finally, the monk who had held out yielded to the abbot, who succeeded in bringing the dogs back to life. Out of gratitude to that abbot, male dogs to this day pee on three legs.

Tricks

A key example of a trick story involving poop is the very well-known (in Cambodia) folk story of Thnon Chey (or Thmenh Chey) who was an indentured servant to a rich merchant (Chigas 2005). Thnon Chey used passive aggressive ways to oppose the merchant, whom he thought had unfairly entrapped him. One of the ways was to obey each of his commands very literally. One day the merchant was going to meet some of his wealthy merchant friends, and he told Thnon Chey to follow him as he rode on his horse to the meeting. The merchant instructed Thnon Chey to "pick up anything that falls along the way" (since he is carrying valuable items to give as gifts to his merchant friends as a way to impress them) and put them in a box that he gave Thnom Chey to carry. As they walked to the meeting, the horse pooped and Thnon Chey collected the poop and put it into the box, unbeknownst to the merchant. When they arrived at the meeting, Thnon Chey gave the box to his master. The master then presented the box to his friends who upon opening the box found horse poop and were upset and insulted and forbade the merchant from joining their group in the future.

Another trick story (Chigas 2005) deals with a marriage ritual. In brief, in the "old days" the prospective husband was expected to spend time living with the family of the prospective wife doing chores, etc., in order for the family to assess his worthiness. In this story, the prospective husband became very nervous one night and had diarrhea. He did not have time to go outside to the outhouse, so he pooped in his prospective father-in-law's hat. The next morning, when they prepared to leave the house to work in the rice fields, the prospective father-in-law put on his hat without noticing it was filled with poop.

In the published collection of stories, *The Blind and The Cripple*, a honey collector substitutes his own shit for honeycombs, but this is a very minor part of the story. In *One Crow Turns Out to be Ten Crows*, one man traded a jar of his own shit for another man's defective very short knife. The knife man's wife sampled the shit and vomited. The jar man tried to kill a dog that peed on a candle but discovered that the knife he traded the jar for was too short to be effective. Both men recognized that their opponent was as clever in the trade as they themselves were and teamed up to cheat a widow and her children out of their possessions. In pursuit of food, they separated and killed each other in an effort to claim all the goods for themselves. A third man happened on the goods and tested his wife by telling her a story about how a crow came out of his anus. He said that she must not tell anybody about that. Of course, she did anyway, but she exaggerated, and, subsequently, a sequence of gossips did the same until the one crow became ten. That man wound up splitting the goods with the king.

Symbolic of, Associated with Wealth

Chaov Archses (The Horse Shit Man) is a story about a man who always tried to remember the Buddha's kindness. He tended horses and kept all their shit in bags, which he put on a boat sailing for China. When the Chinese king opened the four hundred sacks, he found gold. The king was surprised by this unexpected gift from someone he did not know—he had never gone to the Khmer country. But he was also delighted and sent his daughter back to Chaov Archses in a drum. Eventually they married and lived in a palace, thanks to the man's remembering the kindness of Buddha.

The Four Sons who did Not Serve their Father is a story of an old man who gave everything to his sons only to have their wives starve him in return. A stranger found him starving and told him to play a trick on his family. The stranger instructed him to fill a jar with shit and piss and bury it. Then he was to tell his family that it was filled with gold and silver and would be given to the kindest, most grateful son. The old man did so and the wives started offering good food and new clothes to their father-in-law. The old man recovered. When he eventually died, the four sons did not trust each other to divide up the buried treasure and enlisted another man (a distributer) to do this for them. The jar was dug up in front of many people and the excrement was emptied on the head of the distributer.

SYMBOLISM AROUND FECES: A CULTURAL UNIVERSAL?

This symbolic factor of poop is interesting. Several members of the Southeast Asian communities talked about how it has superstitious value connecting it with wealth, a superstition shared by other Asian cultures (e.g., Korean), as we will see. This symbolism of poop and wealth is shared in Western cultures as well. While few currently available American or European folktales include the explicit mention of poop, not all writers from such backgrounds have been so fastidious. In fact, Freud, in his seminal work, *Interpretation of Dreams* (19, 439), wrote:

> Dreams with an intestinal stimulus throw light in an analogous fashion on the symbolism involved in them, and at the same time confirm the connection between gold and faeces which is also also supported by copious evidence from social anthropology.

Freud discusses the symbolic meaning of defecation in dreams throughout that book.

Dundes (1962) talked of the symbolism of throwing money into wells to make wishes come true—found in surprisingly far-flung areas all over the world and far back in time. "Folklore of Wishing Wells" He expressly connected these reflections to the ideas of Sigmund Freud regarding how in being toilet trained, children learn to deposit feces to gain parental approval.

Mentions of Poop in Folktales from Other Countries

Lao Focus. In the focus group to collect folktales from Laotian elders, we also encountered the mention of poop, and the functions of the scatology were similar to what we have just covered in the Cambodian context: fear response, symbolism of wealth, and trickery.

One elder told us a story called *The Greedy Dog and Meat.* That individual mentioned that she had "learned [the story] at school very young." It goes like this:

Once there was a dog who traveled from his home. He found a small piece of meat in the road. The dog was excited, "I'm going to take this meat! I am going to find a safe place to eat the meat." The dog walked on with the meat in his mouth. He came upon a bridge. He came to the middle of the bridge. The sun was shining brightly. He looked in the water under the bridge.

He saw another dog reflected in the water, and the dog had a very big piece of meat in his mouth. He thought to himself, "I am going to get that big meat. I am going to take it from that other dog." (It never occurred to him that it was his reflection.) He dropped his little piece of meat and jumped into the water to get the big piece of meat.

Oh dear! The dog looked for the meat but there was no piece of meat in the water. He did not think about the fact that he could not swim. He did not know what to do. His greed had pushed him to want more. He began to feel sorry for himself. He did not know how he was going to cross the river.

All of a sudden, he saw an alligator swimming toward him! The dog began to shake in fear. He was afraid the alligator would eat him for a meal. He thought, "I am going to die surely." As the alligator came closer, it asked, "Hi Dog. Do you need some help? Just tell me how I can help." The dog felt happy and said, "Yes, I would like for you to help me get to the other side." The alligator replied, "Hop on my back and I will help you across the river." So the dog hopped on the alligator's back and rode across the river to the other side. The alligator kept opening his mouth to talk to the dog and the dog was afraid that the alligator was going to eat him up. As he approached the riverbank, the dog jumped off the alligator's back quickly. He was so afraid that he pooped on the alligator's head as he was getting off.

Our group informed us that the moral of the story was: Those who want too much will end up getting nothing. And: Don't poop on those who help you. Show respect and be thankful.

Another story told in the Lao group was one that supposedly took place a long time ago in the heritage city of four kings. One of the kings was sleeping and he was dreaming that he was crossing the river and eating poop. He woke up. He went to the temple and talked to the monk. The monk interpreted the dream for him and said, "Oh you're going to have good luck. Now you need to travel up north by canoe." The monk instructed him to resist the lesser amounts of gold he would first find along the way—gold that was not his—until he arrived at his destination. That would be where he would find masses and masses of gold. The man did as the monk told him and built a temple that is now eight hundred years old. As one elder explained,

"There's a lot of people have dreams like that in my country. . . . If you crave the poop—if you have a dream you crave the poop, you have good luck."

He went on to offer an example from his own life,

"Before I came to U.S. I submitted my application for my doctoral degree and. . . . about like two days before I heard from the university, I dreamt of a bathroom, like toilet full of poop and I felt really bad and then I told my grandma, "I dreamt this.""

And she said, "You're going to get a lot of money," and two days later I heard from the university that I got the scholarship.

A tale of poop trickery is known as *The Lazy Novice* (a published version is available on Kindle and is called *A Sticky Mess*, which differs in some details but not in essence) and involves a lazy but clever boy who was always getting into trouble. His parents sent him to the wat (temple), where he had many chores to do, including sweeping up the wat. The head abbot got angry at the boy because there was still some chicken poop on the floor of the wat. In the print version, the boss said that if he found more poop on the ground the next day, the abbot would make the boy eat the poop. Disgusted by this thought, the boy made a batch of *mieng*—a delicious Lao snack—which resembles poop. He spread this around. When the abbot found it, he made the boy lick it up, which the boy did, declaring it delicious. The abbot became curious and tried a piece, which he also declared delicious. The abbot ordered the boy to sweep all the poop in the yard and put it on a plate for him to eat. The boy was very happy when the abbot spat out the first bite in disgust. The boy said, "What did you expect. You are eating chicken poop."

Censorship?

Some of the differences between Eastern and Western folktales may well be the result of the extensive editing of the latter that has taken place over the centuries. Folktale scholars (e.g., Harries 2001; Zipes 1983) have documented how carefully scrubbed of bawdy or scatological context Western folktales were in the many iterations in print they underwent. Evidence that such laundering occurred appeared in 2009. Nineteenth-century folklorist Franz Xaver von Schönwerth (2015) collected Bavarian folktales—different ones and/or different versions of those collected by the Grimms, and this collection was not bowdlerized due to the fact that it disappeared for so long. For example, in the tale of the tailor who killed seven (flies) with one blow, the flies hover over poop instead of jam, as they do in the Grimms' version. In fact, 5 out of 72 (6.9%) of the tales in Schönwerth's collection (2015) contained such matter-of-fact off-hand mentions of cow or horse or rooster dung; this is remarkably similar to the 6.6% of Cambodian folktales that did (see table 6.1). In *Hans the Strong Man,* however, poop played a slightly more complicated role in making a messy trap for farmhands he was competing with. Harries (2001, 96) notes that Andrew Lang made mention of the difficulty he had in finding a "good version" of *Jack the Giant Killer*, meaning one that did not contain bawdy and scatological references.

The folklorist D. L. Ashliman collected many folktales over the years, and these are available online. Among these are what Ashliman called "Underground People Disturbed by Farm or Household Waste" (https://www.pitt.edu/~dash/type5075.html#stocksee). He presents eleven such folktales (ATU Type 5075) from Germany, Wales, Scotland, Sweden, and Denmark. Most involve human or animal waste falling into the underground homes of wee folk, who kill the culprits. The wee folk explain that if people move the animals, there will be no more problem. The animals subsequently live and thrive.

Not only were Western folktales cleaned up, there was a similar effort by one of the compilers of the ATU index. As Dundees (1997, 198) put it, "Thompson indulged in what can only be described as absurd and excessive prudery." Dundes notes that in an obscure footnote, Thompson acknowledged "Thousands of obscene motifs" and left space in his Motif Index for them to be catalogued in the future.

The prominent sociologist, Norbert Elias (1939/1976), catalogued the changes many individuals recommended for the behavior of the secular upper classes in the West, prominently led by Erasmus (1466–1536). There was a calculated effort to "civilize" people, which meant, paradoxically, explicitly informing them of unacceptable behavior. "It is impolite to greet someone who is urinating or defecating (Elias 1939/1976, 129)," for example. "Let no one, whoever he may be, before, at, or after meals, early or late, foul the staircases, corridors or closets with urine or other filth, but go to suitable, prescribed places for such relief (Elias 1939/1976, 131). Elias (1939/1976, 134–141) mentioned that bodily functions that were viewed with only slight, if any, embarrassment before Erasmus came to be viewed with increased embarrassment and shame over time. We will need to consider whether this cultivation of shame regarding bodily functions in the West was entirely worthwhile. Some (Bauman and Briggs 2003) argue that this effort is part and parcel of the larger and international effort of modernization, not just civilization, of cultures.

The movement to sanitize folktales in Western culture was never completely successful, as attested to by the Schönwerth and Ashliman collections. Furthermore, in a landmark essay, Alan Dundes (1966) discussed the fact that in men's restrooms all over America, there are many inscriptions, which he call "latrinalia," which he likened to "fecal smearing." Instead of talking or hearing about poop in folktales, men write or read about it on public restroom walls.

CONCLUSIONS

So what have we learned from consideration of the subjects mentioned in Cambodian and other Asian and Southeast Asian folktales that Westerners consider taboo subjects? Poop and pee (and adultery and nakedness and many other supposedly taboo subjects from the very-much-manufactured Western point of view) are facts of life all over the world and always have been. In consideration of Schönwerth's uncleansed tales, we found just as many references, proportionally, to scatology as in the larger Cambodian collection. To ignore, to censor references to poop ourselves and to refuse to allow our children to talk about such things perhaps allows these subjects to assume more psychological importance than need be. The cultivation of embarrassment and shame around bodily functions by Western writers (Elias 1939/1976) did eventually result in a cleaner, tidier world, but at a big price. Many people— children, adults, especially elderly people--suffer toileting accidents. In addition to their discomfort, many experience shame, sometimes crippling shame.

There are alternatives to avoiding an unpleasant subject, most notably by confronting it—by means of what psychologists call desensitization therapy, where people are encouraged to confront that which they fear in order to conquer that fear (Wolpe 1961). What if the man who was afraid of poop had undergone desensitization therapy? He wouldn't have been on that elephant in the first place. What if the man who was afraid of lawsuits had undergone the same? He would not have been living and farming in the tree and slipping to his peril. In our strenuous efforts to avoid something, we do often encounter it much more forcefully and problematically than we would have had we taken a less emotionally avoidant approach. For example, a time-honored rule about sensing that you are about to fall is "not to fight the fall" because that will make it worse. In a sense, then, *What You Hate Becomes Your Fate* can be thought of as a caution against avoiding poop in life in general. After centuries of shame and embarrassment in the West surrounding this very human bodily function, perhaps we all should reverse that trend. In that sense, confronting poop in fairy tales might well become preemptive desensitization, helping to reverse that Western effort. Jen (2017) explores the idea that encouraging people to embrace alternate—and superficially competing—Eastern and Western values may well be a healthier path for us all, a goal we heartily endorse.

Meanwhile, we must not lose focus on the most important message of this folktale, namely that our hatreds warp us in a paradoxical way. Our hatreds impel us to contort ourselves to avoid them in such a way that we actually encounter them face-to-face, up close and personal. In a world that seems overwhelmed with festering hatreds that provoke acts that engender even more hatreds, we could only wish that this folktale's wisdom would reach a wider audience.

REFERENCES

Bauman, Richard & Briggs, Charles L. 2003. *Voices of Modernity: Language Ideologies and the Politics of Inequality.* Cambridge: Cambridge University Press.

Buddhist Institute. 1968. A *Collection of Khmer Folk Stories in Simple English*, translated by Chhim Chanbora. Cambodia: Mores and Customs Commission.

Bunly, Than. 2004. "The Status of Oral Folktale Narration in Contemporary Phreah Theat Thmor Da Village." Unpublished master's thesis, Royal University of Phnom Penh.

Chandler, David. 1972. "Cambodia's Early History." In *The Land and People of Cambodia*, 39–49. Lippincott: J. B. Lippincott Company.

Chigas, George. *Tum Teav: A Translation and Analysis of a Cambodian Literary Classic.* Documentation Center of Cambodia (DC-Cam), Phnom Penh, 2005.

Dy, Khing Hoc & Mak, Phoeun. 1989. "Cambodia." *Southeast Asia, Languages and Literatures*, 1989.

Dundes, Alan. 1997. "The Motif-Index and the Tale Type Index: A Critique." 34. *Journal of Folklore Research.*

Dundes, Alan. 2007. "Theses on Feces: Scatological Analysis." In *Meaning of Folklore*, edited by Simon J. Bronner, 352–81. Boulder: University Press of Colorado.

Elias, Norbert. 1939/1976. *On the Process of Civilisation.* Dublin: University College Dublin Press.

Freud, Sigmund. 1965. *The Interpretation of Dreams.* New York: Avon Books.

Harries, Elizabeth. 2001. *Twice Upon a Time.* Princeton: Princeton University Press.

Jacob, Judith. 1996. "The Genres." *The Traditional Literature of Cambodia*, 13–52.

Jen, Gish. 2017. *The Girl at the Baggage Claim: Explaining the East-West Culture Gap.* New York: Knopf.

Malterude, Kirsti. 2001. "Qualitative Research: Standards, Challenges, and Guidelines." 358: 483–488. *The Lancet.*

Pavie, Auguste. *Contes Populaires du Cambodge, du Laos et du Siam.* Leroux, 1903.

Sanavongsay, Nor. 2013. *A Sticky Mess.* Kindle edition.

Schönwerth, Franz Xaver von. 2015. *The Turnip Princess and Other Newly Discovered Fairy Tales.* New York: Penguin Group.

Wolpe, Joseph. 1961. "The Systematic Desensitization Treatment of Neuroses." 132: 189–203. *Journal of Nervous and Mental Diseases.*

Zipes, Jack. 1983. *Fairy Tales and the Art of Subversion.* New York: Routledge Classics.

EDUCATIONAL PERSPECTIVE

Chapter 7

Japanese Language Socialization through Folktales

Masahiko Minami

Adults implement their goals for child development in a wide variety of ways. As a result, in addition to basic grammar and vocabulary, children acquire knowledge of the appropriate social use of language beginning in early childhood. Thus, culture-specific patterns of communication play a pivotal role in children's interpretation of how to interact with the people around them.

It is well known that the Japanese communication style is intuitive and indirect and that interpersonal communication, at times, relies on intuition, empathy, and feeling. Previous studies (e.g., Minami 2002; Minami and McCabe 1991) have demonstrated that the structure of Japanese children's narratives can be understood within the larger context of *omoiyari* "empathy" training of Japanese children (Clancy 1986). Empathy training nicely accounts for the production, comprehension, and appreciation of implicit discourse favored in Japanese society.

Through the examination of retellings of Japanese folktales, this chapter reveals how Japanese children learn an intuitive, indirect style of communication. The study introduces several popular folktales but focuses on a story entitled "Gongitsune" ("Gon the Fox"), a longtime staple in national-language readers for elementary school children. This famous children's story written by Nankichi Niimi is said to be based on a folktale from the author's hometown of Yanabe, in Central Japan. However, Niimi's additions have altered the content to make it more of a story of guilt and apology, which fits adults' expectations of how Japanese children should behave, and how their language and social development should proceed.

LANGUAGE AS A SOCIOCULTURAL PRODUCT

A Definition of Culture

People in different societies have different beliefs and systems of belief, and language can be thought of as not only a manifestation but also a product of culture. At the same time, no culture is static. For instance, the culture of Japan has changed greatly, particularly in the Meiji period (1868–1912) and also in the post–World War II era. Yet culture consists of many complicated factors, some of which have remained stable in Japan. According to Matsumoto (2000: 24), culture can be defined as

> a dynamic system of rules, explicit and implicit, established by groups in order to ensure their survival, involving attitudes, values, beliefs, norms, and behaviors, shared by a group but harbored differently by each specific unit within the group, communicated across generations, relatively stable but with the potential to change across time.

Because values, beliefs, and norms are cognitive products, we can view culture as cognitive. In other words, cultures are actually knowledge/cognitive representations translated into certain norms, opinions, attitudes, values, and beliefs (Matsumoto and Juang 2008).

Socialization is the process of learning to behave in a way that is acceptable to society, whereas enculturation means the gradual acquisition of the characteristics and norms of a culture by an individual. Matsumoto's (2000) above definition of culture also illustrates the nature of cultural psychology, the central tenet of which rests on the "constructivist" conception of meaning, stipulating that social interactions are culturally constrained. That is to say, in different cultures, children's lives are shaped in different ways in consonance with adults' models and expectations of what the children's development should be. Following specific cultural norms, distinct goals and plans for child development are implemented in a wide variety of ways. As noted, we call this process socialization or sometimes enculturation, that is, the process by which young children learn and adopt the ways and manners of their culture. As agents of socialization or enculturation, adults, especially parents, in each culture socialize their children differently. Through the process of socialization, children engage in cultural learning; they acquire the ability to recognize and interpret the variety of activities that take place in their socioculturally specific environments. Consequently, children growing up in different cultures have particular experiences through which they develop diverse expectations, preferences, and even beliefs.

Omoiyari (Empathy) as a Representation of Japanese Culture

From an early age on, Japanese children go through the enculturation process of *omoiyari* (empathy) training, which is embedded in the larger context of Japanese culture (Doi 1973; Lebra 1976). Furthermore, this enculturation continues into the school setting, and, in this sense, children's homes and the school constitute a continuum. As Clancy (1986) argued, a Japanese individual who is truly empathic does not rely on explicit verbal cues to understand someone's wishes because these should be intuited through more subtle cues of gesture and tone. This elliptical, affect-oriented style, which is also favored by Japanese mothers, illustrates that they are sensitive to their children, an approach that helps their children acquire and develop this subtle communicative style at home (Azuma 1986; Shigaki 1987), in case they need to apply it in the school setting.

Enculturation is apparently related to strategies for controlling children's behavior. According to Hess, Kashiwagi, Azuma, Price, and Dickson (1980), for example, in comparison to US mothers, Japanese mothers tend to think that in the preschool period of development children mature emotionally and learn to be polite and obedient. In this way, Japanese mothers believe that even preschool children should be capable of reading the minds of others and putting themselves in another person's position in order to understand that person's feelings.

As Clancy (1986) reported, as a control strategy, Japanese mothers appeal to the feelings of others and even of inanimate objects, such as "This broccoli wants to be eaten so badly." From an early age on, therefore, children go through the process of empathy training highly valued in Japanese society. In Japanese there is an idiom *ishin-denshin*, which literally denotes what the mind thinks, the heart transmits, that is, "I understand instinctively what you have in mind." The idiom emphasizes the existence of a sort of mental telepathy between individuals. Verbosity is traditionally frowned upon in Japanese society, and proverbs like "Silence is golden," "Still waters run deep," "The mouth is the source of misfortune," and even "A talkative male is embarrassing" are often cited. Mothers, as primary caregivers, thus induct their children into a subtly interactive communicative style.

High-Context Cultures versus Low-Context Cultures

We (sometimes unknowingly) understand that there exist cultural variations in the world. According to Hall (1976), some cultures favor high-context communication, whereas others prefer low-context communication. Note that high-context communication refers to "one in which most of the information is either in the physical context or internalized in person, while very little is in the coded, explicit, transmitted part of the message"; on the other hand, low-context communication means "the mass of the information is vested in the explicit code" (Hall 1976: 79). High-context cultures (including much of the Middle East, Asia, Africa, and South America) are relational, collectivist, intuitive, and contemplative. In contrast, low-context cultures (including North America and much of Western Europe) are logical, linear, individualistic, and action-oriented. These low-context traits are very different from those of communicators in high-context cultures who depend less on verbal precision and legal documents. It is worth noting that Hall considers context as a continuum, with high context on the one end and low context on the other; cultural groups are situated at a variety of points along this continuum. Following Hall, Western cultures tend to be situated on the low-context end of the continuum, whereas Asian cultures tend to fall on the other end.

Cultural differences are identified at the individual's psychological level as well. Markus and Kitayama (1991) proposed two fundamentally different senses of self—the Western or individualistic construal of self as an independent, separate entity on the one hand, and an interdependent construal of self, which is common in many non-Western, collectivistic cultures on the other. The individualistic construal of self is more likely to be found, for instance, in US society, where individuals are socialized to be unique, to express themselves, to realize and actualize the inner self, and to promote their own goals. Thus, standing out and asserting oneself is a virtue, so it is "the squeaky wheel that gets the grease." In contrast, the interdependent construal of self is more common, for instance, in Japanese society where individuals are socialized to adjust themselves to an attendant relationship or a group to which they belong, to try to read each other's minds, to be sympathetic, to occupy and play their assigned roles, and to engage in appropriate actions. Thus, the individual is viewed as inherently connected or interdependent with others and inseparable from a social context. In this way, Markus and Kitayama's illustration shows how these divergent forms of self are tied to differences in what people notice and think about, what they feel, and what motivates them.

Social Relativism

As seen in the discussions by Hall (1976) and Markus and Kitayama (1991), it is important to understand the guiding beliefs or ideals that characterize a community, nation, or ideology. However, we should avoid unnecessarily emphasizing the dichotomy between low-context, individualistic Western cultures and high-context, collectivistic non-Western cultures. To begin with, non-individualistic cultures do not necessarily fall under the category of collectivistic culture; there are cultures that may be defined as non-individualistic and yet also non-collectivistic. It is also noteworthy that individualism-collectivism orientations are setting-specific. According to Hofstede's (1984: 157) worldwide survey of employee values (a range between 0 and 100), for example, the highest individualism index values were found for the US (91) and Australia (90) and the lowest for Venezuela (12) and Columbia (13), with Japan (46) in the middle. Second, in the West at least, whereas the word "individualism" is likely to connote positivity, the word "collectivism" may not (Azuma 1996). Indeed, as Gardner (1989) reported, in China a prescribed series of basic skills lessons is valued highly, whereas American children are more imaginative and, moreover, creative in storytelling. As Gardner (1989: 7) puts it, "China and the United States turn out to embrace two radically different solutions to the dilemma of creativity versus basic skills." Moreover, the Confucian paradigm (e.g., malleability of human behavior) that has supported East Asian cultures still underlies contemporary Japanese culture (Feiler 1991; Lebra 1976; Miyanaga 1991).

If the distinction between individualism and collectivism were dichotomous, on the other hand, Chinese culture and Japanese culture would be categorized to belong to exactly the same group of collectivistic, group-oriented cultures. Nonetheless, Japan and China differ greatly in various ways (e.g., Tobin, Wu, and Davidson 1989), although they are both Asian societies in which group-oriented norms prevail and they might be both categorized as high-context cultures, to borrow Hall's (1976, 1989) term. When comparing mathematics learning, for example, in Japanese, Chinese (Taiwan), and US elementary school classrooms, Stigler and Perry (1988) concluded that whereas Western educators tend to rely on nativism (children's inherently unique limitations), Asian educators are more comfortable with the principle of empiricism (all children have potential, and with proper efforts can attain almost anything). In spite of such similarities between Japan and China (emphasizing effort as opposed to emphasizing ability), these researchers also pointed out a crucial distinction between them, stating that "Chinese classrooms are more performance oriented and Japanese classrooms more reflective" (Stigler and Perry 1988: 40). This contrast suggests that Japanese classrooms tend to value the problem-solving process at least as much as, if not more than, the ability to arrive quickly at a solution, a feature not generally observed in Chinese pedagogy. Thus, not only in Japan but generally in other Asian cultures as well, less emphasis is placed on creativity and/or imagination; at the same time, however, Asian cultures, which are often considered to fall under the category of high-context cultures and/or collectivism in terms of describing beliefs about child-rearing and education, should not be lumped together in one category.

Unlike the Western notion of individualism, the Japanese counterpart connotes that an individual can only claim his or her own will and personality
within the framework of social relativism (Lebra 1976), an ethos in which
the individual is defined by the reference groups to which he or she belongs,
including household, residential area, school attended, or place of employ-
ment (Holloway and Minami 1996). As mentioned above, in accordance
with Markus and Kitayama (1991), the Western self is characterized as independent, self-contained, and autonomous, whereas the non-Western—mostly
Asian—self is characterized as interdependent, relational, and collectivistic.
Social relativism is the norm in Japanese society, and this is reflected in certain linguistic devices and strategies (Minami 2009). Under social relativism,
an individual is defined in terms of the referential groups to which he or she
belongs. One derives one's primary identity from the school one attends when
one is young; when one is older, one identifies with the company for which
one works. Being unique (e.g., too creative/imaginative) is often equivalent
to being weird and, consequently, unacceptable. In the context of social relativism, therefore, individualism and creativity are vulnerable to suppression.

To illustrate the differences between the United States and Japan, for
instance, Lebra (1976) argues that American culture is characterized by an
ethos dominated by the pursuit of individual autonomy and self-interest,
which stands in sharp contrast to the social relativism of the Japanese. As
Maynard (1992: 16) aptly summarized, "In Japan, there is a tradition of defin-
ing self on the basis of the human relationship within the society of which the
self is part." In other words, social relativism recognizes diversity within a
society. Also, while in Western cultures individualism is generally connected
with creativity, it is somewhat difficult for an individual to nourish a Western
sense of individuality in Japanese soil that is influenced by aforementioned
Confucian beliefs; referring to social relativism, Miyanaga (1991: 4) called
the Japanese type of individualism "passive individualism." In order to maintain good relationships with others in Japanese society, each individual is
expected to follow a quasi-parent-child relationship and to be sensitive to the
cues given by other members in the so-called family.

Interaction of Culture and Language

It is important to understand the characteristic spirit of a culture and community as manifested in its beliefs and aspirations, and it is imperative to
understand the relationship between culture and language. Recall that Hall
(1976) suggested that cultures can be differentiated along a dimension of
contextualization. High-context cultures, Hall argued, foster differential
behaviors according to the specific context within which the behavior occurs.

Low-context cultures, in contrast, minimize differences in behavior due to context.

The idea presented by Hall (1976) is similar to that of Bernstein's (1971) conception of elaborated code (context free, universalistic in meaning) versus restricted code (i.e., context dependent, particularistic in meaning, used in relatively informal situations, and stressing the speaker's membership in a group), which has stood as a major contribution to various fields (sociology, psychology, linguistics, to name a few) in terms of increasing our awareness of the influence of social class differences on individual behaviors. As seen above, high-context cultures rely comparatively less on explicit, spoken language in order to transmit meaning; instead, they rely on the interpersonal relationships among the speakers/listeners and the history of previous discussions. Bernstein asserted that lower-class families' communication in England should be characterized as restricted code. While Bernstein's claim that there was substantial evidence suggesting the effects of sociocultural variables is understandable, it may not apply to other cultures. The Japanese language is a highly contextualized language. Nevertheless, according to Azuma (1996), in Japanese communication, regardless of the social class, meanings/intentions are understood without excessive information.

Many studies have looked at language-cognition issues since Sapir (1921, 1929) and Whorf (1956) proposed their hypothesis that speakers of different languages think differently, as demonstrated by the structure and function of their language. Many studies have continued to provide a wealth of support for linguistic relativity. For instance, comparing American English with that of the Yucatec Maya in southeastern Mexico, Lucy (1992) identified distinctive patterns of thought relating to differences in the two languages. Likewise, Lin and Schwanenflugel (1995) examined English and Taiwanese Chinese and demonstrated the close relationship between language structure and the structure of category knowledge in American and Chinese speakers. However, it is culture that has a pervasive influence on the language we use—an influence on vocabulary as well as the rules by which words are put together to construct meaningful phrases, sentences, and discourse. That is, the linguistic relativity hypothesis itself is nothing but a manifestation of culture's deep relationship with cognition. Culture influences pragmatics, the rules that govern how language is used and interpreted in different sociocultural contexts.

As can be easily imagined, the Japanese language itself is a highly contextualized language; the speaker must be fully aware of (1) whether the relationship with the listener is intimate, or (2) whether the communication is impersonal. Certainly, sources of diversity within Japanese society should be recognized. Given the presence of Korean and Chinese minorities in Japan, the portrayal of monolithic collectivism within a framework of a completely homogeneous society is overly simplistic. Nonetheless, Japan is a relatively homogeneous society, and in such a milieu, even if a speaker is not explicit but ambiguous, the similarity of background allows for more accurate inferences on the part of the listener. At least Japanese people believe so.

As we grow, we acquire the particular language use that reflects our cultural norm. As Azuma (1986: 9) aptly mentioned, "In contrast to the West, where it is the sender's responsibility to produce a coherent, clear, and intelligible message, in Japan, it is the receiver's responsibility to make sense out of the message." This Japanese belief that the burden is always on the listener/reader and not on the speaker/writer is cultivated by the previously mentioned *omoiyari* (empathy) training. Ambiguous utterances may result in successful communication in Japan because interlocutors believe that they have the shared experience necessary to make sense out of the ambiguous uses of the language (Donahue 1998). In Japan, as opposed to the United States, for instance, ambiguous communication can and does play a different role in the interface of orality and literacy. Many cultural differences in pragmatics can be summarized in the light of communication style. It is thus critical to examine how the language used in a society reflects widely accepted social norms and, conversely, how the social norms shape that language use.

FOLKTALES AND CHILDREN'S LITERATURE

Sazanami Iwaya and His Fairy Tales

The political reforms of 1868 that accompanied the enthronement of Emperor Meiji are called *Meiji Ishin* in Japanese. The word *Ishin* comes from Chinese classical literature and basically means renewal, connoting the arrival of something that is novel or new. After Japan abandoned the feudal system and entered the Meiji period, the multitalented Sazanami Iwaya (1870–1933), who was a novelist, editor, playwright, critic, and storyteller, became a pioneer of Japanese children's literature. Iwaya was interested in folk literature, that is, stories transmitted orally throughout generations, and was concerned that Japanese cultural tradition might become extinct if people relied on oral literature alone. In keeping with modernizing trends in Japan and concomitant developments in the literary arts, Iwaya decided to spread traditional fairy tales for the education of young children (Saito 1974) and published a volume entitled *Old Tales of Japan* in 1896 (Meiji 29). Below are synopses of some of the well-known stories included in that volume. Iwaya and others involved in children's literature did not necessarily emphasize children's implicit learning of morals. But reflecting the goal of children's socialization, children's literature gradually integrated an implicit, empathic style of discourse. Analyzing children's literature thus indicates how adults see their children, and how these adults want their children to grow.

Issun-bōshi

Fairy tales, because of their roots in oral tradition, have multiple versions, some of which were not necessarily intended for children. "Issun-bōshi" ("Inch Boy" or "The Inch-High Samurai," which depicts a figure reminiscent of Tom Thumb in English folklore) is one such story with several versions, but the ending unequivocally tells us how the god's magical powers fulfill the wishes of worshippers:

> Once upon a time, a childless old couple went to Sumiyoshi Shrine and prayed to the god to be blessed with a child. "Just one little child of our own, no matter how small," they pleaded, and so the woman gave birth to a little baby boy. However, since the child was very little—only one inch tall—and never grew taller, he was called Issun-bōshi. One day, Issun-bōshi told his parents that he wanted to go the capital to become a samurai warrior. With the permission of his parents, he embarked on his voyage with a bowl as a boat, a chopstick as a paddle, and a needle as a sword. When Issun-bōshi reached the capital, he came upon the home of a wealthy lord. Issun-bōshi convinced the lord that he could do anything, and the lord agreed to employ him. When a girl of the lord's family went on a journey to a faraway palace, an *oni* (ogre) kidnapped her. To save the girl, Issun-bōshi stabbed the *oni* with the needle. The *oni* cried, dropped an *uchide no kozuchi* (a mallet of luck, or magic wooden hammer) and ran for its life. The girl said, "Any wish you make with this mallet will come true! What do you wish for, my hero?" When the mallet was shaken, a miracle happened—with each shake Issun-bōshi grew taller, and he became a big, fine man. He eventually married the girl, and—as the story goes—he was able to use the mallet to conjure food, treasures, and other things, so that the family prospered for generations.

The god enshrined in Sumiyoshi Shrine has long been believed to have a remarkably miraculous efficacy for various things, such as smooth pregnancy and delivery, and healthy growth of the child. The tale of a tiny child is said to have already existed by the end of the Muromachi period (1336–1573), but in the adult version, Issun-bōshi was depicted as a monster in the original folktale (e.g., because Issun-bōshi never grew taller, the old couple thought that he was some kind of freak; he also cruelly framed a lord's daughter in order to gain her hand). It was Iwaya in the Meiji period who removed the wickedness from the original and turned Issun-bōshi into a more lovable figure. Iwaya furthermore focused on the god's miraculous power to grant children's universal wish to grow big, and, at the same time, created a culturally unique world based on Japan's indigenous beliefs.

Momotarō

Momotarō ("Peach Boy") is arguably the most popular hero of Japanese folklore. His story is also one of the best-known traditional folktales commonly read to preschoolers using a popular art form called *kamishibai* (which literally means "paper drama"). Historically, *kamishibai* was used by monks, who used picture scrolls to tell stories with moral lessons to illiterate audiences. This ancient Japanese art form continued to serve as a highly useful tool during the postwar period in Japan, until the advent of television. In many *kamishibai* folktales, the protagonists are nameless, good-natured, childless old couples; both "Issun-bōshi" and "Momotarō" start with similar openings, "Long, long ago, in a certain place," which flavors storytelling with some authenticity in various places including classrooms (Norton 1991). Likewise, both stories end with Heaven's reward for the good. Note that "Hanasaka jī-san" ("The old man who made flowers blossom"), another well-known traditional folktale, follows the same story schema (i.e., a virtuous human goes a certain way and finds fortune whereas a selfish human goes the same way but ends up with the exact opposite) (Sakade and Kurosaki 1958).

Iwaya likewise included a version of "Momotarō" in his series, *Old Tales of Japan*. In the folktale in the Edo period (1603–1867), "Momotarō" was born to an elderly couple who ate a peach and regained their youth. Departing from this "rejuvenation" type, Iwaya chose to retell a version in which Momotarō was born from a peach, so that the story might have more appeal as a fantasy for young children.

> Long, long ago, in a small village, there lived an old, childless couple. One day when the old wife was washing clothes in the river, a giant peach came tumbling down the stream. When the woman and her husband tried to open the peach to eat it, they discovered a baby inside. The couple named the baby Momotarō, from *momo* (peach) and *tarō* (eldest son in the family), and brought him up with love and care. Momotarō grew up rapidly into a strong boy, and left the couple to fight against evil *oni* (ogres) who dwelled in a place called *Oni-ga-shima* (Ogres' Island). En route, Momotarō met and befriended a dog, a monkey, and a pheasant, who agreed to help him in his quest in exchange for a portion of his *kibi dango* (millet dumplings). On the island, Momotarō and his animal friends beat up the ogres and made them surrender, and returned home with the treasure that the ogres had stolen from people.

Iwaya was not only the author of the "Momotarō" tale in the afore-mentioned folktale collections, but he was also a major contributor to the elementary-school textbook versions. In fact, "Momotarō" was the first tale to be incorporated by the Meiji government into nationalized textbooks for elementary school.

Gon the Fox

In addition to Iwaya, many other writers contributed greatly to folktale-based children's literature in the Meiji period. Among them, the novelist Miekichi Suzuki (1882–1936) was a pioneer who elevated folklore and children's stories into a respected literary genre. Suzuki launched a children's literature magazine entitled *Akai tori* ("Red Bird") which played an important role not only in pioneering literary movements but also in establishing and developing new frontiers in children's fiction, poetry, and songs (Saito 1974).

The Story

"Gongitsune" ("Gon the Fox") is a children's story about the life of a little fox called Gon, written by Nankichi Niimi (1913–1943), who was born in Yanabe, in the City of Handa, Aichi Prefecture (located in Central Japan). The masterpiece, which he wrote at age eighteen, appeared in the journal *Akai tori* ("Red Bird") in 1932. Niimi is sometimes called the Hans Christian Andersen of Japan, and the story of "Gon the Fox" brings to mind such sad stories as "The Little Mermaid" and "The Little Match Girl." Unfortunately, since Niimi died of tuberculosis at the age of twenty-nine, he published only a few works. "Gon the Fox" consists of six scenes, as summarized below:

SCENE 1

This is a story that Mohei, an old man in my village, told me when I was little. Once upon a time, in a place called Nakayama, there was a small castle, where a feudal lord named Nakayama lived. A short distance away, a mischievous little fox named Gon lived all alone in a small hole he had dug in a forest filled with ferns. Day and night, Gon went out to a nearby village and caused mischief, annoying the villagers.

One day, Gon walked out of the forest and reached the bank of a small river, where he saw Hyōjū, a young villager, shaking a net in the rain-swollen stream in order to catch fish. Inside the net, Gon saw a fat eel and the shining bellies of fish. As soon as Hyōjū left his fishing basket behind, Gon bounded out from tall grass and ran straight to the basket. Unable to restrain his mischievous nature, Gon took the fish out of the basket one by one and threw them back into the stream. He almost emptied the basket, and tried to grab the fat eel, but the eel was so slippery that he could not grab hold of it. Just then, Hyōjū came back and saw Gon. "Hey, you, thieving fox!" he screamed. With the eel still wrapped around his neck, Gon jumped up in surprise and ran away. Hyōjū did not chase him. With a sigh of relief, Gon gnawed on the eel's head and killed it. He finally managed to unwrap the dead eel from his neck, and put it on the grass near the entrance of his hole.

SCENE 2

Ten days later, Gon found the villagers making preparations for an event, and he saw a funeral procession enter the graveyard. Hyōjū was wearing a ceremonial white kimono, holding the mortuary tablet of his mother, and Gon learned that the event was a funeral for Hyōjū's mother. Hyōjū usually had a bright happy face, like a red sweet potato, but that day he looked sad and withered. That evening, Gon sat in his hole, thinking, "Hyōjū's mother must have said that she wanted to eat some eel on her deathbed. That is why Hyōjū took out the net and went fishing. If only I hadn't ruined it!" Realizing the consequences of what he had done, Gon repented his behavior and was burdened with guilt toward Hyōjū.

SCENE 3

One day, Hyōjū—who had always lived with his mother—was washing barley by his red-bricked well. "Now, Hyōjū is all alone just like me," thought Gon to himself as he watched Hyōjū from behind a shed. As Gon started to leave, he heard a peddler's call, "Sardines for sale! Fresh sardines for a bargain!" The sardine seller parked his wagon on the side of the road and carried some shiny sardines to his village customer's house. While the peddler was not looking, Gon went to the cart, took five or six sardines from the basket and ran back to Hyōjū's house, imagining this act would make amends for his previous behavior toward Hyōjū. "This is one good deed for penance," thought Gon.

The next day, Gon gathered loads of chestnuts in the mountains and took them to Hyōjū's house, and noticed that Hyōjū had some scratches on his cheek. Wondering what had happened, Gon heard Hyōjū mumbling to himself, "Who in the world threw those sardines into my house? The sardine seller got angry with me. He thought I had stolen the fish, and he beat me up." Gon realized that his attempt to perform a good deed had only made matters worse for Hyōjū, and felt even guiltier toward Hyōjū, whom he had harmed even further. Afterward, Gon only gathered chestnuts and matsutake mushrooms and took them to Hyōjū's house.

SCENE 4

One beautiful autumn evening, Gon went out for a stroll and headed toward Nakayama Castle. As he walked up the path leading to the castle, he heard voices coming from the opposite direction. It was Hyōjū and another farmer named Kasuke. "Recently, strange things have been happening around me," said Hyōjū. "Ever since my mother died, someone has been giving me chestnuts and mushrooms and other things every day. I have no idea who it could be. Somebody just puts the things in my house and leaves." While Hyōjū was grateful for the gifts that Gon had collected in the forest, he did not know where they came from. Upon arriving at another villager's house, Hyōjū and Kasuke walked straight inside. After a while, three more men went into the house. Gon heard a Buddhist priest rhythmically pounding the temple drum and chanting a sutra.

SCENE 5

Gon squatted down near the well until the priest had finished chanting. Then, Hyōjū and Kasuke came out of the house. Since Gon wanted to hear the rest of their conversation, he followed them. When they came near the castle again, Kasuke said all of a sudden, "I bet the chestnuts and mushrooms must have come from the god." Hyōjū was surprised and said "What?" "Yeah," Kasuke replied convincingly. "The god knows you are all alone now, and feels pity for you. Every day you should thank the god." Overhearing this conversation, Gon thought with mixed feelings, "I'm the one who brought the chestnuts and mushrooms to Hyōjū. He should thank me, not the god. It's not fair."

SCENE 6

The next day as well, Gon took some more chestnuts to Hyōjū's house, where he was making rope in his shed. Noticing that Hyōjū was home, Gon crept around to the back door, and slipped silently into the house. But Hyōjū saw him sneaking around, and thought, "That must be the fox that stole my eel. He must be here to cause more mischief." Hyōjū took his gun and crept up behind Gon. Just as Gon was about to leave, Hyōjū shot him. Gon fell down with a thud. Hyōjū stepped inside the house and glanced toward the entrance, where he saw the chestnuts stacked in a pile. "What?" Hyōjū was shocked to see the chestnuts. "It was you that was bringing me the chestnuts!" Gon, lying on the ground, nodded wearily. The gun slipped out of Hyōjū's hands. A thin wisp of blue smoke rose from the gun.

Different Versions

The story of "Gon the Fox" has at least three versions. The original version is solely folklore passed down by hunters from generation to generation. Since this version is supposed to end at the scene of the funeral of Hyōjū's mother (i.e., Scene 2), there is no mention of Gon being shot by Hyōjū. Version two is the one written by Niimi when he was eighteen years old. Using his collection of interviews with hunters, Niimi created the continuation of the story beyond the funeral scene. Version three is the "Red Bird" edition, which was adapted by aforementioned Miekichi Suzuki, to be published in the magazine *Akai tori* ("Red Bird") in 1932.

The three versions differ greatly in content. As seen in version one, which existed as an oral tradition, it must have been a common occurrence that wild animals ravaged the fields and stole fish that villagers had caught, so in this sense the folktale reflects historical reality. In folktales, as stated above, foxes are described as being intelligent but sometimes cunning figures; when the funeral took place at a villager's house, the villagers might have felt as if the animals had quit their mischief because of repentance. Of course, this is only a human interpretation of animal behavior, but in the context of folklore, the ending of version one is understandable. However, it must be noted that Gon the fox engages in remarkable empathy in connecting the death of Hyōjū's mother to his own theft of the eel.

Versions two (a story prepared by Niimi) and three (an edited story for children by Suzuki), in contrast, belong to the stories of animals returning favors to human beings (A-T-U type B336)—Hyōjū was grateful for the gifts he received, but he did not know where they came from. Based on his personal experience of losing his mother when he was four years old, Niimi expanded the folktale and added the tragic ending, which fascinated readers—Hyōjū failed to comprehend Gon's clumsy attempts at friendship until it was too late. One could read this tragic ending as a failure of empathy on Hyōjū's part; unlike Gon the fox who connected the funeral with the theft of the eel, Hyōjū fails to imagine that the unforeseen gifts were a form of atonement by the eel-thief.

Note that the story that has appeared in school textbooks is version three, the "Red Bird" version. While the majority of the changes may be subtle, Suzuki is said to have made corrections and changes in as many as thirty places. For Suzuki, a talented, proud novelist who had studied English literature at Tokyo Imperial University (now the University of Tokyo) and launched a children's literature magazine, it might have been somewhat distasteful to publish a work as it had been prepared by an eighteen-year-old substitute teacher in a rustic elementary school. However, he seems to have been relatively broad-minded for a man of his times, in his position. The majority of his editing in thirty places focused on scenic simplifications and the elimination of non-standard dialectal vocabulary, such as the word meaning "shed" (this may reflect the Meiji government's policy of language assimilation, intended to make Japan catch up with the West). However, the most important change Suzuki made was in shifting the emphasis to the theme of guilt and repentance. Arguably, the most significant difference from the earlier version comes at the very end:

> Assailed by guilt, Gon tried to make amends by stealing sardines, gathering chestnuts and mushrooms, and leaving them all for Hyōjū. Toward the end, Hyōjū saw Gon sneaking around, recognized him as the eel thief, and shot him to death out of anger about the death of his mother. Only afterward did he realize to his horror that the fox he just shot had given him all the mushrooms and nuts.

Recall the aforementioned Japanese idiom *ishin-denshin* (i.e., 'transmitting heart to heart'), which symbolizes a form of interpersonal communication through unspoken mutual understanding (between a human being and an animal, in this case). It was just before the death of Gon, whom Hyōjū shot with his gun, that the two creatures—the human being and the animal—finally arrived at perfect sympathy with each other. This tragic ending has impressed people of all ages, from elementary school children to adults, even from before the story appeared in *Akai tori* ("Red Bird"). In fact, it is reported that Niimi, who was an elementary-school substitute teacher, used to tell the story to his students in the classroom (Saito 1974).

As mentioned above, however, there is a difference between the versions in terms of the perspective they adopt. In version three (i.e., Suzuki's edits) the story develops from the perspective of Gon, but shifts abruptly at the very end to that of Hyōjū. While the ending of version two (i.e., Niimi's) explicitly states that Gon felt happy while lying wearily—dying, in fact—(hearing Hyōjū say "It was you that was bringing me the chestnuts!"), version three (i.e., Suzuki's) does not describe how Gon felt. This leaves room for readers to imagine Gon's feelings, an important lesson for an elementary-school *kokugo* (Japanese/national language) reader, which is reviewed in the section below. Comparing the three versions, and versions two and three in particular, we can see the progressive transformations toward the emphasis on the empathic style of discourse.

Educational Implications

Emphasis on Empathy

In terms of educating young readers, "Gon the Fox" received favorable reviews in the US as well as in Japan. A couple of reviews appeared in 2015, in response to the publication of an English edition of the picture book. A US reviewer named Taniguchi (2015: 90) wrote, "This poignant tale will resonate with older readers, who will empathize with the struggles of a lonely outsider." Kirkus Reviews (2015: 172) wrote, "The startling and violent ending may make it difficult to find an audience, but it is a valuable introduction to a non-Western storytelling aesthetic," and further praised the story, "A lot of information about Japanese culture and custom is imparted in the course of this telling." Another reviewer, Jorden (2015) warned readers of the dangers of thoughtless, hasty decisions, which might lead to an unwanted ending, Gon meeting the end of his life in this case:

> "This story is a valuable read for young people (it is geared towards children ages seven to ten) because of all the lessons mentioned. In addition to the negative consequences of juvenile acts and the possibility that you can always redeem yourself after childhood blunders, kids learn that you might not get the credit you deserve. Gon is angered when he overhears Hyoju thanking God for the items delivered to this house ..." (jetwit.com/wordpress/2015/05/10/jq -magazine-book-review-gon-the-little-fox/)

It is necessary here to revisit cultural differences in the light of education. American elementary school textbooks tend to instruct the child to take an objective and analytical view of the story, the situation, and the actions of the characters in order to evaluate the effectiveness of their actions. Japanese elementary school language textbooks, in contrast, tend to encourage "the child to imagine the feelings of another and merge his or her identity with that of the character, even if that character should happen to be an animal" (Gerbert 1993: 161). Japanese teachers and textbooks ask students to do empathic reading, using prompts such as "What do you think Character X really felt like at this point?"

"Gon the Fox" appears in the official fourth-grade *kokugo* (Japanese/ national language) textbook. In the 1992 version of the textbook, the following questions are posted at the end of the story (Kurihara et al. 1992):

- In scenes 1 through 5, what did Gon do, what did he see, and what did he think? Let's read how his feelings shifted through each scene.
- In scene 6, what did Hyōjū know and what did he think? Let's read how Hyōjū's feelings changed by considering the differences between his three utterances.

The 1999 version (Kurihara et al. 1999) further asks scene-by-scene questions, after posing the overall question "How did you feel when you read this work? Discuss the story with your classmates and compare your impressions":

- In scene 1, Gon was so mischievous that he ended up stealing an eel. What effects did this mischief have on the feelings of Gon and those of Hyōjū after that?
- Scene 2 describes one particular day. Why was the scene divided into morning, noon, and evening?
- Scene 3 depicts Gon's actions such as "throwing sardines into Hyōjū's house" and "going to the shed and leaving chestnuts at the entrance." Why did Gon change the places he left the gifts and the ways in which he placed them?
- Scenes 4 and 5 are mainly conversations between Hyōjū and Kasuke. Gon was eager to know what they were talking about. How is Gon's eagerness described?
- In scene 6, how did Hyōjū's feelings change as reflected in his utterances toward Gon?

This feature of encouraging discussion is not limited to "Gon the Fox," although the story has continuously been adopted in *kokugo* textbooks. Throughout all grade levels, Japanese education encourages children to empathize with others (and personification is sometimes used for this empathy training, as seen in "Gon the Fox"). As explained earlier, according to Lebra (1976), unlike the Western notion of individualism, the Japanese counterpart connotes that an individual can only claim his or her own will and personality within the framework of social relativism. As Lebra (1976: 13) states, furthermore, "For Japanese, guilt seems to stem at least in part from one's empathic feelings for the pain and sacrifice suffered by another person." The lesson of "Gon the Fox" is to teach the reader to understand and sympathize with feelings of regret and guilt, and this lesson appeals to the Japanese ethos in a society where social relativism is dominant.

This emphasis found in Japanese school education parallels the strategy taken by Japanese mothers, who appeal to the feelings of animals and even inanimate objects when providing their young children with explicit training in empathy (Clancy 1985, 1986). In these respects, therefore, professional theories are in line with the folk psychology reflected in Japanese mothers' concerns; continuity exists from home to school. It is particularly noteworthy that "Gon the Fox" is the only folktale that has continued to appear in post–World War II *kokugo* textbooks. Empathy training through literature has been one of the main goals of *kokugo* textbooks, and "Gon the Fox" is the epitome of the folktales that reflect it.

Historical Perspective: From Morale to Moral Education

The choice of materials for *kokugo* readers mirrors the times and national politics. As introduced earlier, in the Meiji period (1868–1912), Sazanami Iwaya not only authored the "Momotarō" tale for his commercially successful folktale collections, but also contributed greatly to the textbook versions. The "Momotarō" tale was first incorporated into the nationalized textbooks for elementary schools by the Meiji government in 1887, after which it continued to appear in the National Language Reader (*kokugo tokuhon*), except for a brief hiatus. This continued appearance of the tale reflects the spirit of the times in Japan during its period of modernization. Momotarō can be seen as a metaphor of a military soldier or commander of Great Japan, whereas the ogres are the evil beings who devour poor people and plunder treasures from the Emperor's land of Japan. Momotarō's expedition is thus morally justifiable. The years surrounding the "Momotarō" tale's publication (i.e., the Iwaya versions) and its continued appearance in the National Language Readers coincided with the Sino-Japanese War (1894–1895) and the Russo-Japanese War (1904–1905), a seeming invitation to imagine that the ogres represented the neighboring big countries—the Qing dynasty of China and the Russian Empire. Broadly speaking, before World War II, Japanese, particularly the government, placed a strong emphasis on ways to raise the people's "morale," that is, the mental or emotional state of the nation's individuals.

In contrast to "morale," emphasis in the post–World War II years shifted to "morals," the concept that an individual's action or objective should be ethical or virtuous. Educators and publishers who created *kokugo* textbooks tried to include stories that could tell ethical lessons. While some classic literary texts still continued to be adopted in *kokugo* textbooks after World War II, the majority of folktales, including Iwaya's "Momotarō," tale were not. One exception was Niimi's "Gon the Fox," a sad or even painful story, which has survived for more than the past four decades and enjoyed longevity while other folktales have disappeared or been removed from the *kokugo* readers.

One can indeed find many sad stories in *kokugo* textbooks, which may make children feel discomfort, pain, and even anguish when they are required to read them aloud in the classroom. This is because postwar *kokugo* education has played the role of moral education in the schools. It is important to note here that moral education is included in Japanese compulsory education. A glance at the Education Ministry's curriculum guidelines reveals that empathy occupies an important part of the following four core items (self-discipline, relationship with others, community and society, and the sublimity of life and nature):

A. Self-discipline: mainly about oneself—self, autonomy, freedom and responsibility, aspirations, growth of individuality.
B. Relationship with others: mainly about human relations—friendship and trust, kindness, compassion (empathy), courage, mutual understanding, tolerance.
C. Community and society: mainly related to groups and society—fairness, respect for rules, social justice, working, public spirit, family love, enhancement of family life, respect for tradition and culture, love for one's country and hometown, international understanding and international friendship.
D. The sublimity of life and nature: mainly related to preciousness of life and nature.

"Gon the Fox" is not the only sad story used to promote moral education in Japan. Japanese elementary school *kokugo* readers include many sad, war-time stories such as the following:

- "Kawaisōna zō" ("Faithful elephants"), which appeared in 2nd graders' *kokugo* texts in the 1980s, is a story about the elephants that were killed in a Tokyo zoo in the aerial bombings near the end of World War II.
- "Chīchan-no-kageokuri" ("Chii's moving her shade to vast sky"), which appears in 3rd graders' *kokugo* curriculum, tells the story of a small girl who died during World War II (Miyaji et al. 2004).
- "Hitotsu no hana" ("One flower"), which depicts how a family is torn by war, appears in 4th graders' *kokugo* books (Miyaji et al. 2007).

Why are sad stories used in *kokugo* readers for teaching morality? It would seem that stories about good and evil might be sufficient for this purpose. Another alternative might be to use stories of just retribution, such as a story about a fox who has stolen and killed an eel, but then is magically transformed into an eel and suffers the same fate. We must ourselves exercise empathy to address this question.

We note that those who experienced World War II and had vivid memories of it were active during the time when these works were adopted as textbook readers. We suggest that there remains a question as to how many Japanese war survivors felt (and still feel) guilty toward those who died in the war, enemies and allies alike. Perhaps it is this guilt—and the hope that young readers will learn to resonate with it—that underlies the *kokugo* readers' editors' choice and redaction of these sad stories.

Even if there was a stigma of defeat in the background of adopting these war-time stories, it would be more natural to assume that these works continue to be supported because they stir up the reader's emotions regardless of prior war experience. Painful, pessimistic, and sad stories are preferred in *kokugo* readers because, for self-reflective Japanese people, a sense of guilt stems from empathy. This preference mirrors the Japanese people's gnawing distress and regret stemming from a sense of guilt for their past wrongful deeds, including wartime brutality. Domestically, these painful sentiments encompass adults' traumatic feelings about sending young people into war, sympathy with those who suffered from the dropping of the two atomic bombs on Hiroshima and Nagasaki, and good intentions to create an antiwar mindset in their children. Internationally, regrets and guilt also include empathic feelings for the pain felt by the people in neighboring Asian countries due to Japan's expansionist policy and resultant aggression.

Internationalization: Current and Predicted Future Trends

For almost the past four decades, the number of literary narrative materials and the time spent on teaching them have decreased, whereas the number of expository materials and the time spent on teaching them have increased. Since the dawn of the new millennium, furthermore, the internationalization of Japanese education has been a buzzword, particularly in the early 2000s. Internationalization is closely associated with raising intercultural competence (Matsumoto 2000), that is, successful collaboration toward a shared set of goals between individuals with different cultural backgrounds.

Reflecting this international orientation, the Education Ministry of the Japanese government has claimed that *kokugo* textbook readers must be revised so that they develop children's logical thinking and communication skills, which have been regarded as increasingly important. These skills are surely indispensable in today's global society, particularly for interacting with people with low-context cultural backgrounds. According to Aridomi (2014), in the academic years from April 2006 to March 2011, expository materials, especially task-based ones, became the mainstream of *kokugo* textbooks, shifting the emphasis from empathy training to the logical thinking and communicative skills that are critical for completing expository reading and writing tasks. Note that, in this period, "Gon the Fox" continued to appear in textbooks, but without the aforementioned lead-questions asking about Gon's and Hyōjū's feelings (Miyaji et al. 2004, 2007). This was presumably a reflection of the Education Ministry's intent to teach students to exchange their ideas freely, believed to be a necessary skill for internationalization.

Despite such recent trends, empathy training has continued to be the goal of teaching when literary narrative materials are used in the *kokugo* curriculum, and this emphasis has continued throughout the other shifts of the past four decades. As Minami (2009) claims, traditional empathy training through literary materials can go hand in hand in *kokugo* education with developing logical thinking and communications skills through expository materials (which is required particularly in low-context societies), as both— one for tradition and the other for internationalization—play important roles in *kokugo* education. The introduction of folklore elements and narrative techniques can be used to elicit reader participation and, at the same time, to preserve the succession of traditional literary techniques from ancient times to the present. Thus, it may be safe to assume that empathy, the core of the identity of a Japanese individual who lives in a social-relativism dominant society, will continue to serve as an important component of Japanese culture, and that it will be passed on to future generations.

CONCLUSION: EMPATHY-ORIENTED CULTURE REVISITED

This chapter has repeatedly emphasized that a set of similar features might exist among Western cultures; likewise, a different set of similarities might exist among Asian cultures. Taken together, certain contrasting features might be identified between Western and Asian cultures. Western cultures, however, should not be lumped together in one category; neither should Asian cultures. Japanese culture shows behavioral patterns that differ greatly from those identified in Western cultures and might be categorized as a collectivistic Asian culture. The guiding principle of the Japanese, however, can be better characterized as social relativism, within which the individual is defined by the reference groups to which he or she belongs (Holloway and Minami 1996).

Social relativism, which is characterized as being relational and interpersonal, does not necessarily imply that the Japanese lack the notion of independence or individualism. Rather, they have traditionally defined each individual, and his or her function, on the basis of the human relationships within the society of which he or she is a part; each individual is thus allowed to enjoy individualism and independence within the framework of the group. As discussed earlier in this chapter and in other chapters as well, the model of an absolute dichotomy between the East and the West, then, does not necessarily work; nor does an absolute dichotomy between individualism and collectivism. Instead, Japanese culture and its traditions should be understood in the context of an empathy-oriented society where social relativism prevails.

To conclude, this chapter has investigated Japanese culture through folktales. We understand culture through the lens of "human behavior." Culture is an abstract concept; although we see manifestations of our cultural heritage, we do not think about our culture every day, nor do we necessarily ever clearly "see" culture. We use the concept of culture as an explanatory construct to help us understand and categorize: (1) similarities within a group and (2) differences between groups. As discussed earlier in this chapter, a culture consists of a certain set of shared beliefs, customs, and values. Developmentally, from early childhood on, people have to learn the rules preferred in their cultures. In this sense, culture serves as one of the most important determinants and influences on our lives. This chapter has revealed that a continuity exists, in the light of empathy, between oral language traditions and school literacy practices, and has further confirmed that a continuity does exist between home and school practices.

REFERENCES

Aridomi, Yumiko. 2014. *How Japanese National Language Textbooks (kokugo) Have Changed Their Goals.* Unpublished master's thesis, San Francisco State University.

Azuma, Hiroshi. 1986. "Why Study Child Development in Japan?" In *Child Development and Education in Japan*, edited by Harold Stevenson, Hiroshi Azuma, and Kenji Hakuta, 3–12. New York: Freeman.

Azuma, Hiroshi. 1996. "Cross-national Research on Child Development: The Hess-Azuma Collaboration in Retrospect." In *Japanese Childrearing: Two Generations of Scholarship*, edited by David W. Shwalb and Barbara J. Shwalb, 220–240. New York: Guilford Press.

Bernstein, Basil. 1971. *Class, Codes and Control: Vol. 1. Theoretical Studies Towards a Sociology of Language.* London: Routledge & Kegan Paul.

Clancy, Patricia M. 1985. "The Acquisition of Japanese." In *The Crosslinguistic Study of Language Acquisition, Volume 1: The Data*, edited by Dan Isaac Slobin, 373–524. Hillsdale: Lawrence Erlbaum Associates.

Clancy, Patricia M. 1986. "The Acquisition of Communicative Style in Japanese." In *Language Socialization Across Cultures*, edited by Bambi B. Schieffelin and Elinor Ochs, 373–524. New York: Cambridge University Press.

Doi, Takeo. 1973. *The Anatomy of Dependence* (John Bester, Trans). Tokyo: Kodansha International. (Original work published 1971)

Donahue, Ray T. 1998. *Japanese Culture and Communication: Critical Cultural Analysis.* Lanham: University Press of America.

Feiler, Bruce S. 1991. *Learning to Bow: An American Teacher in a Japanese School.* New York: Ticknor & Fields.

Gardner, Howard. 1989. *To Open Minds: Chinese Clues to the Dilemma of Contemporary Education.* New York: Basic Books.

Gerbert, Elaine. 1993. "Lessons from the *Kokugo* (national language) Readers." *Comparative Education Review, 37*(2): 152–180.

Hall, Edward T. 1976. *Beyond Culture.* New York: Anchor.

Hall, Edward T. 1989. "Unstated Features of the Cultural Context of Learning." *The Educational Forum, 54*(1): 21–34.

Hess, Robert D., Kashiwagi, Keiko, Azuma, Hiroshi, Price, Gary G., and Dickson, W. Patrick. 1980. "Maternal Expectations for Early Mastery of Developmental Tasks and Cognitive and Social Competence of Preschool Children in Japan and the United States." *International Journal of Psychology, 15*: 259–271.

Hofstede, Geert. 1984. *Culture's Consequences: International Differences in Work-related Values*. Beverly Hills: SAGE Publications.

Holloway, Susan D., and Minami, Masahiko. 1996. "Production and Reproduction of Culture: The Dynamic Role of Mothers and Children in Early Socialization." In *Japanese Childrearing: Two Generations of Scholarship*, edited by David W. Shwalb and Barbara J. Shwalb, 164–176. New York: Guilford Press.

Jorden, Rashaad. 2015. "Gon, the Little Fox" Japan Exchange & Teaching Programme Alumni Association of New York (JQ) Magazine. Retrieved from jetwit.com/wordpress/2015/05/10/jq-magazine-book-review-gon-the-little-fox (last access: 08.14.2019).

Kirkus Reviews. 2015. "Gon, the Little Fox." *Kirkus Reviews, 83*(6): 172.

Kurihara, Kazuto, et al., eds. 1992. *Kokugo 4, part 2 Habataki*. Tokyo: Mitsumura Book Publishing (certified by the Ministry of Education in 1991).

Kurihara, Kazuto, et al., eds. 1999. *Kokugo 4, part 2 Habataki*. Tokyo: Mitsumura Book Publishing (certified by the Ministry of Education in 1995).

Lebra, Takie Sugiyama. 1976. *Japanese Patterns of Behavior*. Honolulu: University of Hawaii Press.

Lin, Pei-Jung, and Schwanenflugel, Paula J. 1995. "Cultural Familiarity and Language Factors in the Structure of Category Knowledge." *Journal of Cross-Cultural Psychology, 26*(2): 153–168.

Lucy, John Arthur. 1992. *Language Diversity and Thought: A Reformulation of the Linguistic Relativity Hypothesis*. New York: Cambridge University Press.

Markus, Hazel R., and Kitayama, Shinobu. 1991. "Culture and the Self: Implications for Cognition, Emotion, and Motivation." *Psychological Review, 98*(2): 224–253.

Matsumoto, David. 2000. *Culture and Psychology: People Around the World* (2nd ed.). Belmont: Wadsworth/Thomson Learning.

Matsumoto, David, and Juang, Linda. 2008. *Culture and Psychology* (4th ed.). Belmont: Thomson Higher Education.

Maynard, Senko K. 1992. *Discourse Modality: Subjectivity, Emotion and Voice in the Japanese Language*. Amsterdam: John Benjamins.

Minami, Masahiko. 2002. *Culture-specific Language Styles: The Development of Oral Narrative and Literacy*. Clevedon: Multilingual Matters.

Minami, Masahiko. 2009. *Language and Culture: Understanding Language Variations from the Viewpoint of Linguistic Theories* (Original title: *Gengo to bunka: Gengogaku kara yomitoku kotoba no bariēshon*). Tokyo: Kurosio Publishers.

Minami, Masahiko, and McCabe, Allyssa. 1991. "Haiku as a Discourse Regulation Device: A Stanza Analysis of Japanese Children's Personal Narratives." *Language in Society, 20*(4): 577–600.

Miyanaga, Kuniko. 1991. *The Creative Edge: Emerging Individualism in Japan*. New Brunswick: Transaction Publishers.

Miyaji, Yutaka, et al., eds. 2004. *Kokugo 3, part 2 Aozora*, Mitsumura Book Publishing (certified by the Ministry of Education in 2001).

Miyaji, Yutaka, et al., eds. 2007. *Kokugo 3, part 2 Aozora*, Mitsumura Book Publishing (certified by the Ministry of Education in 2004).

Norton, Donna E. 1991. *Through the Eyes of a Child: An Introduction to Children's Literature* (3rd ed.). New York: Macmillan.

Saito, Toshiko. 1974. "The Meaning of Tradition in Children's Literature and Nankichi Niimi" (Original Title: *Jidōbungaku ni okeru dentō no igi to Niimi Nankichi*). *The Otani Gakuho, 54*(2): 54–65.

Sakade, Florence, and Kurosaki, Yoshisuke, eds. 1958. *Japanese Children's Favorite Stories*. Tokyo: Charles E. Tuttle.

Sapir, Edward. 1921. *Language: An Introduction to the Study of Speech*. New York: Harcourt, Brace and Company.

Sapir, Edward. 1921 [1929]. "The Status of Linguistics as a Science." *Language, 5*: 207–214.

Shigaki, Irene S. 1987. "Language and the Transmission of Values: Implications from Japanese Day Care." In *Home and School: Early Language and Reading*, edited by Bryant Fillion, Carolyn N. Hedley, and Emily C. DiMartino, 111–121. Norwood: Ablex.

Stigler, James W., and Perry, Michelle. 1988. "Mathematics Learning in Japanese, Chinese and American Classrooms." In *Children's Mathematics: New Directions for Child Development, 41*, edited by Geoffrey B. Saxe and Maryl Gearhart, 27–54. San Francisco: Jossey-Bass.

Taniguchi, Marilyn. 2015. "Gon, the Little Fox." *School Library Journal, 61*(5): 90.

Tobin, Joseph J., Wu, David Y. H., and Davidson, Dana. H. 1989. *Preschool in Three Cultures: Japan, China, and the United States*. New Haven: Yale University Press.

Whorf, Benjamin Lee. 1956. *Language, Thought, and Reality: Selected Writings*, edited by John B. Carroll. Cambridge: MIT Press.

Chapter 8

Educational Implications of Buddhist Values in Vietnamese Folktales

Tham Tran and MinJeong Kim

Folktales have long been recognized as a source of learning (Hanlon 2000) and a means of transmitting moral values from generation to generation (Leimgruber 2010) in countries in Southeast Asia, as well as the rest of the world. As folktales depict the cultural, social, and moral values of the countries (Shaŵa and Soko 2013; Hourani 2015), people have used folktales as a tool to educate young minds about traditional values and to set behavioral expectations (Hourani 2015). Under a long and profound influence of Buddhism on Vietnamese culture since the first century (Nguyễn 1993), Vietnamese folktales have been commonly used for educational purposes in order to emphasize the importance of valuing individuals' moral attitudes for reciprocal social relationships in accordance with Buddhist values (Cao 2019).

In the current national Vietnamese educational curriculum, based on students' psychological features, folktales are being used in teaching literature to students from preschools to high schools (Ly 2014; Nguyen 2020; Vu 2017; Vu 2020). Folktales are great sources of nurturing children's morality and character (Nguyen 2017). Each tale is imbued with human values and has a profound educational meaning, which helps children develop healthy and ethical viewpoints. Teaching folktales helps foster students' true aspirations and love toward family, homeland, and country. The lessons drawn from the stories of folktales help contribute to personality development, forming kindness and compassion in students (Ly 2014; Nguyen 2020; Vu 2017; Vu 2020).

Central to teaching folktales as tools to help students develop healthy identities is the collectivist perspective that emphasizes the importance of ethical and responsible members of the society. This view leads students to thinking of their identities in relation to their social relationships with significant others around them. Two basic principles in Buddhism, interdependent co-arising (*Lý Duyên Sinh*) and karma (*Nghiệp*) are closely related to what it means to be a good member of society in Vietnam. In other words, the two concepts provide students not only with moral lessons but also with behavioral guidelines for identity development in a collectivistic society.

The principle of karma, referring to the law of cause and effect, is depicted in many Vietnamese folktales as a means of teaching people to avoid doing evil things and to encourage them to do good deeds. Vietnamese folktales bring out the Buddhist moral lessons of the cause-and-effect law which is expressed in famous Vietnamese proverbs "those who do good deeds will have good outcomes" and "who sows the wind will reap the whirlwind." Folktales based on the Buddhist principles are known for nourishing compassion and kindness in order to attain a good life with peace and happiness in the present and the future. Evil characters with bad qualities (such as being greedy, harsh, or unsympathetic) usually end up with adverse consequences because of their evil behaviors and mindset. In contrast, righteous characters who are usually poor or orphaned with good personal qualities (such as being kind, hardworking, diligent, honest, helpful) go through adverse life experiences, but finally are blessed with happy and successful endings at the end of the story. Karma refers to an individual's present life being decided by what they did in the past, and what the person does in the present life will affect his next life.

Buddhism also emphasizes the value of interdependence. Buddhism proposes interdependent co-arising of all phenomena, which can be briefly explained that "everything is a result of multiple causes and conditions" (Thich 1998, 370), or everything depends on something else to exist. Aligning with this Buddhist notion, Vietnamese folktales emphasize ethics and values individuals need to learn to maintain healthy social relationships (co-exist), in which social relationships themselves are the priority. Individuals are willing to sacrifice their own benefits for collective benefits. Individuals tend to perceive themselves as a part of a larger social whole. Therefore, they tend to be harmonious toward others to maintain social relationships. Harmony is emphasized in the interactions of Vietnamese people in most social contexts.

This chapter conducts a content analysis of two Vietnamese folktales for children, focusing on educational themes related to the two Buddhist values of karma and interdependent co-arising ingrained in the folktales. The two folktales examined in this article include *The Starfruit Tree* and *The Story of Tấm and Cám*. These folktales are among the most popular educational folktales used to teach kindergarten and elementary students. These folktales were elicited from Vietnamese American families in Lowell, Massachusetts, who participated in the *Southeast Asian Folktale Project*.

EDUCATIONAL VALUES IN VIETNAMESE
CURRICULUM TAUGHT THROUGH FOLKTALES

In the Vietnamese educational curriculum, folktales are used as mentor texts for Vietnamese Language Arts, Literature, and Ethics from PreK-12 (Ly 2014; Nguyen 2020; Vu 2020). The goals of teaching folktales are to transmit Vietnamese traditional culture, to educate students about ethical values, and to provide students with moral lessons that individuals need to learn to maintain healthy social relationships.

One of the major goals of Vietnamese education is to raise a member of the country who values social relationships that build on ethics and traditional values of a collectivist society (Nguyen 2020). Vietnamese folktales provide moral lessons that emphasize the importance of self-cultivation to become a good person in the society and to behave ethically in family and social relationships. Through the narration of different characters and the social relationships they have, the folktales give students exemplary lessons of "loving people as you love yourself," being filial to their parents, and loving other people in the family like grandparents, brothers, and sisters (Ly 2014). These folktales uphold and praise good moral and social sentiments accord-ing to their aesthetic points of view. There can be the faithful husband and wife relationship (e.g., the Legend of Vong Phu Stone, the Legend of Horse Shoe Crab, the Story of Betel Nut and Areca), the passionate friendship (e.g., the Legend of Mattocks, the Three Friends), the brotherly love, a benevolent love (e.g., Sugar Cane Grower and Passerby) (Nguyen 2020).

Folktales also criticize and condemn unethical things in society. In these cases, the stories provide useful lessons as a way of warning the wicked and evil that are raging in society: at the end of the folktales, the wholesome person will get good results, and the wicked or evil are always properly pun-ished. People also want to consider folktales as reminders and admonitions for those who have been and are deliberately forgetting the relationships between brothers, spouses, parents, and neighbors, to strengthen and culti-vate good sentiments in families, villages, and society. The moral concep-tions expressed in folktales are distilled from actual behavioral experiences and, at the same time, are the ideal morality that people want to cultivate. Therefore, such moral conceptions are both familiar and strange, both close and sublime, at the same time ordinary and holy. It is not only what is inherent in the community but also what will be needed to make life better (Nguyen 2020).

These goals are closely related to Buddhist values, especially karma and interdependent co-arising which are explained in the following section. The two Buddhist values are highlighted in the Vietnamese folktales that are commonly used for educational purposes in order to emphasize the importance of valuing individuals' moral attitudes for reciprocal social relationships.

KARMA AND INTERDEPENDENT CO-ARISING

According to Buddhist doctrine, the law of cause and effect is an axiom that explains the relationship between an action and its corresponding result. The law entails a basis of the causes of each thing—why each thing comes into existence. The law of cause and effect governs all existence. This law is impartial; it takes no sides. No one can deny or change the inevitable law of cause and effect.

Karma is a Sanskrit word meaning "actions" including actions of body, speech, and thought (Geshe Kelsang Gyatso 2001). Karma in Buddhism means action driven by intention which leads to future consequences. A person's karma will determine how he or she is reborn in samsara, the cycle of rebirth. According to Mackenzie (2013), karma is a semantically complex and contextually fluid notion. In other words, karma refers to the law of cause and effect in which our volitionally motivated acts cause a certain consequence (Goldstein 2008). If we do wholesome deeds motivated by kindness, compassion, and generosity, we will earn happiness, peace, and wealth. In contrast, if our conduct is motivated by greed, anger, or delusion, we will face suffering sooner or later. If we plant a seed of cherry, we will get cherry fruits in the future. We cannot expect it to produce apples. Karma, therefore, is the law of nature and of cause and effect on the psychophysical world (Goldstein 2008).

Buddhist teachings explain that the effect we see in this life may be brought about by its cause from a previous life or one of many past lives. The cause that is created in this life may take effect in the next life or many of the subsequent lives to come. Beings are driven from life to life in samsara depending on the nature of karma in their present life as well as previous lives (Wilson 2016). Samsara is a never-ending cycle of life, birth, death, and rebirth. Only enlightened ones are free from Samsara. There are six realms of reincarnation including hells, hungry ghosts, animals, humans, asuras (i.e., demons), and heavenly beings.

Another important characteristic of the law of cause and effect is that a cause itself cannot form an effect, but it needs other supporting factors. The cause and supporting factors are interdependent to generate an effect. The absence of other factors can cause change or distortion of the result. For instance, an apple seed cannot grow without supporting factors such as water, soil, sunlight, air, and so on. This characteristic refers to the notion of inter-dependent co-arising. Interdependent co-arising is generally defined such that the arising of everything is dependent upon many causes and conditioning factors (Thich Nhat Hanh 1998).

The second basic principle of Buddhism, interdependent co-arising, or dependent origination, refers to a process in which suffering can arise and can end in our lives. Interdependent co-arising is considered as the essence of Buddhist teaching. It expresses an understanding of life in which everything is interconnected. Nothing can stand alone or separate as in, "we are part of this process of dependent origination—causal relationships are affected by everything that happens around us and, in turn, affect the kind of world that we all live in inwardly and outwardly" (Feldman 1999, 37). According to Bloom (2018), in the religious aspect, the teaching of interdependent co-arising underscores the doctrine of karma which explains suffering existing in humans and the world. At the same time, the teaching of interdependent co-arising confirms the composite nature of phenomena. In other words, people can actively change their destiny, bettering their lives and society by avoiding non-virtuous deeds and doing virtuous deeds.

TWO FOLKTALES

Two folktales were selected for analysis for this chapter from the Southeast Asian Folktale Project (See Introduction in this book for more information about the project). Specifically, we selected the two tales published in the children's book our research group prepared, *A Long Long Time Ago in Southeast Asia*. The two tales, *The Starfruit Tree* and *The Story of Tấm and Cám* were selected by Vietnamese American families who told the stories published in the book as the most typical educational texts to teach children Vietnamese values.

The Starfruit Tree

The law of cause and effect in interdependent co-arising is evident in many Vietnamese folktales (Thích Thái Hoà 2011). According to this law, everything is a result of multiple causes and conditions (Thich Nhat Hanh 1998). One thing to note is that the obvious effect of wholesome or evil conduct permeates each folktale so that people can witness it. Reflecting on the law of karma, *the Starfruit Tree* is one of the typical folktales glorifying gratitude and affirming a strong belief that those who conduct wholesome deeds will in turn experience good luck and wholesome consequences, while those who do bad deeds will in turn experience miserable results.

Once upon a time, there was a very rich man who lived in a village. When he died, he left his two sons a huge fortune. The two brothers were entirely different from each other. The elder brother was greedy while the younger one was very kind. The elder brother claimed the whole fortune and left his younger brother only a starfruit tree. Both brothers got married. The elder brother with his inheritance had nothing to worry about. Meanwhile, the younger brother who only had the starfruit tree was very worried. Thus, he took good care of his tree, hoping that it would give him a lot of fruit so that he could make a living by selling it. The tree grew bigger and bigger. It had a lot of fruit. When the starfruit was ripe, a raven flew by and stopped in the tree to eat a lot of starfruit. The younger brother was very sad to see this happen every day, but he did not know what to do. One day, he decided to stand beneath the tree and talk to the raven: "Raven, please don't eat my fruit. This fruit tree is my only fortune."

"Don't worry," the raven replied. "I'll pay you back with gold. Make a two-feet long bag. Tomorrow morning, I'll come back and take you to get the gold." Next morning, the raven really did come back. He let the younger brother sit on his back and flew over the sea to an island filled with gold. The younger brother gathered all the gold he could fit into the bag that he had made. Then he flew back home on the raven's back with a lot of gold. He was very happy and became very rich.

The younger brother invited the elder one to come over. The elder brother said, "No, I don't want to go to your shabby house." The younger brother kept inviting his elder brother to visit him. "I have something for you, Brother." Finally, the elder brother gave in. He visited his brother and found to his surprise that his brother had all sorts of riches—a very big house, lots of beautiful furniture, lots of money.

"How did you get all these riches, Brother?" the elder one asked. The younger brother told him about the starfruit tree, the raven and the trip to the island filled with gold. The elder brother offered to trade all his fortune for the starfruit tree. The kind younger brother gladly accepted the offer. The raven came as usual and ate a lot of starfruit. The elder brother spoke to the raven the same words as his younger brother did. He received the same answer from the raven. But he was so greedy that he made a six-foot long bag instead of a two-foot long bag. The next day, the raven came to take him to the island of gold. After he filled the bag with gold, he put the gold into all of his pockets, too. Then, he climbed onto the raven's back to go home. But the load was so heavy that when they flew over the sea, the raven tilted his tired wings. "Let go! Let go of the gold!" the raven screamed. But the elder brother did not want to let go of the gold. Finally, the raven had to drop him into the sea. Back at home, the younger brother waited for the elder one for a very long time. "Why is it taking so long for my brother to come back?" The next day, the younger brother met the raven and asked where his brother was. The raven told him that the elder brother would not let go of the gold and fell into the sea and died.

The *Starfruit Tree* depicts the elder brother as being greedy and selfish toward his own younger brother while the young brother is characterized as poor and humble. As brothers, they were supposed to love and help one another, but the elder one did not do that. Greed and selfishness made the elder brother treat his younger brother poorly. The elder brother took almost all inherited fortune from their father and just left his younger brother a small hut with a starfruit tree. Being greedy, the elder brother was so glad to discover from his brother that the bird repaid starfruit with gold. He asked his brother to exchange the starfruit tree with his own fortune so the raven would take him to the island of gold too.

The elder brother displayed his greed again when he substituted a larger bag for one with the size the raven specified. The bad consequences that the elder brother received were not due to the bird but because of his own limitless covetousness. The bird reminded the elder brother twice to let go of the gold because it was too heavy for it to carry, but he did not. Finally, the bird had to drop him into the sea along with his gold. The six-foot-long bag was a semiotic image reminding people not to desire excessively. We should not let greed and desire control our life, which could lead to evil and misfortune.

Meanwhile, the younger brother was depicted as having virtuous traits. He was so kind and obedient that he accepted and agreed to all arrangements from his elder brother. He worked very hard to support his family without any complaint. Because he was honest, the younger brother told his elder brother everything about the raven eating starfruit and repaying it with gold. Being honest, too, the younger brother prepared the bag with the size exactly as the bird told him. He was also willing to exchange the starfruit tree with his elder brother's fortune as the elder brother asked him. In the end, the younger brother had a prosperous and happy life. This character emphasizes the lesson that we should do good deeds, living a life morally to attain happiness and wealth.

In addition, as the raven stopped by and ate the starfruit, a notable detail was that the raven said it would repay the fruit with gold. The younger brother thought that the bird just said that and might not keep its promise. Surprisingly, one day later, the bird came back and flew the younger brother to the island of gold. This detail emphasizes the virtue of keeping promises and being grateful to those who help us.

The folktale the *Starfruit Tree* reflects the characteristic of karma mentioned above that any cause will create a corresponding effect. Every single volitional act gives rise to its own effects. As our acts are motivated by greed, anger, and ignorance, we are creating the karmic conditions for suffering to come. As our acts and speech are motivated by generosity, loving-kindness, and understanding, we are creating the fruit of wealth, peace, and happiness in the future.

In terms of co-arising, the kindness and the good deeds and wholesome actions that the younger brother accumulated through most of his life situations are the supporting factors that brought about his prosperous and happy life in the end of the folktale. In the case of the elder brother, with his nature of greed and covetousness (the cause), he treated his younger brother badly and did not change his evil attitudes and behaviors (supporting factors), which finally led to the detrimental consequence of death and misfortune (effect).

In the same vein but having a different motif than *the Star Fruit Tree*, *the Story of Tấm and Cám* is another Vietnamese fairy tale. There are different versions of this story with different endings. This story reveals the Buddhist influence in this country, especially karma and samsara. Vietnamese people's dreams of social justice and the ultimate victory of goodness are also addressed through this folktale. The following version of the story was collected from the interview data of our Southeast Asia Folktale Project in Lowell for the children's book, *A Long, Long Time Ago in Southeast Asia*.

The Story of Tấm and Cám

Tấm and Cám were stepsisters. Tấm's mother died when Tấm was young. Her father then remarried, but he passed away not long after that. Tấm had to live with her stepmother (Cám's mother). The stepmother was so jealous of Tấm's beauty that she forced her to do all chores. Meanwhile, she adored her daughter, Cám, and did not let her do anything.

One day, Tấm and Cám went fishing to get a reward from their mother for the one who caught the most fish with a new "áo yếm" (a Vietnamese traditional undershirt). While Tấm was working hard to catch a basket full of fish, Cám was just playing around. Then Cám tricked Tấm and took all the fish Tấm had caught. Being tricked by Cám, Tấm sobbed uncontrollably.

Bụt (Buddha) appeared and told her to look into her basket and find a little goby fish left and to carry and release it into the well in her backyard. Tấm carefully followed Buddha's instructions. She fed it with cooked rice every day. Tấm's stepmother and Cám noticed that and wanted to kill her fish. One day, the stepmother asked Tấm to feed a buffalo in a faraway field; then she and her daughter went to the well to catch and eat Tấm's little fish.

When Tấm discovered her fish was dead, she burst into tears. Buddha appeared again and told her to put the fish's bones into four separate jars and bury them under the four corners of her bed.

A short time later, the King proclaimed a big nationwide festival to look for a wife. Tấm asked for permission to join the festival, and her stepmother ordered

Tấm to sort out one big basket of mixed white rice and paddies into two separate baskets before she could go. Tấm knew that she could never finish the job in time, and she cried.

Then Buddha appeared again and sent hundreds of birds to help her. Buddha then told her to dig up her four jars to get a beautiful gown, golden slippers, a saddle, and a horse to go to the festival. On the way to the festival, Tấm dropped one of her slippers in the stream. One of the King's servants caught it and showed him the golden slipper. The King was amazed by the beauty of the slipper and sent his word that the one whose feet would fit in this shoe would become the new Queen. No one could fit into that small shoe but Tấm.

The King immediately asked her to be his Queen and took her to the Palace.

On the anniversary of Tấm's father's death, she went home to prepare an offering for her father's altar. Her stepmother asked Tấm to climb the areca tree to pick some fruit. The stepmother then cut down the tree to make Tấm fall and die. By tradition, Tấm's sister, Cám, would marry the King in her place.

Tấm's soul turned into a beautiful nightingale and flew to the Palace. Recognizing the spirit of his beloved late wife through the beautiful songs it sang, the King loved the bird very much. Cám was very jealous and angry. On her mother's advice, she waited until the King was out and she killed the bird. Then she burned and buried the bird's feathers in the Palace garden. From the feathers grew two beautiful sapele trees under which the King loved to hang his hammock to lie on. Cám and her mother cut down the trees to make a loom for Cám to weave fabrics. When Cám was weaving, Tấm's voice spoke out of the loom and made Cám afraid. Cám burned the loom into ashes and threw the ashes far away from the Palace. From the ashes grew a "thị" tree that had only one golden fruit with a very sweet, pleasant smell.

One day, a poor old woman walked by the tree. She adored the smell of the fruit and asked the tree to drop it in her bag. She promised that she would keep the fruit on her bed and only smell it. The fruit then fell into her bag. When she brought the fruit home, Tấm secretly appeared from the golden fruit to tidy and prepare hot meals for the old woman every day.

One day, the old woman pretended to go out but came back early, hiding herself behind the door, waiting for Tấm to walk out from the golden fruit and clean the house. She ran in and tore up the fruit so Tấm had to stay as her adoptive daughter. After that, the King stopped by the hut when he got lost while hunting. The old woman offered him an areca nut, wrapped in betel leaves. The King was surprised to see the betel had been skillfully rolled, exactly the way his wife did. He asked to see who prepared the betel. Tấm came out, and the King immediately realized that the girl was his late wife. He was overjoyed and took her back to the Palace. Knowing the truth, the King sentenced both the stepmother and Cám to death for their evildoing.

However, Tấm asked him to forgive them. The King agreed but ordered them to get out of the Palace. On the way home, a sudden storm arose with fierce thunder. Lightning struck the stepmother and Cám, and both died in pain.

This folktale is considered a Vietnamese version of Cinderella among many variations of Cinderella around the world. Just in Europe, more than 500 versions of this folktale have been found (Northup 2007). These stories tell about orphaned, but hardworking and kind-hearted, girls. Usually, the Cinderella folktale versions from the West end when Cinderella marries the prince (or the King) after putting on the lost slipper, and the couple live happily ever after. Unlike those stories, the story of Tấm and Cám has a second part, depicting Tấm's arduous and fierce fight against evil to attain her worthy happiness. Both parts of the story reflect the law of karma (or cause and effect) in Buddhism, as well as the dreams of happiness and social justice of working Vietnamese people in the past.

The story started with describing Tấm as a beautiful, beloved girl who endured misfortunes in her childhood: her mom passed away; her dad remarried an evil woman; then her dad passed away. Tấm lived with her wicked stepmother and stepsister. The stepmother was so jealous of Tấm's beauty that she not only forced Tấm to do all the chores but also did various malicious things to harm and kill Tấm. The magnitude of the stepmother's and Cám's evil increased over time. First, the stepmother demanded Tấm catch fish; then Cám tricked Tấm to take Tấm's basket full of fish. When Tấm was taking care of the goby (the only fish left from her basket), loving it as her only friend, her stepmother and Cám tricked her into herding the buffalo in a faraway field so they could catch and eat Tấm's goby. Then, the stepmother prevented Tấm from joining the national festival by ordering her to sort out white rice from paddies. Furthermore, the stepmother and Cám killed Tấm by cutting down the areca tree after asking her to climb up to the top of the tree to pick the fruit to offer to her father's altar on the anniversary of his death. Tấm died and Cám took Tấm's place to go to the palace to marry the King. The stepmother and Cám's evils did not stop there. After Tấm was reincarnated as a nightingale, Cám killed the bird, then burned and buried the bird feathers. The burned feathers grew to be two beautiful sapele trees under which the King liked to hang his hammock to lie on. Out of jealousy, again, Cám cut down the trees to make a loom upon which to weave fabrics. Cám then burned the loom into ashes and threw the ashes far away because she heard Tấm's voice coming from the loom. Cám and her mother's level of evil deeds continuously increased. Their malicious intent and hatred multiplied. But in

Tấm's late reincarnation as a girl stepping out of the "thị" fruit, Tấm reunited with the King and came back to the palace. She became the Queen and lived happily with the King ever after.

We can see the chain of events that follow the law of cause and effect and the interdependent co-arising in the story of Tấm and Cám. The main characters' actions (causes) and their effects are contiguously linked to results in the particular ending of this first version of the story. It indicates that a present cause itself is generated from an effect of a previous cause, and the effect itself can be the cause of a future effect. Tấm's diligence and kindheartedness is the cause of the effect that Buddha appeared and asked her to find a goby left in her basket and then take good care of that goby. Tấm's caring for her goby made her stepmother and Cám trick her so they could kill the goby, eating it and leaving only fish bones. Tấm put the fish bones into four separate jars and buried them under the four corners of her bed, where they became her beautiful clothes, slippers, horse, and saddle so that Tấm could join the festival with Buddha's help. Tấm came to the festival and lost one of her slippers, which eventually caused her to meet with the King and become Queen. When Tấm became Queen, this triggered jealousy and greed in her stepmother and Cám. They committed many evils to kill her multiple times. Longing for her lover and suffering from being killed and having her happiness taken away caused Tam to be reincarnated into a nightingale, two sapele trees, a loom, and a "*thị*" fruit so that she could live for her own happiness.

Tấm's happy life clearly shows the principle of cause and effect with the medium of supporting factors of interdependent co-arising in between the cause (Tấm's good heart) and the effect (her happy life). Tấm did various continuously wholesome deeds, and she finally attained happiness and prosperity as the consequence of her morally just behaviors. She fulfilled all tasks assigned to her by her stepmother without complaint: catching fish, sorting grains, herding buffalo, and picking up areca fruit. After becoming the Queen, she still remembered her dad's death anniversary and went back home to help her stepmother prepare for the anniversary. Although her stepmother and Cám had treated her cruelly before, Tấm treated them kindly. Even after experiencing so much torment from the stepmother and Cám, she was forgiving them. She asked that the King not kill them as punishment and instead let them go back home to be ordinary people. Karma, however, struck them down on the way home. In contrast, Tấm's wholesome virtues finally paid off with a happy life with the King in the palace.

On the other hand, the consistent characteristics of cause and effect and the interdependent co-arising are confirmed through the stepmother's and Cám's deaths as consequences for their many malevolent acts toward Tấm. Their evil thoughts and actions (cause) kept Cám and her mother from ever feeling happy even when they succeeded in doing harm to Tấm (effect). They repeatedly faced fear that Tấm would come back and found evil ways to harm Tấm (supporting factors). They had to find ways to lie to the King about Tấm's disappearances. Even though Cám replaced Tấm's position as the Queen, she did not receive love from the King. After being forgiven and ordered to go out of the palace, on the way back home, they painfully died as fierce lightning and thunder hit them. The end of the story reflects a corresponding trait of the law of cause and effect that *"gieo gió gặt bão*—who sows the wind will reap the whirlwind" (Vietnamese proverb). Those whose actions are motivated by greed, hatred, and evil will get their painful consequences, sooner or later. No one can avoid the effect of karma. As the Buddha taught in the *Upajjhatthana Sutta* (Subjects for Contemplation), "I am the owner of my karma, heir to my karma, born of my karma, related to my karma, abide supported by my karma. Whatever karma I shall do, for good or for ill, of that I will be the heir." Among different versions of the end of the story of Tấm and Cám, this version dignifies the value of Tấm's wholesome virtues and indicates the consistency of the characters' traits in the story. Tấm's nature is kindhearted and forgiving, even forgiving her stepmother and stepsister for the evils they had done to her. The stepmother and Cám, however, still paid for the evil sins they did with their painful death, which again is in accordance with the law of cause and effect. This ending is considered to have the highest educational meaning (Thích Thái Hòa 2011).

In addition to the end of the story of Tấm and Cám mentioned above, there are some other, different versions of the ending. There is one version collected by Minh Long (2014), Literature Publishing House, stating that:

> Tấm came out to greet the King. The King joyfully recognized Tấm. The King took Tấm back to the Palace and they lived a happy life. Knowing Tấm had come back, the stepmother and Cám were scared and ashamed, so they ran far away, and nobody saw them after that.

This ending also expresses the moral lesson of cause and effect, the one who does good deeds will get good consequences and the one who does bad deeds will get bad consequences. Feeling scared and ashamed and running away from the palace was in this version the bad consequence for the stepmother and Cám.

In still another, contrastive version of the end of this story, it describes how Tấm took revenge on Cám:

> Tấm became Queen again and lived happily with the King. Wondering why Tấm had been loved by the King so much, Cám came to ask her how to have

skin as fair as hers. Tấm told Cám to take a bath in boiling water, which she gleefully did, and died a painful death in the hot water. After finding this out, the stepmother wept and died not long after that. (Nguyễn Đổng Chi 1975)

And there is yet another version of the end of this story that increases the level of Tấm's revenge toward her stepmother and stepsister. This version was collected by Nguyễn Văn Ngọc (2003).

Later, when Tấm has returned to the palace, Cám asks Tấm about her beauty secret. Tấm does not answer, but instead asks back: "Do you want to be beautiful? I'll help you!"

Cám immediately agrees. Tấm tells her to jump down a hole and she does so. Tấm then commands the royal soldiers to pour boiling water onto her, killing Cám and using her corpse to make fermented sauce (in the same way fish sauce is made). Tấm then sends the sauce to her stepmother, saying it is a gift from Cám.

The stepmother believes so and eats it every day. One day, a crow flies by the stepmother's house and rests on her roof and cries out:

"Delicious! The mother is eating her own daughter's flesh! Is there any left? Give me some."

The stepmother becomes angry, but when she finally reaches the bottom of the jar, she discovers a skull inside. Realizing it is Cám's, the stepmother immediately dies of shock.

From the perspective of folk beliefs, this ending shows the folk concept of "One doing good deeds will get good results (*ở hiền gặp lành*)" and "Sow the wind and reap whirlwind (*gieo gió gặt bão*)." Tấm is the character representing the good, fighting for legitimate happiness and finally getting her desired reward. The stepmother and Cám are characters representing evil, constantly using many evil tactics to deprive Tấm of something she values, and their inevitable consequence for this is paying with their lives. Folks believe that evil people deserve catastrophic punishment.

Some may consider that the way Tấm took revenge on Cám was too cruel and not in line with Tấm's personality throughout the story and does not reflect the compassion value in Buddhism. However, the characteristics of characters in folklore function to represent and transcend the wishes of folks. Living under the oppression of a feudal society, folks always dreamt that good people would be happy, and those who caused suffering to others would be punished. Stepmother and Cám have caused Tấm so much suffering, so the final punisher for those sins must also be Tấm. That ending expresses the dream of justice of Vietnamese people in the past. Folks strongly believed that good would overcome evil, and justice would be executed. Although evil can be powerful and overwhelming, the victory of good is absolute. Tấm's punishment for Cám is the most powerful one exemplifying that strong belief because it entirely eradicates the seeds of evil. This ending does not reflect the Buddhist substance which proposes no killing for any reasons, but it does reflect the wishes of working-class people in the past in the revolution against the evil of their oppressors (Lê 2009, 35).

In light of karma in Buddhism, with evil intentions and acts to avenge Cám and the stepmother, Tấm herself made a new bad cause such that she would continue to meet her stepmother and Cám in future lives to pay for her own bad deeds. The samsara of cause and effect never ends if we are not aware of it and stop making bad causes. Regarding the end of this folktale, venerable Thich Thai Hoa (2011) explains that

> If Tấm were a well-educated Buddhist, when she is free from bad karma to be Queen, she would silently thank her stepmother and Cám and find ways to help them see cause and effect, to practice transforming bad and evil causes, to bring about peaceful results. The story of Tấm and Cám, in that case, would be upgraded to a high level of education dignifying wisdom and compassion in Buddhism. However, the story of Tấm and Cám [with this ending] has helped people see that after death, karma is still there with us; and karma can itself re-create the cycle of samsara (i.e., the cycle of death and rebirth) in cause and effect. We will reap the fruit of what we have sown.

CONCLUSION

Both *The Starfruit Tree* and *The Story of* Tấm and Cám have profound educational meanings in Vietnamese contexts. *The Story of* Tấm and Cám highlights the direction of goodness for each human being. The tragic consequences of the stepmother and Cam may serve as a warning for anyone who intends to do something evil toward others. This consequence is central to its moral lesson for children, which is closely related to the concept of Karma. The happy ending of Tam presents an example and encouragement for those who try to do good things, that they will eventually get favorable results. Furthermore, the image of a bird in *the Starfruit Tree* gives us a lesson of keeping our promises. The bag of gold that the bird told the brothers to carry reminds us to live morally and not let greed control us. If we lose ourselves out of greed or because of greed, we will fall into the abyss of evil which will lead us to dissatisfaction and misery. In contrast, when we do good deeds, living a gentle and virtuous life, we will surely have good luck and happiness in life.

The chapter has elaborated the karma and interdependent origination in Buddhism and how these two concepts are embedded in several Vietnamese folktales. Through various characters, the two folktales profoundly depict moral lessons that evil results always come from evil causes going along with evil supporting conditions, and good causes with the medium of wholesome supporting factors will always lead to good results. We should not do evil deeds in order to avoid adversity, and we should live a virtuous life in order to give rise to happiness, peace, and richness for ourselves and others. Being aware of the law of karma helps us to be in control of our life and take responsibility for our own acts. Understanding the law, we shall not blame ourselves or others for our adversity but start to improve our behaviors to attain good results. We know that how we are today is the result of our past actions, so we shall be able to control results by controlling causes and the supporting factors. To have good results, we need to be diligent in committing actions that benefit not only ourselves but also others. These lessons were exquisitely expressed through various depiction of characteristics and plots in the two aforementioned folktales.

REFERENCES

Bloom, Alfred. 2018. "The Central Concept of Buddhism: The Teaching of Interdependent Co-arising." *Shin Dharma Net*, August 20, 2020. bschawaii.org/s hindharmanet/studies/coarising.

Cao, Thao H. 2019. "Tư tưởng Phật giáo trong truyện cổ tích Việt Nam." February 4, 2019. phatgiao.org.vn/tu-tuong-phat-giao-trong-truyen-co-tich-viet-nam-d3376 0.html.

Feldman, Christina. 1999. "Dependent Origination." *Insight Journal*, Spring 1999, 37–42.

Geshe, Kelsang Gyatso. 2001. *How to Transform Your Life—a Blissful Journey*. New York: Tharpa Publications.

Goldstein, Joseph. "Cause and Effect Reflecting on the Law of Karma." *The Buddhist Review Magazine*, August 29, 2020. tricycle.org/magazine/cause-and-effect.

Hanlon, Tina. 2000. *General Guidelines for Teaching with Folktales, Fables, Ballads and other Short Works of Folklore*. Ferrum: Ferrum College.

Hourani, Rida Blaik. 2015. "Folktales, Children's Literature and National Identity in the United Arab Emirates." *Looking Glass: New Perspectives on Children's Litera-ture*, 18(1). https://ojs.latrobe.edu.au/ojs/index.php/tlg/article/view/598.

Lê, Thị Huệ. 2009. "Tư Tưởng Phật Giáo Trong Truyện Tấm Cám" [Buddhist Conception in the Story of Tấm and Cám]. *Journal of Religious Research*, 4: 30 – 45.

Leimgruber, Walter. 2010. "Switzerland and the UNESCO Convention on Intangible Cultural Heritage*." Journal of Folklore Research*, 47 (1–2): 161–196.

Ly, Huong Ai. 2014. "Phát triển hứng thú đọc truyện cổ tích cho học sinh Tiểu học - Tài liệu text." *123doc*, July 18, 2014. text.123docz.net/document/1892716-phat-t rien-hung-thu-doc-truyen-co-tich-cho-hoc-sinh-tieu-hoc.htm.

MacKenzie, Matthew. 2013. "Enacting Selves, Enacting Worlds: On the Buddhist Theory of Karma." *Philosophy East and West*, 63(2): 194–212.

Minh, Long. 2014. *Truyện Cổ Tích Việt Nam Dành Cho Thiếu Nhi – Tấm Cám* [Vietnamese Folktales for Children—Tấm and Cám]. Literature Publishing House: Ho Chi Minh city.

Nguyễn, Đổng Chi. 1975. *Kho Tàng Truyện Cổ Tích Việt Nam* [Treasure of Vietnamese Folktales]. Episode 4. Ha Noi Social Science Publishing House: Ha Noi.

Nguyen, Hang. 2017. "Một Số Biện Pháp Đưa Truyện Cổ Tích Việt Nam Vào Trong Hoạt Động Giáo Dục Cho Trẻ 5-6 Tuổi." *123doc, November* 16, 2017. text.123do cz.net/document/4587825-mot-so-bien-phap-dua-truyen-co-tich-viet-nam-vao-tr ong-hoat-dong-giao-duc-cho-tre-56-tuoi.htm.

Nguyễn, Lang. 1979. *Việt Nam Phật Giáo Sử Luận* [History of Vietnamese Buddhism]. Ha Noi: Literature Publishing House.

Nguyen, Nhung Thi Tuyet. 2020. "Dạy học truyện cổ tích Tấm Cám trong chương trình Ngữ Văn 10 THPT theo định hướng phát triển năng lực học sinh." *THPT Nguyễn Thái Học*, April 29, 2020. thptnguyenthaihoc.vinhphuc.edu.vn/mon-ng u-van/day-hoc-truyen-co-tich-tam-cam-trong-chuong-trinh-ngu-van-10-thpt-theo -dinh-huo-c22044-264559.aspx.

Nguyễn, Văn Ngọc. 2003. *Truyện Cổ Tích Việt Nam* [Vietnamese Folktales]. Ha Noi: Literature Publishing House.

Thich, Nhat Hanh. 1998. *The Heart of the Buddha's Teachings*. New York: Broadway Books.

Thích, Thái Hòa. 2011. *Truyện Tấm Cám Trong Con Mắt Thiền* [The Story of Tấm and Cám Through the Meditative Eyes]. Ho Chi Minh city: Publishing House of Culture and Art.

Thích, Thiện Hoa. 2006. *Phật Học Phổ Thông* [Fundamental Buddhism Studies]. Ha Noi: Religious Publishing House.

Vu, Ha Thi. 2017. "Một số kinh nghiệm dạy học truyện cổ tích trong chương trình sgk Ngữ văn 6 cho học sinh trường thcs và thpt Nghi Sơn." *sangkienkinhnghiem.net*, May 15, 2017. sangkienkinhnghiem.net/skkn-mot-so-kinh-nghiem-day-hoc-truyen -co-tich-trong-chuong-trinh-sgk-ngu-van-6-cho-hoc-sinh-truong-thcs-va-thpt-nghi -7397/.

Vu, Oanh Thi Kim. 2020. "Vai trò của truyện cổ tích đối với việc giáo dục trẻ mầm non*." Trường Mầm Non Hoa Hồng*, November 19, 2020. mnhoahong. tpbacgiang.edu.vn/truyen/vai-tro-cua-truyen-co-tich-doi-voi-viec-giao-duc-tre-ma m-non.html.

Wilson, Jeff. 2016. "Saṃsāra and Rebirth". Oxford Bibliographies in Buddhism. Accessed March 20, 2021. www.oxfordbibliographies.com/view/document/obo -9780195393521/obo-9780195393521-0141.xml.

Chapter 9

Learning *Nunchi*

Folktales as Tools to Teach Emotional Competence in Literacy Learning in Korea

MinJeong Kim and Min-Young Kim

When the snow is falling outside on a winter's night, little children start to gather around a *Hwaro* (a traditional charcoal brazier) with chestnuts roasting to listen to tales from their grandma. When the children all settle in their spots, the grand opening of an old tale begins, "A long, long time ago in a small village far, far away in the woods . . ." Folktales have been passed down by word of mouth since time immemorial and this example provides a picturesque image of traditional storytelling in Korea. Even very young children in Korea today who do not know what a *Hwaro* is might come across this picture in a storybook or a reading app. These folktales, as instances of ritual practices in families, schools, and communities, are reflections of Korean customs, traditions, cultural, and educational values. Folktales have been used as socialization tools at home and in schools for educational purposes to teach these values (Canonici 1995; Mantra and Maba 2018; Minami and McCabe 1995; Moore 2011).

It is commonly believed that folktales are typically used in educational settings to teach moral lessons (cf. Rahim and Rahim 2012). While moral lessons (e.g., good deeds are rewarded and bad deeds are punished) are presented in most Korean folktales in a quite explicit and clear way, Korean children are taught in school to reflect largely on the emotional status of the main characters in the story rather than the moral per se. For example, the national Korean Language Arts textbook for Grade 3 includes a unit titled *Reading to Understand Characters' Emotions,* and it is one of the five major lesson units for achieving the Korean Language Arts standards which highlight emotional well-being and empathy development of the readers as part of language and literacy learning (Ministry of Education 2016).

We view the emphasis on emotion in teaching of narrative (folktale) as a culturally distinctive feature of the Korean National Language Arts curriculum. In contrast, the US English Language Arts standards (e.g., Common Core Standards suggested by the Massachusetts Department of Elementary and Secondary Education) mainly suggest that teachers teach cognitive strategies to examine structural aspects of narrative texts (e.g., teaching summarization and inference strategies to retell beginning, middle, and end in proper order). Contrary to that of the US English Language Arts curriculum, one of the most commonly asked comprehension questions of a folktale in the national Korean Language Arts textbook is as such: "summarize important events of the story based on how the main characters would 'feel' about what happened." This kind of question asks children not only to "summarize" the structural components of the story (e.g., 6 W's questions such as *who, what, when, where, how, and why*), but also helps them learn socially and morally acceptable behaviors and emotions that foster empathy toward people in trouble, which we view as a language socialization process (Ochs 1988). More importantly, children, through this process, learn a culturally specific way of evaluating a morally complicated situation by attending to the feelings and intentions of people involved rather than judging these people only based on dry facts of the event.

In this sense, we view folktales in the Korean national textbook as narrative discourse that needs to be understood in its own sociocultural and socioemotional context (Heath 1983; Michaels 1981). As textbooks provide milestones for acquisition of cultural values and societal norms practiced by the members of the society (Curdt-Christiansen 2017), textbooks are one of the important resources and a medium for cognitive, linguistic, cultural, and emotional socialization. Therefore, folktales in the Korean textbooks are tools to socialize children to use empathetic language, and to become morally conscious and empathetic through such language use.

In this chapter, we describe ways children in Korea are encouraged to be linguistically and emotionally competent by understanding how *nunchi*, a form of social sensitivity unique to Koreans, works for successful communication and problem solving in narrative texts. Possibly because of its entertaining nature as a trickster story, *The Hare's Liver* has been widely incorporated in children's books and textbooks in the forms of both drama (plays) and prose (short stories). Particularly in this textbook, the story has been dramatized in a way that foregrounds the intentions, feelings, and communicative actions of the characters to achieve the goal of the lesson unit: "to empathize with the characters' emotions." The particular goal is also evident in the ways that the prompts and the comprehension questions that follow the text are formulated in the textbook.

Our analysis focuses on two key aspects of the folktale *The Tale of Hare's Liver*. First, we analyze the content and structure of the play script (e.g., the main plot of each scene and stage directions), focusing on the emotional and symbolic aspects of the main characters' behaviors, specifically how they use *nunchi* to resolve the main problem associated with the Dragon King's illness (e.g., obtaining a hare's liver as a cure). Second, in addition to the analysis of the characters' behaviors related to *nunchi*, we analyze the prompts and questions for comprehension following the play script.

NUNCHI AND EMOTIONAL COMPETENCE

We chose to focus on *nunchi* as an essential component of emotional social-ization to develop emotional competence in Korean contexts for two reasons. First, we found it intriguing to see the term *nunchi* directly used in the stage directions and the dialogues of the characters as a communicative strategy in the textbook. In addition to the direct use of the term, behaviors that cause or are caused by *nunchi* are prevalent in the dialogues. Second, due to its ever-changing nature, *nunchi* is considered as a major determinant for successful communication with others (Kim 2003) and is particularly valued as a com-municative skill in collectivistic societies such as Korea, Japan, and China where there is more emphasis on the individual's self-control and ability to collaborate with others than on self-expression in problem solving.

The literal meaning of *nunchi* is "eye-measure" or "sense of eye" that captures what is hidden between the lines of the uttered words by observing and feeling the air of the scene without explicit verbal and nonverbal cues. *Nunchi* is a multilayered concept that can be practiced at multiple levels within different contexts. For example, building on the study of Heo et al. (2012), we classify *nunchi* in two different ways to conceptualize its functions in different contexts: (1) its existence in the individual's attitudes toward others (e.g., whether one has or lacks *nunchi*), and (2) the interlocutors' behaviors with *nunchi* (e.g., whether the individual looks at *nunchi* of others or gives *nunchi* to other individuals (See table 9.1 for types of *Nunchi*).

When one has *nunchi* he or she is able to easily sense others' intentions, desires, and feelings. As a result of this ability, one can support others better in many kinds of social situations (e.g., families, communities, workplaces, etc.). On the other hand, if one lacks *nunchi* it means he or she is likely to be viewed as socially inept. Another way to conceptualize *nunchi* is to use it as a verb describing whether the speaker is giving *nunchi* to others or looking at *nunchi* of others. When one looks at others' *nunchi* it has a negative con-notation that he or she feels a bit daunted trying to sense others' intentions and feelings. This type of *nunchi* often occurs in a hierarchical relationship. For example, mostly younger people in lower social positions look at *nunchi* of older people and others in higher social positions. If one gives *nunchi* to

Table 9.1　Types of *Nunchi*

	Forms of Nunchi	Context	Participants
Existence	Having nunchi (눈치가 있다)	One behaves properly, responding to others' feelings and intentions.	Anyone with shared social identities such as friends, families, colleagues, neighbors, etc.
	Lacking nunchi (눈치가 없다)	One is lacking the ability to sense what goes on among people and does not behave properly in the social context.	Anyone with shared social identities such as friends, families, colleagues, neighbors, etc.
Behavior	Looking at nunchi (눈치를 보다)	One feels and looks daunted, sensing others' negative intentions and feelings. This type is reserved for negative feelings.	Anyone in the context. But mostly younger people in lower social positions look at nunchi of older people and others in higher social positions.
	Taking care of nunchi (눈치를 살피다)	One tries to sense other people's needs, feelings, and intentions to make them feel comfortable in the context. This type is reserved for both positive and negative feelings.	Anyone with shared social identities such as friends, families, colleagues, neighbors, etc.
	Giving nunchi to others (눈치를 주다)	One implicitly warns others about a lack of nunchi.	Mostly older people and people in higher social positions give more nunchi to younger people and others in lower social positions.

Source: Adapted from Heo, Park and Kim (2012).

someone, he or she gives implicit and indirect warning (e.g., silently staring at the person who behaves inappropriately in the social context) to someone about lack of *nunchi*.

Fostering Social Sensitivity through the National Curriculum in South Korea

Due to its highly instructive nature with clear moral lessons and distinctive linguistic features, folktale literature has been traditionally used in schools as a tool to teach children the Korean language, morals, traditional values, and wisdom to make good judgments. *Jeonrae donghwa* (Korean traditional tales for children) is a genre to foster children's literacy development and moral education in Korea. *Jeonrae donghwa* is pervasive in Korea's national elementary curriculum for the subject of Korean Language Arts. Folktales are presented as mentor texts in textbooks for children to analyze their linguistic forms, narrative symbols (e.g., objects, gestures, characters, backgrounds, etc.), and structural characteristics (e.g., understanding components of play scripts).

The national curriculum in South Korea has held authoritative power in many facets of education: the ways that textbooks are developed, the ways that instructional contents are delivered in the classrooms, and the ways that teaching and learning are evaluated and assessed (Chung 2005; Kim 2015). Seven curricular reforms have occurred since the first national curriculum was released in 1955. The last reform, the seventh national curriculum, has been revised three times (2007, 2009, and 2015) since it was initially released in 1997. Throughout the reforms and the revisions, the nature and the goals of the Korean national curriculum have been adapted to meet educational and societal needs (So et al. 2012; So and Kang 2014). For example, responding to the demands of the changing workplace and economic landscape, the latest revision of the seventh Korean Language Arts curriculum in 2015 asserts that one of the goals of the subject of Korean Language Arts is to help students raise their critical thinking skills in the twenty-first century, which was largely missing in the first iteration of the seventh curriculum in 2007.

While the national curriculum was adjusted to meet educational needs, the foundational view of the characteristics and the goals of the Korean Language Arts (KLA) curriculum have stayed mostly the same. The national curriculum has prescribed that the subject of KLA performs the functions of (1) a tool for thinking and communication; (2) a tool for enculturation and transmission of national ideologies and core values; and (3) a tool for humanity education. Of interest is the characterization of the Korean language as a tool for enculturation and humanities education. In fact, the first national curriculum of the KLA (1955) asserts that the Korean language is inseparable from one's personality, thus the ongoing effort to use a correct and standardized language would help one's emotional and character development, which is the key value of the KLA education.

In addition to emotion and character development, the curriculum highlights its functions of building relationships with others and developing a sense of community, closely aligned with characteristics of the high-context society (Hall 1976). For example, in the latest version in 2015, the curriculum characterizes the six competencies as an outcome of the Korean language education. The competencies include "critical and creative thinking competence," "data and information literacy competence," "communicative competence," "community and interpersonal competence," "enculturation and cultural literacy competence," and "reflection and self-improvement competence."

Of relevance to this study is the *community and interpersonal competence*, defined in the curriculum (2015) as "the competence of respecting both the values the community upholds and the diversity the community embraces, and the competence of collaborating with others and resolving interpersonal conflicts." The emphasis on the relationships and the community accounts for, and manifests, the values widely held in the KLA curriculum, including fostering social sensitivity, developing emotional competence, and promoting empathy. These values of high-context cultures (Hall 1976) such as Korea, Japan, China, and more are explicitly taught as subject matter in school as part of the students' language socialization process (Ochs 1988). Learning cultural codes by reading culturally specific texts and vice versa in these high-context cultures is quite contrary to how reading is taught in American schools. American elementary textbooks based on the current common core standards, for example, place more emphasis on the students' ability to analyze and understand the factual relationships among the characters and events (Minami and McCabe 1995). In contrast, designated space exists in the KLA curriculum for study units closely and explicitly related to understanding emotions of others through reading.

Teaching *nunchi* by understanding others' emotions is explicit in the 2016 version of the KLA textbook for third grade used in this chapter. A set of two KLA textbooks for third grade was used for the two semesters of the school year, in which nine study units are included. The study units in the third grade first semester KLA textbooks are: (1) Reading Fun, (2) Spacing in Writing, (3) Summarizing a Text, (4) Listen to Write, and (5) Forms of Words. In the second semester textbook, the units include: (6) Emotions Reflected in Texts, (7) Feeling Inspired Through Reading, and (8) Speak Realistically. As in Study Units 6, 7, and 8, one of the major study units is about emotions of others in the text. While students are instructed to develop reading fluency (e.g., Reading Fun) and cognitive skills for comprehension (e.g., Summarizing a Text), they are also socialized to learn how to understand and use implicit and highly contextualized language to grasp others' intentions and emotions. This study unit is well aligned with the goals of the national KLA curriculum that highlights the inseparable relationships between language acquisition and socioemotional development of students.

Teaching *Nunchi* through the Tale of *The Hare's Liver*

The Tale of The Hare's Liver

The Hare's Liver is based on a story of a sea turtle that deceives a rabbit to obtain his liver to cure his *Yongwang* (Dragon King). When *Yongwang* gets seriously ill, his subjects find that rabbit livers will cure the king's illness. So the turtle, one of the king's royal subjects, is sent off to the land to find a rabbit. When the turtle finds a rabbit, he tricks him into going with him to meet the Dragon King in the East Sea. Upon their arrival, the rabbit soon realizes that his life is at risk. When the king's subjects try to kill the rabbit to take out his liver, he comes up with a trick. The rabbit tells the Dragon King that he will need to go back to the land to bring his liver back because he left it there. Having believed the rabbit, the king orders the turtle to take the rabbit back to the land. As soon as the rabbit gets off the turtle's back on the dry land, he teases the turtle, "Who could take his liver in and out of his body? You stupid turtle!" and hops away.

The Hare's Liver is classified as type KT 39 in the Korean type index. This old folktale from seventh-century Korea is one of the most beloved folktales. This tale has been commonly used in *Pansori* performances. Pansori is a traditional musical storytelling genre that is characterized by its "expressive singing, stylized speech, and a repertory of improvised texts and gestures" (UNESCO n.d.) involving a singer and a drummer. *Pansori* is rooted in the Joseon Dynasty period (1392–1910) of Korea and is inscribed on the UNESCO's list of Intangible Cultural Heritage in 2008 (UNESCO n.d.). *The Hare's Liver* is a popular tale that has been adapted in *Pansori Sugungga* (Song of the Sea Palace).

The Tale of Hare's Liver *in the Textbook*

In the third-grade KLA textbook, the tale of *The Hare's Liver* is presented as a play script in the unit of "Emotions Reflected in Texts." The goal of the unit is listed on the first page as "Inferring Main Characters' Feelings." Instruction for reading the script such as "Read the text thinking about expressions you can use to infer a character's feeling" is also given. The play script has two acts. The first act includes two scenes with a comprehension prompt that instructs students to "imagine" the five main characters' feelings. The second act contains six scenes with two prompts for comprehension, one of which is to summarize the main plot of the story and the other is to find lines that express feelings of the main characters.

Analysis of The Tale of Hare's Liver[1]

The first act includes two scenes that illustrate the search for a cure for the Dragon King's illness. On a surface level, the main function of these first two scenes seems to be to inform the audience of what the cure for the king's illness is and how his subjects get to find it out. It certainly is part of the original tale. But, what is interesting is how the story then unfolds by focusing on the emotional tensions and argument between two of the king's servants,

Table 9.2   Themes of the *Hare's Liver* Play Script

Act	Scene	Main Themes
I	1	The royal subjects of *Yongwang* worried about the king's illness.
	2	*Yongwang* ordered the turtle to bring the hare's liver.
II	3	The turtle looked for the rabbit on the land.
	4	The turtle tricked the rabbit into going with him to meet *Yongwang*.
	5	The rabbit tricked *Yongwang* to find a way out of the predicament. Turtle brought the rabbit back to the land.
	6	The rabbit hopped away into the woods, laughing at the turtle.

Commodore Crab and General Octopus, who had very different perspectives and personalities during the process of looking for the cure for their king.

Act I Scene 1

Yongwang (Dragon King) is lying in bed and his anxious servants are talking to each other.

Commodore Shark: (stroking his beard) "Well, this is a big challenge. *Yongwang* is not getting well. I'm seriously concerned that this only gets worse."

Commodore Crab: (giving a sideways glance at General Octopus who was frantically going back and forth) "Look, General Octopus, please stop moving. You make me feel restless."

General Octopus: "What? You think I want to do this? My anxiety eats me alive from the inside! Why don't you stop bugging me and go figure out how to cure *Yongwang*'s illness?"

Commodore Crab: "Are you saying I have been useless?"

Commodore Shark comes over to Octopus and Crab, bawling them out for quarreling.

Commodore Shark: "Look. How dare you two behave disrespectfully in this palace? Leave off, right now."

All servants startled and lowered down their upper bodies.[2] *Yongwang* got up, opening his eyes.

Yongwang: "Why is everyone making a noise?"

Commodore Cutlass: "Yes, Your Majesty, nothing to worry about. We were just talking, worrying about your illness."

Yongwang: (sighing) "How come we don't have a doctor who can take care of my illness? Ah, I don't think I can live any longer."

Servants: (in a quavering, united voice) "My apologies, your highness."

Commodore Blowfish comes in, lowering his head.

Commodore Blowfish: "Your Majesty, Dr. Sea Bream from the faraway sea has been waiting to see you since early morning. He came a long way to cure your illness."

Commodore Crab: (bluntly) "Did you just say Dr. Sea Bream? I've never heard of such a name before? Just tell him not to bother and leave."

General Octopus: (quickly waving arms out) "No. He came all the way to us from the faraway sea. He should know a cure. Bring him in now."

Commodore Crab: "How come you always object to my ideas? Do you have any bad feelings about me (showing anger by throwing up his pinchers)?"

General Octopus: "I am just telling the truth! You are just picking on me."

Commodore Shark: "Here you go again. Stop, please. Why don't we meet Dr. Sea Bream now?"

Scene 2

Dr. Sea Bream with his glasses on is checking Yongwang's pulse.

Yongwang: "Did you figure out my illness?"

Dr. Sea Bream is silently tilting his head.

Commodore Shark: "Why don't you tell him right away?"

Dr. Sea Bream: "There is no cure in the sea because *Yongwang*'s illness is very rare."

Yongwang: "What should I do about this? I still have a lot to do for my people in the sea."

Servants: "Our sadness is immeasurable, Your Majesty."

Dr. Sea Bream: (raising his glasses) "Your Majesty, do not worry too much. There is no cure in the sea. But there is a cure on land."

Yongwang: (opening his eyes widely) "What did you just say? Is there a cure for my illness? What is it?"

Dr. Sea Bream: "Yes, it is a liver of an animal called a hare."

Yongwang: "A hare's liver? Then go to the land to catch a hare."

Dr. Sea Bream: "But it is hard even for people on the land to catch one because hares are very fast and clever."

Yongwang: (looking at his subjects) "Who will get a hare?"

Servants remain silent, looking at others' *nunchi.*

Yongwang: "Why are you not answering? Commodore Shark, can you go?"

Commodore Shark: "Your Majesty, my deepest apologies. But I cannot survive outside the water."

Yongwang: "Then, no one can go?"

General Octopus: (making sly facial expression) "Your Majesty. I believe Commodore Crab can go. I heard that he went on a picnic to the land before."

Yongwang: (looking at Commodore Crab with a happy face) "Oh, is that right? Commodore Crab, can you go?"

Commodore Crab: (startled) "Ah, no Your Majesty. Although my grandfather often visited the land, I have never set foot on the land."

General Octopus: "Commodore Crab, just be honest and admit that you are scared instead of using your grandfather as an excuse. Aren't you ashamed?"

Commodore Shark: "Ah, stop there. We have no time to waste. (After thinking for a bit) Your Majesty, why don't we send a turtle?"

Commodore Blowfish: "That's a good idea. I heard that turtles can freely travel between land and sea."

Commodore Shark: (in a loud voice) "Bring the turtle in."

A moment later, the turtle came in and lowered his head in front of *Yongwang.*

Yongwang: (looking at the turtle) "Can you bring a hare from the land?"

Turtle: "I will risk my life to get a hare, Your Majesty."

Yongwang: "You are truly praiseworthy. You are my loyal servant."

Most of the two scenes are used to describe how Commodore Crab and General Octopus argue over each other's different perspectives and behaviors. In addition, the scene displays how they behave to resolve the problem (their argument). Throughout the script there are stage directions in almost every line, indicating how the acting characters feel and behave. For Act I there are five highlighted lines in the textbook for which students are expected to infer how the characters feel. The five lines selected for comprehension activities are the following:

1. Commodore Shark: (*stroking his beard*) "Well, this is a big challenge. *Yongwang* is not getting well. I'm seriously concerned that this only gets worse."
2. Commodore Crab: (bluntly) "Did you just say Dr. Sea Bream? I've never heard of such a name before? Just tell him not to bother and leave."
3. Yongwang: (opening his eyes widely)
4. Servants remain silent, looking at others' *nunchi.*
5. General Octopus: (making sly facial expression) "Your Majesty. I believe Commodore Crab can go. I heard that he went on a picnic to the land before."

All five prompts for comprehension check above certainly require the readers to have in-depth knowledge about multilayered meanings of paralinguistic cues across time and space. In line 1, Commodore Shark is stroking his beard worrying about the king's illness. One might easily say that Shark is simply worried about the king. It is true. But, the stage direction "stroking his beard" adds more layers to his behavior. The behavior of stroking one's beard is a gesture of deep thinking by a thoughtful high-ranking officer in a monarchy. This nonverbal cue implies that Shark is not only worried about the king but is also actively searching for a solution. Indeed, this calm and reserved behavior is recognized as trustworthy, as Shark is the one the Dragon King turns to when he has concerns throughout the script. The same stage direction "stroking his beard" is given to *Yongwang* in Scene 5:

Yongwang: (stroking his long beard) "I sent my turtle to the land to get you here because I heard that your liver would cure my chronic illness." The "stroking his long beard" stage direction indicates, again, thoughtfulness (although in this case for a selfish cause) and a high social position. This kind of nonverbal cue/action is contrary to the frantic and argumentative behaviors of General Octopus and Commodore Crab.

In line 2, Commodore Crab responds impolitely and bluntly to the suggestion of Blowfish about Dr. Sea Bream, indicating that only famous doctors can work for the king. This behavior is a reflection of his loyalty to the king: He, as a loyal servant, only wants the best for his king. In fact, the argument between Octopus and Crab is a result of their competition over their loyalty to the king. Each of them thinks he is a better servant and that therefore his idea is better. This competitive behavior and argument are a reflection of 군신유의 (*Kunsinyueui*), one of the five Confucian codes of conduct, meaning loyalty between a king and his subjects (Kim 2003).

Kunsinyueui is the most important code of conduct to the king's subjects and this explains their behaviors in line 4 looking at each other's *nunchi* and remaining silent instead of actively volunteering for going out of the sea to get the hare's liver for the king. They, as the Dragon King's servants, feel the pressure to be loyal and want to live up to that expectation; however, they are scared to risk their lives, which causes them to look at each other's *nunchi*. They are looking at each other's *nunchi* because they neither want to volunteer (as they will die out of water) nor do they want to give up the opportunity to save the king as fiercely loyal servants. So, they are looking at each other's *nunchi* to decide how they will behave based on what other servants feel, say, and do. General Octopus takes advantage of this moment to challenge Commodore crab's loyalty, suggesting he could go. The stage direction in line 5, "making sly facial expression" indicates his negative intention that resulted from his previous argument with Crab.

Act II consists of four scenes (Scene 3, 4, 5, and 6). Act II is mostly about the processes of the turtle going to the land to get the hare and how the hare tricks the king and escapes the scene. In Act II, three prompts are given to reflect on how three main characters would feel in the scenes.

1. Turtle: (happy to find the hare under the tree) 'Great, this guy must be the hare'
2. Hare: Blank (students are expected to find lines that are reflective of the Hare's feelings).
3. Yongwang: (suddenly in a tender voice) "Mr. Hare! Are you sure you will get you liver?"

Act II Scene 3

The turtle is looking at the animals playing in the forest in bloom.

Turtle: (taking a glance at the picture of a hare in his hand) "Um, this will take forever. I'd better ask the animal with horns over there (showing the picture of a hare). Hey there, you with horns! Have you seen this animal?"

Cow: (slowly blinking) "I'm not sure. He looks familiar. . . . Wait, he must be Mr. Hare who lives over the pine tree hill."

Turtle: (talking to himself) "Hmm, Mr. Hare must be the one I am looking for."

Cow: "By the way, who are you? You look strange" (looking over the body of the turtle).

Turtle: (startled) "Ah, I am a friend of Mr. Hare and I am on my way back home from a long distance trip."

The turtle stretched his neck to say thank you.

Scene 4

The turtle is approaching the hare who is dozing off under the pine tree.

Turtle: (happy to find the hare under the tree) 'Great, this guy must be the hare'

Turtle: (waking up the hare). "Hey look, Mr. Hare! How are you?"

Hare: (startled) "Who are you?"

Turtle: (greeting politely) "I am Turtle from the ocean palace. I am thrilled to meet you, the famous Mr. Hare."

Hare: (taking a step closer to the turtle) "How come my name has become known to the ocean palace?"

Turtle: (hiding excitement) "Of course. Everybody is eager to meet you, the smart and handsome Mr. Hare (raising his shoulders)."

Hare: "Everyone knows me here but I'm surprised to hear that I am also famous in the ocean palace."

Turtle: "Mr. Hare, how do you find living here?"

Hare: "Well, my life is not luxurious here, but I live a comfortable life. I love this place full of azalea, forsythia, dancing butterflies in spring and cicada sounds under the pine trees in summer. I really can't ask for more!"

Turtle: (shaking his head and raising his voice) "No, Mr. Hare! You are a good liar. Think about this. You are too busy to enjoy the flowers in spring hiding from the scary hawk trying to catch you after spending winter in the dark cave. And the farmers will shoo you away if you try to drink from the stream, which makes your heart pound. Aren't you just too busy running away from everything? I wonder if there's even one day when you don't need to worry about these things?"

Hare: (silent for a while) "How do you know so much about my life? Really, I feel anxious all the time just to survive. That's how my eyes got red from the tiredness from looking at this *nunchi* and that *nunchi*."

Turtle: "I just heard from the grapevine that everybody is trying to leave because it's getting more tough to live in the forest. May I ask why you are not leaving?"

Hare: (making worried facial expression) "I do not have too many friends and I am not sure where to go."

Turtle: (as if he caught a good chance) "Ah, Mr. Hare, don't you worry. Come with me to the sea palace. You have beautiful snowy white fur and your eyes are like rubies. Dragon King will adore you."

Scene 5

The turtle is standing in front of *Yongwang* with the hare.

Yongwang: (stroking his long beard) "I sent my turtle to the land to get you here as I heard that your liver would cure my chronic illness."

Hare: (startled) "What? You want to eat my liver?"

Turtle: (with an apologetic facial expression) "Mr. Hare, I'm sorry. But you should feel honored as a little animal to give your life to *Yongwang*. Don't be too distressed."

Yongwang: (with a loud voice toward the servants) "Tie up the hare."

Hare: (hiding fear with a calm voice) "Wait, as a humble little animal I will be honored to die for you. But I have something very important to tell you."

Yongwang: (waving his hand to his servants who were coming to the hare) "Really? Let me hear what you have to say. Go on."

Hare: (coming closer to Yongwang) "I drink morning dew for breakfast and ginseng for dinner unlike other animals. That's why my liver is a cure all. So, there are so many animals asking for my liver that I always hide my liver in narrow gaps in the rock when I have to go out."

Yongwang: (surprised) "Then, does that mean you don't have your liver with you now?"

Hare: "Yes, because Sir Turtle did not tell me about your illness, I just left it in the rock and followed him."

Turtle: (in an angry voice) "You are such a sly lad. How can you possibly take your liver in and out? I cannot forgive you as you are lying to *Yong-wang*. Tie up the hare."

Hare: (trying to laugh it off) "Your Majesty, please consider it carefully. Your illness will never be cured if there's no liver when you open up my belly."

Yongwang: (hesitantly) "What do you all think about this?"

The subjects whisper briefly to each other and become silent.

Commodore Shark: (coming forward) "Your Majesty, you'd better believe the hare."

General Octopus: "The hare sounds quite suspicious. But you'd better let him go with the turtle to bring his liver here."

Yongwang: (suddenly in a tender voice) "Mr. Hare! Are you sure you will get your liver?"

Hare: (hiding the joy and in a serious voice) "Your Majesty, you should not worry. My liver is useless to me. Why should I save it for nothing? I will go get my liver and I will forever serve you."

Yongwang: (moved) "Oh, you are praiseworthy! I will raise you to the highest rank."

Scene 6

As soon as they arrived on the land, the hare got off the turtle's back and started to jump and sing happily.

Turtle: (giving the hare a strange look) "Hey Mr. Hare! We have a long way to go and *Yongwang*'s illness is severe. Let's hurry up to go back to the sea palace."

Hare: (laughing out loud) "You stupid turtle, how can I take my liver in and out of my body when it's always inside my body? I could have died because you tricked me and I wanted to call all my friends to take revenge on you, Turtle. But you worked hard to give me a piggyback ride. So I will let you go. Go back to the palace quickly and tell *Yongwang* not to waste his time anymore, but instead just wait till the time comes to die."

The turtle stares blankly at the hare as he hops off to the forest laughing. Curtains come down with the sounds of sea waves and birds chirping from the forest.

In Scene 3 and Scene 4, the turtle is excited to find the hare dozing off under the tree. But, the turtle, throughout the scene, tries to hide his excitement and guilt, looking at the hare's *nunchi* to deceive him. The turtle's intention is well reflected in the stage directions. For example, he startles whenever he is asked questions by the cow and the hare. He is aware of his unethical behavior of deceiving the hare and his conscience causes him to look at the hare's *nunchi*. In its simplest meaning, looking at *nunchi* is to try to grasp another person's feelings, desires, and intentions. More recently, however, the notion of *nunchi* has been extended to include one's conscious efforts to figure out one's positionality in the situation and behavioral decisions made as a result of such realization and looking at *nunchi*. The turtle behaves more carefully and politely, looking at the hare's *nunchi* not just to deceive the hare but to justify feelings of guilt despite his higher social position (e.g., The turtle later tells the hare to take it as an honor to die for the king as a "little" animal). His behaviors stem from his conscious decision as a result of looking at *nunchi*.

This becomes more obvious in Scene 5. The turtle apologizes with "an apologetic facial expression" when the hare finds out the king's agenda to kill him. Even though the turtle no longer has a reason to treat the hare nicely he continues to be nice only until the hare ruins the turtle's *che'myeon*. *Che'myeon* is "a codified set of social norms in Korea that dictates one's place within society, as well as how one is perceived by others" (Armstrong 2016, 21). Keeping *che'myeon* is one of the important goals for looking at or giving *nunchi* in Korea. In Scene 5, the hare tries to escape the scene, blaming the turtle for not informing him of the king's illness, which causes the turtle to stop looking at the hare's *nunchi* and to try to punish the hare. *Che'myeon* is similar to "keeping face." There is, however, a difference in nature between *che'myeon* and keeping face. Keeping face is to maintain respect from and dignity in front of other people one is interacting with. It is closer to keeping pride of self. *Che'myeon* involves keeping both one's and other's pride. In a Confucian society, it is critical for people in high social position to keep their *che'myeon*.

In Scene 5, the turtle's *che'myeon* is ruined by the hare in front of the king; he seems to be a less loyal servant. But the turtle's order is ignored when the Dragon King changes his condescending attitude toward the hare. Dragon King, suddenly in a soft voice, asks the hare if he will be able to get his liver. This is prompt 3 in the textbook for Act II, asking students to infer how the king feels at this moment. The stage direction "suddenly in a soft voice" indicates that now the king is looking at hare's *nunchi*, asking a favor.

In Scene 5, the hare constantly has to look at other animals' *nunchi* based on his understanding of the situation he is involved in in order to escape the scene, hiding both his emotions and scheming to trick the king. In Scene 6, the hare finally escapes the chaos and changes his position, mocking the turtle for his stupidity. The hare, however, keeps the turtle's *che'myeon* at the end by letting him go instead of taking his revenge.

CONCLUSION

Children's socioemotional development and literacy learning are inseparable processes in Korean contexts as inscribed in its national curriculum and the emotional nature of teaching narrative texts. The concept of *nunchi* is ubiquitous in narrative texts for children in Korea. *Nunchi* in the play script of *The Tale of Hare's Liver* functions as a means for various purposes: a motif to cause or resolve conflicts among characters, a tool to regulate emotions key to successful communication, and, most importantly, an emotional system that socializes readers to understand and use verbal and nonverbal linguistic codes relevant to their sociocultural contexts.

Contrary to the unilateral perspective on *nunchi*—that it is mainly for understanding others' feelings—intersubjectivity is key to understanding and practicing *nunchi* in context. In other words, *nunchi* is multidimensional and interactive. *Nunchi* is used to understand one's own positionality in the social relationship, as well as that of others. It also includes behavioral expectations for socially acceptable behaviors and responses in the immediate context. In other words, children in Korea, through literature, are exposed to the notion of *nunchi* as an action-oriented, not other-centered, concept. Finally, *nunchi* involves attention to social hierarchy in a way that is most distinctive.

NOTES

1. Minjeong Kim translated the transcript from the 2016 version of Grade 3 Korean Language Arts textbook.
2. In a gesture of deference that is not as deferential as a bow.

REFERENCES

Armstrong, Michael J. "Role-playing Game Based Learning, EFL Curriculum" (Culminating Projects in English. St. Cloud University, 2016), 68.

Canonici, Noverino N. 1995. "Folktale Performance as an Educational Experience." *Southern African Journal for Folklore Studies, 6*(1), 13–23.

Chung, Hye S. 2005. "Analyzing Critically the 7th Curriculum for the Department of the Korean Language and Searching the Alternatives to It: Centering on its Contents." *Journal of Korean Language Education, 23*: 53–89.

Curdt-Christiansen, Xiaolan. 2017. "Language Socialization Through Textbooks." In *Language Socialization,* edited by Patricia A. Duff, Stephen May, 195–210. Springer.

교육부[Department of Education] (2016). 국어 3-2 나 [*Korean Language Arts 3-2 B*]. Miraen.

Hall, Edward T. 1976. *Beyond Culture*. New York: Anchor.

Heath, Shirley B. 1983. *Ways with Words: Language, Life, and Work in Communities and Classrooms*. Cambridge: Cambridge University Press.

Heo, Jaehong, Park, Wonju, & Kim, Seungju. 2012. "Conceptualization of *Nunchi*." *Research on Humanities, 33*: 557–581. [Published in Korean]

Kim, Changwon. 2015. "Agendas for Korean Curriculum Revision: Domain and Contents System." *Journal of Korean Language Education, 51*(1): 6–35.

Kim, Suk-hyon. 2003. " Korean Cultural Codes and Communication." *International Area Review, 6*(1): 93–113.

Mantra, Ida B. N., & Maba, Wayan. 2018. "Enhancing the EFl Learners' Speaking Skill Through Folktales Based Instruction." *SHS Web of Conferences, 42*(00017): 1–6.

Michaels, Sarah. 1981. ""Sharing Time": Children's Narrative Styles and Differential Access to Literacy." *Language in Society, 10*: 423–442.

Minami, Masahiko, and McCabe, Allyssa. 1995. "Rice Balls and Bear Hunts: Japanese and North American Family Narrative Patterns." *Journal of Child Language, 22*(2): 423–445.

Moore, Leslie C. 2011. "Language Socialization and Repetition." In *The Handbook of Language Socialization*, edited by Elinor Ochs and Bambi Schieffelin. Massachusetts: Wiley-Blackwell, 209–226.

Ochs, Elinor. 1988. *Culture and Language Development: Language Acquisition and Language Socialization in a Samoan Village*. Cambridge: Cambridge University Press.

Rahim, Husni, & Rahim, Maila D. H. 2012. "The Use of Stories as Moral Education for Young Children." *International Journal of Social Science and Humanity, 2*(6): 454–458.

So, Kyunghee, Kim, Jungyun, & Lee, Sunyoung. 2012. "The Formation of the South Korean Identity Through National Curriculum in the South Korean Historical Context: Conflicts and Challenges." *International Journal of Educational Development, 32*(6): 797–804.

So, Kyunghee, & Kang, Jiyoung. 2014. "Curriculum Reform in Korea: Issues and Challenges for Twenty-First Century Learning." *The Asia-Pacific Education Researcher, 23*: 795–803.

Index

Aarne, Antti, 22
Aarne-Thompson-Uther (ATU) Index, 6–8, 22, 23, 68, 69, 71, 75–78, 83, 87, 88, 90, 91, 95, 111
abstract, 48
action, complicating, 48
aesthetic values, 4, 53
aggression, 8, 83–86, 91, 92, 95
Akai tori ("Red Bird"), 127, 130, 131
Allen, Johnie J., 86, 91
American(s), 37; educational system, 49, 50; folktales, 10, 108; mothers, 59
Anderson, Craig A., 86, 91
anger, 94
Angkor Empire (802–1431), 101
Angkor Wat, 101
animals' behaviors, 73
animation, 38
animism, 73
anti-AAPI movement, 40n1
anti-Chinese movement, 30
Arabic tale-type, 22
Aridomi, Yumiko, 136
Aristotelian ethics, 77
Ashliman, D. L., 90, 91, 111
Asia, 29–30
Asian American, 20; communities, 27; folktales, 37

Asian American Folktales (Green), 37
Asian folktales, 4, 5, 19, 27, 29, 30, 32, 33, 37–39, 40n1, 47, 70, 74, 79
Asian societies, 27, 121
AT Index, 22
ATU. *See* Aarne-Thompson-Uther (ATU) Index
ATU 513 tale type, 75–78
Azuma, Hiroshi, 119, 123, 124

Bacchilega, Cristina, 38
Balázes, Béla, 31
ballads, 36, 52
Bartlett, Frederic Charles, 67
Bascom, William R., 20, 90
Bavarian folktales, 110
bayin (eight-sounds), 78
beliefs, 26–28, 32, 118, 120, 124; religious, 34
Ben-Amos, Dan, 21
Bengtsson, Niklas 88
Bernstein, Basil, 123
Betel Nut and Areca, 143
Bettelheim, Bruno, 8, 88, 92, 93, 95
The Blind and The Cripple, 107
Bloom, Alfred, 145
The Book of Songs (Shi Jing), 36
Bottigheimer, Ruth B., 1
Boudinot, David, 94

175

bowdlerizing, 110
Brentano, Clemens W., 33
Brothers Grimm, 4, 33, 68, 69, 76, 85, 87, 90, 110
Buddhism, 11, 12, 20, 141–42, 144, 145, 150, 154, 155
Buddhist Institute, of Cambodia, 99, 101, 102
Buddhist values, 11, 141, 143–44
Bunly, Than, 103
Burmese folktales, 87, 91, 93, 94

Cambodia(n), 67; Americans, 2; community, 8, 9, 99, 102; folk dances, 102; history, 101–11; literature, 101
Cambodian folktales, 10, 68–70, 78, 101, 104; scatology in, 8, 104–11
The Cambodian Mutual Assistance Association, 3
Canepa, Nancy, 38
Cao, Thao H., 141
cause-and-effect law, 142, 144, 145, 151, 152
cautionary tales, 86–88, 93, 94
CCTV. *See* China Central Television (CCTV)
censorship, 9, 90, 100, 104, 110–11
Chang, Chien-ju, 5
Chang, Lan Samantha, 60
Chaov Archses (*The Horse Shit Man*), 107–8
The Chek Chhvea Banana Tree and the Baymath Tree, 105
che'myeon, 171
cheng-yu (idiom), 6, 47, 51–53, 60, 62, 63
Chīchan-no-kageokuri (*Chii's moving her shade to vast sky*), 135
children: abuse, 85; aggression and violence in, 8, 83–86, 95; behavioral regulations, 59; Chinese, 5, 47, 49, 50; communication skills, 136; emotional and cognitive development, 94–95; Korean, 157,

158, 172; Laotian, 90; literature, 124–25, 127; logical thinking skills, 136; Mandarin-speaking, 63; moral development, 92–93; narration structure in Chinese *versus* English, 47–52; self-esteem, 59; social development, 93–94; socioemotional development, 158, 162, 172. *See also* Japanese children
China, 6, 13, 28, 29, 31, 33–36, 53, 61, 67, 76, 78, 121, 159, 162
China Central Television (CCTV), 62
China Federation of Literary and Art Circles, 36
Chinese: Americans, 31, 33; classrooms, 121; folktales, 5, 6, 19, 27, 29–32, 37, 39, 47, 53, 74–78; history, 77–79; language, 53, 60; mothers, 6; parents, 59, 63; societies, 60; tale-type, 22; textbooks, 61; written records, 34–35
The Chinese Boy and Girl (Headland), 29
Chinese Exclusion Act (1882–1965), 30
The Chinese Fairy Book (Wilhelm), 29
Chinese Fairy Stories (Pitman), 29
Chinese Fairy Tales (Giles), 29
Chinese Fairy Tales and Folk Tales (Eberhard), 30
Chinese Fairy Tales: Forty Stories Told by Almond-Eyed Folk (Fielde), 29
Chinese Idiom Conference, 62
Chinese national spirit (*minzu jingshen*), 79
A Chinese Wonder Book (Pitman), 29
Choi, In-Hak, 22, 71, 74
chop-suey lore, 21
Cinderella, 23, 150
Civil Service Examination, 77, 79
Clancy, Patricia M., 119
classroom teaching, 38
The Cloak of Dreams: Chinese Fairy Tales (Balázes), 31
coda, 48
cognitive practices, 4

cognitive psychology, 37
Cole, Michael, 62
collectivism, 7, 67, 70–73, 76–79, 121, 137
collectivistic societies, 142, 159
colloquialisms, 52
colonial ideology, 30
colonialism, 30
comic books, 84
Commission of Mores and Customs, 102
Common Core Standards, 158
communication, 158, 159; cross-cultural, 5, 19, 21, 31, 32, 34, 37, 39, 40; cultural, 62; high-context, 119–20; interpersonal, 10, 117, 123, 131; Japanese, 10, 117, 123, 124; low-context, 120; oral, 22, 26
communicative competence, 161
community and interpersonal competence, 161, 162
Compendium of Chinese Folk Literature (*Zhongguo minjian wenxue daxi*), 36
The Compulsory Education Chinese Curriculum Standards, 60
Confucian beliefs, 122
Confucian ethics, 20, 28, 74, 77
Confucian society, 74
Confucian values, 78
Confucius, 36, 74, 77
conventional stage, 93
coolies, 30
copying, 70
cosmic views, 32
country (*guo jia*), 79
court music, 78
COVID-19, 40n1
Coyne, Sarah M., 84, 85
Crazy Rich Asians (2018), 38
creativity, 121, 122
critical and creative thinking competence, 161
critical thinking, 93, 161
cross-cultural studies, 37
cross-disciplinary approaches, 20, 39

cultural-based classifications, 27
cultural perspective, 5–7, 24
cultural values, 5, 12, 19, 21, 24, 27, 28, 32, 37, 39, 59, 63, 76, 158; family-centered, 20
culture-centered holistic approach, 29, 32, 34
culture(s): American, 7, 28, 37, 70, 86, 122; Asian, 4, 10, 37, 70, 77, 86, 108, 120, 137; Asian American, 37; Burmese, 91; Cambodian, 9, 100; Chinese, 5, 31, 33, 34, 37, 39, 40, 62, 77, 78, 121; Chinese American, 40; collectivist, 70, 73, 120; concept of, 137–38; Confucian, 71, 73, 76; definition, 118; diasporic, 21, 40; differences, 31, 36, 37, 67, 120, 124, 132; East Asian, 121; Eastern, 70, 76, 79; high-context *versus* low-context, 119–20, 122–23; history, 101; individualistic, 120; Japanese, 118, 119, 121, 132, 137; Korean, 71; and language, 122–24; non-individualistic, 120–21; norms, 118, 124; psychology, 118; Southeast Asian, 5, 11; Taiwanese, 62; universal, 62, 108; Vietnamese, 141, 143; Western, 4, 70, 76, 108, 111, 120, 122, 137
curriculum, 38, 60, 134; Vietnamese educational, 141, 143–44

Dafen Oil Painting Village, 70
data and information literacy competence, 161
death, 91
DeForest, Marsha, 62
desensitization therapy, 112
Deutsch, James, 90
Dickson, W. Patrick, 119
didactic coda, 59
dizi (bamboo flute), 78
Dorson, Richard, 30
double contrastive narrative structure, 74

The Downstairs Girl (Lee), 60
Dundes, Alan, 90, 108, 111
Durkheim, Emile, 13

East Asia, 19, 76, 77
East Asians, 37
The East Asian Story Finder (Elswit), 38
Eastern folktales, 8, 9, 110
Eberhard, Wolfram, 22, 30–31
Edo period (1603–1867), 126
education, 77; Japanese, 133; moral, 5;
    values, 10, 157; Vietnamese, 143
educational perspective, 10–13
Education Ministry of Japan, 134, 136
elaborated code *versus* restricted code,
    123
elementary school: classrooms, 121;
    textbooks, 132
Elias, Norbert, 111
Elswit, Sharon B., 38
emotional competence, 158–62
emotional socialization, 12, 13, 158
emotions, 157, 158, 172
empathy-oriented society, 137
The Emperor's New Clothes, 23
empiricism, 121
enculturation, 118, 119
enculturation and cultural literacy
    competence, 161
English: folktales, 83; grammar, 52;
    speaking children, 48
epics, 36
Erasmus, 111
ethics and values, 39, 142, 143
ethnic genre, 21
ethnic myths, 36
ethnographic research, 100
Eurocentric system, 83
Eurocentric theory, 27, 28
Eurocentric values, 22
Europe, 6, 21, 22, 31, 68, 69
European: ethnocentric superiority, 31;
    folktales, 10, 29, 108
Europeanization, 30
European Russia, 90

evaluation, 6, 48, 53, 59, 67
evil, 8, 11, 12, 31, 71, 74, 88–90, 92,
    93, 135, 142, 143, 145, 147, 148,
    150–55
explanatory tale, 92
The Extraordinary Companions (Zipes),
    7, 68, 74

faeces, 10, 108
fairy tales, 21, 23–24, 30, 31, 85,
    124–25
Fairy Tales Transformed? (Bacchilega),
    38
The Fairy Tale World (Teverson), 38
Family Literacy Nights, 3
fantasies, 31, 36
fear, 95
Feldman, Christina, 145
fengshui, 36
Fielde, Adele, 29
The Fisherman and his Wife, 23
Five Hundred Common Chinese Idioms
    (Jiao, Kubler, and Zhang), 53
Fivush, Robyn, 6, 53
folk genre, 19, 21–22, 35
folk literature, 36
folklore, 23, 25; coloniality of, 30;
    forms, 19; functions in culture, 20–
    21; studies, 25, 26
Folk-Lore, 30
"Folklore of Wishing Wells" (Dundes),
    108
folkloristic approaches, 39
folkloristic perspective, 5, 19
folkloristic studies, 19, 20, 39
folk narratives, 24, 39
folk operas, 36
folk psychology, 133
folksongs, 36
folktale(s), 47, 67, 85; context, 26–27;
    continuity of tradition in China, 34–
    36; definition, 1; in East and West,
    27–34; multi-identity in multicultural
    context, 36–40; studies, 29, 30, 32;
    as ways of communication, 19–26

Folktales of China (Eberhard), 30
folk tradition, 34
fortune-cookies lore, 21
The Four Bald Men, 106
*The Four Sons who did Not Serve their
 Father*, 108
French Protectorate, 101
Freud, Sigmund, 10, 108
friendship, 93, 94
Fu Manchu, 31, 32
Fung, Heidi, 6, 59

Gardner, Howard, 121
Gary, G., 22
gender roles, 94
genres, 26, 27
Gerbert, Elaine, 132
German folktales, 4, 33, 83
Germany, 33
gieo gió gặt bão (who sows the wind
 will reap the whirlwind), 152
Giles, Herbert A., 29
Gleanings from Chinese Folklore
 (Russell), 29
Glenn, Christine G., 50
gold, 10, 69, 87, 107–9, 146, 147, 154
Goldstein, Joseph, 144
Gongitsune (*Gon the Fox*, Niimi), 11,
 117, 127–36
Gottschall, Jonathan, 38
Grayson, James, 71, 72, 74
greed, 11, 106, 109, 142, 144, 146–48,
 151, 152, 154
The Greedy Dog and Meat, 109
Green, Thomas, 37
*The Greenwood Encyclopedia and Fairy
 Tales* (Haase), 38
Grimm, Wilhelm, 89
group, concept of, 76–77
group-priority, 77

Haase, Donald, 38
Haiku, 52
Hall, Edward T., 119–23
Hanasaka jī-san (*The old man who
 made flowers blossom*), 126

Haney, Jack, 90
Hanlon, Tina, 11, 141
Hansel and Gretel, 23, 93
Hans the Strong Man, 110–11
Hanyu cidian (*Chinese dictionary*), 52
Harries, Elizabeth, 111
Headland, Isaac T., 29
Hearn, Lafcadio, 29
Heath, Shirley B., 158
heaven, 32
he'erbutong, 78
Heo, Jaehong, 159
Herder, Johann G. von, 33
Hess, Robert D., 119
high-context cultures, 119–20, 162
*The History of Neak Ta Khleang
 Moeung*, 105
Hitotsu no hana (*One flower*), 135
Hofstede, Geert, 121
Hollywood films, 31
Hourani, Rida Blaik, 11, 141
*How Six Made Their Way in the World/
 Six Soldiers of Fortune* (Brothers
 Grimm), 7, 68–69

ICH. *See* Intangible Cultural Heritage
 (ICH)
identity, 19, 22, 25–27, 38; Chinese
 American, 21; cultural, 25, 28, 34,
 37, 39; diasporic, 36, 37; ethnic, 25,
 36, 37, 39; folkloric, 20, 21, 26, 37;
 group, 20, 25, 28, 34, 36, 39, 40;
 national, 20, 33–36; personal, 21, 25,
 37, 39, 40; racial, 36; reconstructing,
 32; regional, 20, 34–36
idiom storybooks, 62
idiom string-up puzzle, 61
Ikeda, Hiroko, 22
individualism, 7, 67, 70, 76, 77, 79, 121,
 122, 133, 137
individualistic construal of self, 120
Indo-European region, 22
infanticide, 90
Intangible Cultural Heritage, 163
Intangible Cultural Heritage (ICH),
 35–37

interdependent co-arising (*Lý Duyên Sinh*), 11, 142–45, 151, 155
interdependent construal of self, 120
inter-group diversity, 38
internationalization, 136–37
interpersonal relationships, 13, 123
Interpretation of Dreams (Freud), 10, 108
intra-group diversity, 38
ishin-denshin, 119, 131
Issun-bōshi (*Inch Boy/The Inch-High Samurai*), 125–26
Iwaya, Sazanami, 124–27, 134

Jack the Giant Killer, 111
Jameson, R. D., 30
Japan, 13, 33, 121, 122, 124, 132, 136, 159, 162
Japanese: art form, 126; classrooms, 121; education, 133, 136; folktales, 88, 117; language, 123; mothers, 119, 133; society, 117, 119, 120, 122, 123; tale-type, 22
Japanese children, 10; language and social development, 11, 117, 118; *omoiyari* (empathy training), 119
Jen, Gish, 7, 70, 112
Jeonrae donghwa (Korean traditional tales for children), 160–61
Jiao, Liwei, 53
Jin Ronghua, 22
jokes, 21, 37
Jorden, Rashaad, 132
Josen dynasty (1392–1897), 71
Joseon period (1392–1910), 163
The Joy Luck Club (Tan), 33
Judge Rabbit Cambodian stories, 102
Just-So Stories (Kipling), 106

Kambujsuriya (Light of Cambodia), 101
kamishibai ("paper drama"), 126
Karen Storybook, 87
karma (*Nghiệp*), 11, 12, 142–45, 147, 148, 150–52, 154, 155
Kashiwagi, Keiko, 119

Kawaisōna zō (*Faithful elephants*), 135
Khmer civilization, 101
Khmer folktales, 100
Khmer Rouge, 102
Kim, Minjeong, 6, 11, 12
Kim, Minyoung, 12
Kim, Seungju, 159
Kinder- und Haus-Märchen (*Children's and Household Tales*, Brothers Grimm), 33
kindness, 11, 107, 108, 135, 141, 142, 144, 147, 148
Kingston, Maxine Hong, 32
Kipling, Rudyard, 106
Kirkus Reviews, 132
Kitayama, Shinobu, 120, 122
The Kitchen God's Wife (Tan), 33
KLA. *See* Korean Language Arts (KLA)
Kobayashi, Fumihiko, 22
Koh, Jessie Bee Kim, 59
Kohlberg, Lawrence, 93
kokugo (Japanese language) reader, 131, 134–36
kokugo textbooks, 132–37
Kongjwi and Patjwi, 70–74, 78
Korea, 13, 67, 157, 159, 171
Korean: folktales, 70–74, 78, 157; language, 160, 161; national textbook, 158; society, 73; tale-type, 22
Korean Language Arts (KLA): curriculum, 12, 161–63; textbooks, 12, 157, 158, 162, 163
Korean type (KT) index, 163
kowtow/bowing, 32
KT. *See* Korean type (KT) index
Kubler, Cornelius C., 53
Kung Fu Panda (2008), 26, 28, 32
kunsinyueui, 167
Kyongsang Province, South Korea, 71

Labov, William, 47
Lang, Andrew, 111
language: and culture, 122–24; as sociocultural product, 118–24

Lao focus group, 88, 94, 108, 109
latrinalia, 111
Lauer, Gerhard, 67
The Lazy Novice, 110
Lê, Thị Huệ, 154
Lebra, Takie Sugiyama, 122, 133
Lee, Stacey, 60
Legend of Horse Shoe Crab, 143
Legend of Mattocks, 143
Legend of Vong Phu Stone, 143
legends, 21, 29, 36
Leimgruber, Walter, 11, 141
Li, Xiaoyan, 48
Liang, Chung-hui, 6, 59
Lin, Lu-Chun, 59
Lin, Pei-Jung, 123
linguistic relativity hypothesis, 123
Lin Lan ("Grimms of China"), 79
literacy development, 161
literacy learning, 157, 172
literary fiction, 60
literary movements, 127
literary narrative materials, 136–37
literature, 84, 85, 95; Western European, 88
Literature Publishing House, 152
The Little Match Girl, 127
The Little Mermaid, 127
The Little Peasant, 23
Little Snow-White, 23
Liu Bowen, 35–36
Liu Bowen Legends, 35
Liu Ji/Liu Bowen Ancestral Sacrifice, 35
Living Folklore: An Introduction to the Study of People and Their Traditions (Sims and Stephens), 38
A Long Long Time Ago in Southeast Asia, 145, 148
low-context cultures, 119–20
Lowell, Massachusetts, 2, 3, 68, 99, 102, 142, 148
Lowell High School, 2
Lowell Public Schools, 3
Lucy, John Arthur, 123

Luo, Ya-hui, 59
Ly, Huong Ai, 141, 143

MacKenzie, Matthew, 12, 144
Mahler, Gustav, 31
Mainland China, 48, 49, 60, 62, 63, 176
Malinowski, Bronislaw, 20
The Man called Kong Hean, 104
Manchu, 78
Mandarin-speaking children, 48, 49
Mandler, Jean M., 62
Markus, Hazel R., 120, 122
Massachusetts Department of Elementary and Secondary Education, 158
mass media, 31
matricide, 90
Matsumoto, David, 118
Maynard, Senko K., 122
McCabe, Allyssa, 1, 2, 5–8, 10, 48
Meiji (King), 124
Meiji Ishin, 124
Meiji period (1868–1912), 118, 124, 127, 134
melting-pot, 37
Melzi, Gigliana, 53
metaphors, 52, 53
Michaels, Sarah, 158
Middle Period (1431–1863), 101
Miller, Peggy J., 6, 59
Minami, Masahiko, 136
Ming Dynasty (1368–1644), 35
Minh, Long, 152
Ministry of Education, of People's Republic of China, 60, 61
misfortune, 119, 147, 148, 150
Miyanaga, Kuniko, 122
modernization, 111, 134
Momotarō (*Peach Boy*, Iwaya), 126–27, 134
monolithic collectivism, 123
Moore, Leslie C., 157
moral attitudes, 141, 144
moral dilemma, 88–92
morale, 134–36

moral education, 5, 61, 71, 74, 134–36, 161
morality, 93, 135, 141, 143
moral lessons, 53, 61, 71, 142, 143, 152, 154, 157
moral standards, 59, 63
moral suasion, 74
moral values, 74, 102, 141
Morfología del cuento, 24
Morfologia della fiaba, 24
Morphologie du conte, 24
Morphology of the Folktale (Propp), 23, 50
Mosel, Arlene, 33
Motif Index, 111
Motif-Index of Folk Literature (Thompson), 24
motifs, 23–25, 27, 32, 73, 78
movies, 70, 84, 95
Mulan, 77
Mu Lan (1998), 26, 28, 32
Mu Lan/Hua Mulan, 35
multiculturalism, 37
mutual trust, 94
myths, 20, 29
Myths and Legends from Korea: An Annotated Compendium of Ancient and Modern Materials (Grayson), 71

The Naïve Men, 106
naming tradition, 33
narration, definition, 1
narration origins in maternal input, 53, 59–60; idioms in educational context, 60–61; idioms in mass media, 62–63
narrative(s), 10, 33, 36, 47, 48, 50, 52, 117; discourse, 158; economy, 53; personal, 48, 49, 59; skills, 6, 53; structure, 74; techniques, 137; texts, 12, 158, 172
national curriculum, 12, 161, 172
National Intangible Cultural Heritage Bearers, 35
nationalistic spirit, 33

National Language Reader (*kokugo tokuhon*), 134
nativism, 121
Neak Ta Chumteav Mao, 104–5
Nelson, David A., 84, 85
New Khmer Architecture, 102
Nguyen, Hang, 141
Nguyen, Nhung Thi Tuyet, 141, 143
Nguyễn Đổng Chi, 153
Nguyễn Văn Ngọc, 153
Niimi, Nankichi, 117, 127, 130, 134
nunchi, 12–13, 157–72; and emotional competence, 13, 159–62; *The Tale of Hare's Liver*, 162–71

O'Brien, Anne Sibley, 3
Ochs, Elinor, 158, 162
ở hiền gặp lành (One doing good deeds will get good results), 153
Old Tales of Japan (Iwaya), 124, 126
Olympic Games, 77
omoiyari (empathy), 10–11, 117, 119, 124, 132–33, 136, 158, 162
One Crow Turns Out to be Ten Crows, 107
One Hundred Common Chinese Idioms and Set Phrases (Yin), 53
online games, 38
opportunity education, 59
oral exercises, 61
oral folktales, 79, 102–3
oral literature, 19, 124
oral narratives, 21, 22, 24, 34
oral traditions, 5, 34, 35, 47, 79, 130
Orientalist effect, 33
orientation, 48
Oring, Elliott, 20
ostracism, 84

Padilla-Walker, Laura M., 84, 85
Pansori, 163
Pansori Sugungga (Song of the Sea Palace), 163
parenting, 59
Park, Wonju, 159

passive individualism, 122
patriotism, 77
performance-centered approach, 22
Perry, Michelle, 121
Peterson, Carole, 6, 48, 53
physical aggression, 84
Piaget, Jean, 93
Pitman, Norman H., 29
political ideology, 34
Pol Pot, 102
poop, 9, 100, 103–7, 112; censorship, 110–11; in folktales from other countries, 108–10; symbolic factor of, 10, 108
Porquoi Tale, 92
post-World War II, 118, 133–35
Pourquoi tales, 106
The Prasat Way Nokor Temple, 104
pre-conventional stage, 93
Predestined Wife, 35
preschool children, 119
Price, Gary G., 119
Prince Norodom Sihanouk, 101
private schools, 61
problem-solving process, 121, 158
Propp, Vladimir, 23–24, 50, 62
prosocial behavior, 84
proverbs, 21, 36, 37, 142
psychological perspective, 7–10
public schools, 61

Qi, Lianxiu, 22
Qing Dynasty (1644–1911), 78
qin/guqin (seven-string zither), 78
Quinn, Molly, 93

rabbit, 6, 68, 70, 74, 78
race, 37
racism, 4, 37, 40n1
Radcliffe-Brown, A. R., 20
Rapunzel, 23
raven, 146–47
Reading to Understand Characters' Emotions, 157
Reese, Elaine, 6, 53

reflection and self-improvement competence, 161
reflexivity, 100–101
reincarnation, 86, 144, 150, 151
relational aggression, 84–85
Renmin Education Publishing House, 61
Republic of China, 78
resolution, 48, 49, 51, 62, 63
Reynard the Fox, 88
righteous characters, 142
The Robber Bridegroom (Brothers Grimm), 87
role-playing game (RPG), 38
Rollins, Pamela Rosenthal, 49
romantic nationalism, 33
Royal University of Fine Arts, 102
RPG. *See* role-playing game (RPG)
Russell, Nellie N., 29
Russian folktales, 50, 62
Russo-Japanese War (1904–1905), 134

Sagwa, the Chinese Siamese Cat (Tan), 33
salad-bowl, 37
samsara, 144, 148, 154
San Francisco Association of Chinese Teachers, 33
sanitizing, 104, 111
Sapir, Edward, 123
sati, 91
scatology, 8, 103, 104–8
Schönwerth, Franz Xaver von, 110–12
school education system, 38
Schwanenflugel, Paula J., 123
Scribner, Sylvia, 62
SEA. *See* Southeast Asian Americans (SEA)
Seki, Keigo, 22
self, 120, 122
self-priority, 77
self-reported aggression, 84, 85
El-Shamy, Hasan M., 22
Shi, Shi, 52
Shi Jing, 36
Sims, Martha C., 38

Sim Uirin, 71
Sino-Japanese War (1894–1895), 134
snails, 6, 7, 68, 70, 74, 78
Snow, Catherine, 2
So, Kyunghee, 161
social class, 123
social harmony, 59
socialization, 2, 4, 12, 47, 63, 118, 124, 157–59, 162
social justice, 7, 69, 135, 148, 150
social norms, 12, 124, 158
social relationships, 142–44, 172
social relativism, 120–22, 133, 137
social rules, 59, 63
social sensitivity, 160–62
solo performances, 78
Some Chinese Ghosts (Hearn), 29
The Song of the Earth (*Das Lied von der Erde, song*), 31
Sonu, Debbie, 93
Southeast Asia, 76, 77, 83, 141
Southeast Asian Americans (SEA), 2
Southeast Asian Folktale Project, 2–4, 99, 142, 145, 148
Southeast Asian folktales, 2, 9, 11–12, 79
Southeast Asian folktales, violence in, 8, 83–96; cautionary tales, 86–88; developmental psychology research, 83–85; impact on child development, 92–95; moral dilemma/moral forces, 88–92
Southeast Asians, 2
South Korean national curriculum, 160–62
Spanish-speaking children, 48
Square (online game), 38
The Starfruit Tree, 142, 145–48, 154
Stein, Nancy L., 50
Stephens, M., 38
stepmother, 23, 71–73, 89, 90, 148–54
stereotypes, 29–33, 40n1
A Sticky Mess, 110
Stigler, James W., 121
Stockdale, Laura A., 84, 85

story grammars, 50, 62
The Story of Cuckoo Bird, 86–87, 94
The Story of Tấm and Cám, 142, 145, 148–54
storytelling, 2, 4, 19, 22, 25–27, 35, 36, 38, 50, 52, 157
Storytelling Animals (Gottschall), 38
students: multiple identities, 39; school identities, 39
subgenres, 21, 24
Sugar Cane Grower and Passerby, 143
suicide, 86, 91
superhero comics and films, 7, 70
Suzuki, Miekichi, 127, 130–31
Swine, Pig, and Lion, 87–88, 94

taboo subjects, 9, 100, 101, 112
Taiwan, 49, 53, 59, 60, 63
Taiwanese: mothers, 59; narrative conversations, 59; parents, 59
The Tale of Hare's Liver, 12–13, 158–59, 162–72
tale-type folktales, 22–24, 27
tall tales, 21
Tan, Amy, 33
Tang China poetry, 31
Taniguchi, Marilyn, 132
Tan Zhenshan, 35
teaching, 12, 38, 59–61, 136, 141–43, 158, 161
Teaching Fairy Tale (Canepa), 38
television, 83, 85, 95
Teverson, Andrew, 38
text printing/reprinting, 34
texts singing, 36
texture, 26
The Juniper Tree (Brothers Grimm), 90
Theravada Buddhism, 101
Thich Nhat Hanh, 12, 145
Thích Thái Hoà, 145, 152, 154
Third Culture, 33, 40
Thnon Chey story, 106–7
Thompson, Stith, 22, 24, 90, 111
Three Friends, 143

Three Grand Collections, santao jicheng, 1984–2009, 36
The Three Hairs of the Devil, 23
Three Lectures on Chinese Folklore (Jameson), 30
Thumbling (Brothers Grimm), 76
tian (sky/upper world), 32
Tikki Tikki Tembo (Mosel), 33
Ting, Nai-Tung, 22, 76
Total War: Three Kingdoms (online game), 38
traditional Korea, 71, 73, 74, 78
traditional literary techniques, 137
traditional medicine, 32
traditional storytellers, 35
The Traditions of the Dog, 106
Tran, Tham, 11
translations, 28–32, 102
The Travels of Marco Polo (Polo), 29
trick story, 106–8
Ts'u-hai, 52
Ts'u-yuan, 52
A Type Index of Chinese Folktales (Ting), 76
A Type Index of Korean Folk Tales (Choi In-hak), 71, 74

"Underground People Disturbed by Farm or Household Waste," 111
UNESCO, 35, 163
United States, 2, 4, 21, 28, 30, 31, 33, 36, 37, 40n1, 62, 121, 122, 124, 132
University of Massachusetts, 3
Upajjhatthana Sutta (Subjects for Contemplation), 152
US Census Bureau, 2
US English Language Arts curriculum, 12, 158

verbal arts, 22
verbosity, 119
victimhood, 94
video games, 83–85, 95
Vietnam, 142
Vietnamese education, 143

Vietnamese Focus Group, 91
Vietnamese folktales, 141–55; educational values in curriculum, 143–44; karma and interdependent co-arising, 144–45; *The Starfruit Tree*, 145–48; *The Story of Tấm and Cám*, 148–54
virtuous life, 155
Vu, Ha Thi, 141
Vu, Oanh Thi Kim, 141, 143

Wang, Qi, 53, 59
Wang, Yan, 48
Weird Brothers, 74–78
Western Asia, 6, 68
Western audiences, 30
Western folktales, 8, 9, 12, 101, 104, 110, 111
What You Hate Becomes Your Fate, 104, 112
wholesome, 12, 143–45, 148, 151, 152, 155
Whorf, Benjamin Lee, 123
Why the Rabbit Doesn't Drink from the Pond, 6, 68
Wiley, Angela R., 6, 59
Wilhelm, Richar, 29
Wilinsky, Charlotte, 6, 8
Wilson, Jeff, 144
Wilson, William, 25
The Women Warrior (Kingston), 32
World War II, 135
writings, 52
written exercises, 61
written tradition, 34, 35
Wu, Chu-hsia, 47, 52

Xiandai hanyu (*Modern Chinese*), 52
Xiandai hanyu cidian (*Modern Chinese dictionary*), 52
Xiandai hanyu zhishi (*Modern Chinese knowledge*), 52
xiao (filiality/filial piety), 28, 59, 72, 77, 78
Xuanyuan (online game), 38

Ye, Jiaqui, 48
The Year of Fish (2007), 38
Yellow Peril, 31
Ye Xian, 30, 35, 38
Yong, Yin Bin, 53
Yuelao Peihun (Yuelao arranging
    marriage), 35
yuelao tale, 35

Zhang, Fangfang, 48
Zhang, Juwen, 74, 79
Zhang, Weiguo, 53
Zhang, Xin, 52, 53
Zhang, Yehong, 67
zhong, 77
Zhu Yuanzhang (King), 36
Zipes, Jack, 4, 5, 7, 33, 68

About the Editors and Contributors

ABOUT THE EDITORS

Allyssa McCabe received her doctorate from the University of Virginia and is Professor Emerita of Psychology at University of Massachusetts Lowell. She was born, raised, and lives in the United States. She founded and coedits the journal *Narrative Inquiry* and has studied how narrative develops with age, the way parents can encourage narration, and cultural differences in narration, as well as interrelationships between the development of narrative, vocabulary, and phonological awareness (the Comprehensive Language Approach to acquisition of literacy). One of her previous books is *Chameleon Readers: Teaching Children to Appreciate All Kind of Good Stories*. Other books on cultural differences in narration include *Chinese Language Narration* and *Spanish-Language Narration and Literacy*.

MinJeong Kim is associate professor in the School of Education at the University of Massachusetts, Lowell. As a former early childhood educator for deaf children in Korea, her research focuses on ethnographic inquiry of narrative practices and literacy learning of young children with diverse backgrounds including children with disabilities in urban contexts. She recently conducted research on folktales of Southeast Asian American families and published a Southeast Asian children's folktales book for teachers and families. Her teaching in higher education includes sociolinguistic perspectives of literacy development and teacher education focusing on supporting literacy learning of young children from lower socioeconomic status families.

ABOUT THE CONTRIBUTORS

Chien-ju Chang, born in Tainan, Taiwan, is professor of Human Development and Family Studies at National Taiwan Normal University. Her research focuses on language and narrative development in Mandarin Chinese-speaking children, home support for child language, narrative and literacy development, and relationship between early language/cognitive skill and later reading performance in young children. Her recent research projects include longitudinal studies examining (1) narrative development (scripts, personal narratives, and fantasy narratives) in Mandarin-speaking children aged from 3 to 10 in Taiwan and Mainland China, (2) joint book reading of Chinese-speaking mothers and toddlers, (3) predictors of later reading skill in Chinese-speaking preschoolers, and (4) vocabulary and narrative performance in Chinese-English bilingual children and adolescents. She is also the principal investigator of Kids in Taiwan: National Longitudinal Study of Child Development and Care Project and coeditor of Language Studies of Chinese Speaking Children, Language Development in Chinese-Speaking Children: Application of Child Language Data Exchange System (CHILDES) and Chinese language narration: Culture, cognition, and emotion.

George Chigas is associate teaching professor in Cambodian Studies at the University of Massachusetts Lowell, where he teaches courses in Cambodian literature and cultural history. He is the author of *Tum Teav, A Translation and Literary Analysis of a Cambodian Classic*. In the late 1980s, he worked and conducted research in refugee camps in the Philippines and Thailand-Cambodian border. Since the mid-1990s, he has traveled frequently to Cambodia to teach and conduct research for extended periods.

Min-Young Kim is assistant professor of Literacy Education in the Department of Curriculum and Teaching at the University of Kansas. Born in Busan, South Korea, she was a former high-school classroom teacher of Language Arts in Korea. As a teacher educator, she has taught and worked with pre- and in-service teachers in Ohio, Michigan, and Kansas and supported their academic and professional growth. As a transnational researcher, her scholarship centers around literacy education, teacher education, and discourse analysis, mainly focusing on argumentative, dialogic, and translanguaging practices in diverse literacy classrooms.

Masahiko Minami, who received his doctorate from Harvard University, was born in Osaka, Japan, but now resides in San Francisco and teaches Japanese language and linguistics at San Francisco State University. He has also served as an invited professor at the National Institute for Japanese Language and Linguistics in Tokyo (2012–2016). He is currently editor-in-chief of the *Journal of Japanese Linguistics*. His primary research interests are bilingual education and cross-cultural studies. He has written extensively on psycho/sociolinguistics with a particular emphasis on cross-cultural comparisons of language development and narrative/discourse structure.

Tham Tran was born and raised in Vietnam. She received her PhD degree in education, literacy studies, from the University of Massachusetts Lowell. Her research focuses on the bilingual and bicultural identity among Southeast Asian American youths, multicultural literacy, and youth positive development programs.

Charlotte L. Wilinsky is a graduate of Amherst College with a BA in psychology and the University of Massachusetts Lowell with a PhD in applied psychology and prevention science. Her research is focused on applied developmental psychology. She is particularly interested in the impact of trauma on development and the research methodology of narrative analysis. She was born in Connecticut and currently resides in Western Massachusetts where she is an assistant professor of psychology at Holyoke Community College.

Fangfang Zhang was born at Xuyi, China. Right now she resides in Nanjing and is associate professor of School of Foreign Languages and Culture at Nanjing Normal University. Her areas of scholarship include the language development of children and second-language acquisition.

Juwen Zhang is professor of Chinese and folklore at Willamette University, Salem, Oregon. He was born in China and has taught at this current position for twenty-one years after teaching in several universities in China and the United States for more than a decade. He earned his PhD in folklore and folklife from the University of Pennsylvania. He is a fellow of American Folklore Society, and current president of Western States Folklore Society, USA. His research interests include folkloristic theories, rites of passage, folk narratives, folk music, Asian/Chinese American folklore, filmic folklore, and folkloric identity.

www.ingramcontent.com/pod-product-compliance
Lightning Source LLC
Chambersburg PA
CBHW022316280326
41932CB00010B/1120